IF WE BREAK

IF WE
BREAK

A MEMOIR *of* MARRIAGE,
ADDICTION, *and* HEALING

KATHLEEN BUHLE

CROWN
NEW YORK

Published in the United States by Crown, an imprint of Random House,
a division of Penguin Random House LLC, New York.

CROWN and the Crown colophon are registered trademarks
of Penguin Random House LLC.

Hardback ISBN 978-0-593-24105-9
Ebook ISBN 978-0-593-24106-6

Printed in the United States of America on acid-free paper

crownpublishing.com

2 4 6 8 9 7 5 3 1

First Edition

Book design by Jo Anne Metsch

THIS BOOK IS FOR

Naomi, Finnegan, and Maisy

CONTENTS

Prologue   xi

PART I: BEFORE

  1. Portland   3
  2. The South Side   9
  3. Will You Marry Me?   19
  4. It's a Girl   32
  5. Belonging   39
  6. That Girl with Her Trumpet   45
  7. Need   56
  8. Quitting   64
  9. And Did You Get What You Wanted from This Life,
      Even So?   71
10. Crossroads   77
11. You Cannot Tell Anyone   84
12. Quest for Friends   92

13. A Silly Girl from Chicago 99
14. A New Reality 106
15. Biden Blood 113

PART II: DURING

16. The Beginning of What's Next 119
17. My Favorite Person 124
18. Something Shattered 129
19. Are You Okay? 137
20. Seems Lonelier This Time 143
21. Flags 150
22. No Comfort, No Cure 158
23. Drunk at Christmas 165
24. Do You Know Where Hunter Is? 173
25. The Photographs 183
26. My Shame 191
27. The Navy 196
28. Abiding Love 207
29. The Good Wife 211
30. Fireworks 216
31. It's Not About the Chicken 222
32. Why Do You Keep Leaving Us? 231
33. Detective Work 239
34. Emotional Life Support 247
35. No More Secrets 254

PART III: AFTER

36. A New Battle, a New Plan 265
37. Good Friday 271

38. Say Your Life Is Great, and Snap, Something
    Bad Happens   278
39. Trust Me on This   289
40. Reclaiming My Name   295

    Acknowledgments   301

PROLOGUE

NANTUCKET, 2014

E very Thanksgiving we visited the island of Nantucket as a family. In November, when the wind is strong and the island is empty of summer visitors, you can imagine what it was like back when ships left the harbor in search of whales. It's a mystical place in the fall, with a gray morning fog covering the island and the sound of the ocean crashing on the shores. Throughout my marriage, this trip was always our family's favorite. But now I carried a sadness greater than anything I'd ever experienced before.

Every year, on Thanksgiving morning, we drove from our rental to the beach where an unassuming little shingled house sat up on a sand dune, looking out toward the water. The year before, the house had been surrounded by sandbags to protect it from the encroaching ocean. This year, as we drove up to where the house once stood, it was gone. The ocean had taken it over.

We parked our cars and got out. This would be the first

year we didn't stand in front of that little house for a family picture. I imagined the heartbreak of the family who owned it. The house was gone, and that felt like a message from the universe: This chapter is over.

Hunter and I walked down to the beach as all the kids scattered along the shoreline and his parents' dog, Champ, ran among us. I wanted to soak up every minute we had together. At the time, everything in my life felt untethered. My brother-in-law was dying from cancer, my husband was struggling with addiction, and I'd just learned about his infidelity. Nothing felt normal, and yet I clung to this tradition. I clung to my family.

As we stood on the beach, the sky gray and the wind strong, I leaned my head against Hunter. "How far can we step back before we fall?" I said to him as I turned, my head still resting against his. With our foreheads firmly pressed together, we each took a step back. We tried to balance ourselves as we continued to step back to the point where we could still hold each other up without falling.

Our lives were breaking but I desperately wanted us to be okay. I needed him to hold me up and he needed me. That was what I'd based my life on and what I strongly believed—that we needed each other. Neither of us could survive without the other. But in the end, in so many ways, we both broke. The question I couldn't answer then was: How would I survive?

PART I

BEFORE

ONE

PORTLAND

n 1992 I was living in Portland, Oregon, trying to reinvent myself as a social activist and tree-hugging liberal. I barely understood climate change but proudly wore my LOVE PLANET EARTH T-shirt. With my flowing bohemian dresses and Birkenstocks, I pretended I knew something about the alternative music scene that was exploding there at the time. I couldn't name three bands, but I could sway and groove with the best of them. I was twenty-three and working for the year as a volunteer with the Jesuit Volunteer Corps (JVC). Having grown up in working-class Chicago, I had no idea what the Pacific Northwest even looked like before I arrived, and the year in Oregon was as ambitious as anything I'd ever set out to do. I was yearning for new experiences and dreaming about who I could become.

I lived in a rambling Victorian house with seven other volunteers. We were strangers to one another but shared the belief that we could make a difference. I listened to heated discussions about the environment, the impact of logging, and what needed to happen to protect the planet. "Yeah," I would add, nodding along. But I knew as much about logging as I did about space flight—zero. My South Side Chicago neighborhood was populated by Polish and Irish laborers who were busy trying to make a living and weren't talking about carbon footprints. But my roommates taught me to not only recycle but compost. At dinner, we passed a talking stick to make sure everyone was allowed to speak their mind without interruption. During one meal, a roommate commented on how quickly we were going through toilet paper and sug- gested, in all seriousness, that we each use no more than two squares. *You might as well just use your hand,* I thought, se- cretly continuing to make a toilet paper mitt.

When it was time to make the grocery list, we'd all sit down to talk about what we wanted. Gourmet coffee was all the rage in Portland, but I didn't drink it. "If we get expensive coffee, can we also get Diet Coke?" I asked. The answer was a resounding no.

That was the year I learned that beans didn't always come in cans and that you had to be able to tell your organic prod- ucts from your nonorganic. When I inadvertently bought the wrong honey, my roommates delicately explained to me that the nonorganic honey contained pesticides. "Who knew?" I said with a smile. "Honey seems so straightforward." That night I wrote a note and taped it to the honey bear's chest: "I'm sorry I wasn't enough. I was just trying to bring a little sweetness to your lives." The bear, with his note, stayed on the counter all year.

I had been working since I was twelve, but it had been selling hot dogs at Comiskey Park, home of the White Sox, and washing dishes at a party rental store. In Oregon, I worked with adults living with mental illness, and I finally felt I was doing something that mattered. My previous four years at St. Mary's University in Winona, Minnesota, were spent playing pool and drinking cheap beer, not sitting around debating social policy. My roommates now seemed like they'd been in the fight for social justice their whole lives while I was just getting started. But regardless of where we'd come from, JVC put us all on the same playing field. We each had an eighty-dollar monthly stipend and we explored the city together, seeing live music and hiking through the parks.

After a few weeks, I found myself dancing with a shaggy-haired volunteer who came from a little state I'd barely heard of. His name was Hunter Biden. As he swung me around that night, my heart started to beat just a little bit faster. He was shy at first, but I never stopped talking. After that night, whenever I would see him and he'd smile at me, I would feel my entire body respond. I'd never met anyone like him before. Despite the longish hair tucked behind his ears and his ripped-up jeans, he carried himself with the elegance of a movie star.

For weeks he and I found ourselves talking on the porch at every JVC party. When a few of us went to a bar the night after Thanksgiving, my eyes stayed only on Hunter, and at closing time, he walked me home, where all of my roommates were fast asleep. He and I sat in two old armchairs in a living room strewn with mismatched furniture, and I waited for him to make a move. It was our first time alone together, and the room hummed with our energy. After what seemed like hours of talking, I couldn't take it any longer. I stood up and walked over to his chair, climbed onto his lap, put my arms around his neck, and leaned down for a kiss. Fireworks! From that moment on, my life would change in ways I'd never imagined.

Suddenly we couldn't be apart. We walked the city for hours holding hands, and talked on the phone every night we weren't together. I didn't see the point in going anywhere if I couldn't be with him. In the mornings he'd walk with me to the nonprofit where I worked, on the first floor of an Episcopal church across town, and walk home with me afterward.

While I was still trying to figure out who I was, Hunter carried himself with a confidence and maturity I'd never seen before. When he told me about the bond he had with his dad and his brother, I'd never heard a man talk so openly about loving his family. They were not just close but shared an emotional tie that seemed stronger than any I'd heard of before. When I learned that, as boys, he and his brother, Beau, had survived a car accident that killed their mother and baby sister, it felt like one more reason why he was special.

Hunter was effusive about our love too, and when he focused his attention on me, it was intoxicating. For the first time in my life, I believed that I might actually be beautiful and smart and unique, all because he said so. Just a few weeks after our first kiss, we started planning our future over Hefeweizen beer. We sat for hours, scheming about how we'd spend the rest of our lives together. First we'd get married, then I'd find a grad school program in psychology while Hunter went to law school.

We talked about our lives back home, describing every family member, every close friend, in detail. We examined every significant childhood memory and each former sweetheart. We were excited by the parts of our pasts that aligned, celebrating them with all the naïveté of early love. We both had Irish roots? Amazing! We'd both been raised Catholic? Incredible! We both loved to read, we were both idealistic dreamers. And most important, we shared a close relationship with our families. What separated us, though, was significant.

Hunter had grown up the son of a U.S. senator. His girlfriend before me was a DuPont heir. At the old estate where he lived, he had a tuxedo hanging in his closet—a tuxedo he used fairly regularly. Where he came from, lineage was a real thing.

Me? I came from Chicago's working-class streets. I'd always felt loved and appreciated by my parents, but my life had a grittiness to it, and my childhood was more practical than aspirational. Dinner at my house was served with paper towels and often included mac and cheese out of a Tupperware bowl. There was never talk of being special.

Hunter tried to tell me that he came from a middle-class family, but nothing about his life looked remotely middle-class to me. Months later, when I went to his house for the first time, I explained to him that the middle-class families I knew didn't live like this, let alone working-class families like mine. "Hunt," I told him, "a kid from a middle-class family does not have a ballroom."

The night before I flew home from Portland to Chicago to be with my family for Christmas, Hunter helped me drop off gifts to my nonprofit clients living on their own in subsidized housing. He'd bought a beat-up old car, and we drove all over the city making our holiday rounds. It was so late by the time we got back to my house that we decided to stay up all night; my flight was at the crack of dawn. But as soon as we turned on the movie *La Femme Nikita,* we were asleep. When we woke up, I'd missed my plane.

I was panicked, but Hunter was calm. He was going to make sure I got on another one, so we jumped in his car. It wouldn't start. "No problem," he said, and found us a public bus.

When we got to the airport, he walked right up to the United counter in his customary blue blazer and jeans, and I watched as he explained that I'd missed the flight because we'd tried to stay up all night but fell asleep on the couch. The woman behind the counter was so charmed by his story that she handed me a new ticket and even apologized to me.

Hunter and I walked over to the gate and sat down, wrapping our arms and legs around each other's. Then we took a pen from my bag and took turns writing "I love you" on each other's hands. The next time I looked up, the once-crowded gate was empty. Had I actually managed to miss this flight too? When Hunter somehow procured me yet another ticket, my faith that this man could do anything was cemented.

TWO

THE SOUTH SIDE

My three brothers and I are third-generation South Siders—free-range city kids of the seventies and eighties. We often fought, but running to our parents, Jim and Roberta, was never an option. Our small Chicago bungalow was a story and a half, the twin of our neighbors', with a shared side entrance and a small apartment on top where my dad's parents, Grandma Ann and Grandpa Dutch, lived.

My oldest brother, Michael, had auburn hair like my mother and a quick wit. Jimmy, with a wiry frame and wild hair, was my constant ally, while Johnny's smile and easygoing demeanor made him everyone's favorite.

For many years, this little house on Mason Avenue was my entire world. Narrow and deep, it had a tight hallway that led to a small kitchen in the back, with the living room in the front and a stairway that always held a pile of things that needed to go down to the basement or up to the bedrooms.

The rule was never to take the stairs empty-handed, because with eight of us living under one roof, there were always things to put away.

As the only girl, I had my own small bedroom with two tiny closets, one of which my mom turned into a "dressing table" by taking the closet doors off and building a plywood table with a glass top and a skirt. It was my favorite part of the bedroom, and one of the only "feminine" places in the house. For a long time, we had one bathroom off the hallway for all six of us, and a bar of Zest was the extent of our beauty products. If I wanted bubbles in my bath, my mom squeezed in some Palmolive.

While my parents took a hands-off approach to parenting, they were always a united front. I never heard them argue or raise their voices. My older brother Jimmy once said that our parents' marriage was a freak outlier, because marriages are never as harmonious as Mom and Dad's.

"I can't believe your mother and I still have so much to say to each other," my dad often said. When I moved away, every time I'd call home, my mom would put it on speaker and call to my dad, "Jimmy, our girl's on the phone."

Both of my parents grew up on the South Side, my mom in another brick bungalow a few miles east of where we lived, with her two sisters. My grandma Dorothy worked as an executive assistant and my grandfather was a railroad supervisor. Dorothy pushed all three of her daughters to go to college, which was not common in their neighborhood in the 1950s. My mom, Roberta, was the oldest and graduated from high school at sixteen, having never missed a day of school, and went away to college in Dubuque, Iowa. Roberta always did what she was told and worked hard, but she had a lot of nervous energy and she never stopped talking. "We had no idea your sisters had so much to say until you left for college," my grandmother once told her.

When I was growing up, my mom was in constant motion, hammering, painting, gardening, cooking. She always had a project. When my younger brother, Johnny, started kindergarten, my dad was working double shifts most days, and she wanted to contribute. Her first job was teaching at a Catholic school a few blocks from our home. But I barely registered that she was working, because she seemed to always be home for us. After three years of teaching full-time and going to grad school, she got her master's degree. A decade later, at the age of fifty, she received her doctorate. To write her dissertation, she took another door off its hinges, setting it on top of two file cabinets in the basement, and worked down there feverishly.

Mom always said that we were a family of late bloomers, and that gave me great comfort. Later in life, she published articles on literacy in academic journals, and she created an early intervention literacy program that was instituted in schools across the state. Back then, I didn't understand the community of strong professional women my mom had built for herself outside our home or how hard she was working. The only person in the house who seemed to appreciate her was my grandma Ann upstairs. "Go help your mother," she'd say to us daily. "She goes to work and then comes home and never stops." On Sundays, Grandma Ann offered to watch us so my mom could go to Mass. It wasn't until twenty years later that I learned my mom never went to church. Instead, she'd go to Three Sons, a diner in our neighborhood, and eat a cheeseburger while she read her paperback novel.

My dad's father wasn't around while he was growing up, and Dad and his brother lived with different members of his mom's family. But no matter where they were, Grandma Ann would wake my dad for school before leaving for her job as a restroom matron. My dad always understood that the homes they stayed in were not their own, so when my parents bought their first house, with an apartment for Grandma Ann and Grandpa Dutch, Dad said it was the greatest gift he'd ever given his mother—finally, a home of her own.

School was another place Dad felt he didn't belong. On financial aid, Dad worked as a student janitor at his Catholic grammar school. "I'm sorry, Sister," he'd say when the nuns came looking for him. "I can't make it to class today. We've got a plumbing problem."

It wasn't until my dad was in his seventies that he learned his father had been involved in an armed robbery. One of five men who had attempted to blow up a vault, Grandpa Dutch acted as the lookout. He had skipped town and wasn't caught by the FBI until eight months later in a Davenport, Iowa, hotel. Grandma Ann was fiercely private about the matter, and if anyone on the block even asked her how the family was, she just muttered, "They've got nerve." When Grandpa Dutch showed up on the South Side ten years later, he was accepted back into the family without question, simply moving in with his wife and two sons, no questions asked. Family lore said he had been offered military service as the court's alternative to prison, and he had taken it.

Grandpa Dutch was a giant barrel of a man with white

hair and a ruddy complexion, and he wore a suit and a bow tie, working at the racetrack six days a week well into his eighties. When he wasn't at the track, he worked as a bookie in the upstairs apartment at one of the many desks my mother made for our family—this one out of a giant piece of plywood and an old table base. It was always strewn with the bets he'd taken over the phone.

Tall and thin, with coiffed hair and a penchant for cigarette breaks, Grandma Ann took care of their apartment and spent hours smoking and looking out over the neighborhood from her picture window. She wasn't one for talking or displays of affection, but I couldn't get enough of her. She'd make me coffee with cream and extra sugar and put out a plate of graham crackers for dipping. We'd sit on the couch, play gin rummy, and watch our favorite shows: *All in the Family, Family Feud, The Carol Burnett Show*. Grandma Ann wasn't effusive, but she was direct. When I told her that she was my favorite grandma, she gave me a stern look and said, "Don't disrespect your Grandma Dorothy." Then she kicked me out of her house, and I sat on the top step until she finally let me back in.

Telling someone they were special wasn't something people did in our family, and my brothers and I were not spoiled. If I ever asked any of my grandparents to buy me anything, one of them would say, "I'll buy you two and you can run between them." And if I ever dared to ask to be driven somewhere, God forbid, one of the four of them would quip, "Sure. The second Tuesday of next week." In my neighborhood, if you couldn't run fast, you weren't going to be picked for a game of tag. Abandoned houses were meant to be explored, and as long as we were home for dinner, no one cared where we were. My brothers and I walked the mile to and from school, but whenever we could, we'd scratch up a handful of change and take the bus down Austin Avenue. "How much money is that?" the driver would ask suspiciously as the four of us crowded on. "It's all there," answered Michael, the oldest and the most brazen. He'd shove the coins quickly into the fare box as we pushed behind him and took our seats. Once on the bus, I'd bury my nose in a novel.

At home, my go-to fighting strategy with my brothers was to taunt them before quickly running to the bathroom and locking the door. When we sold the house, the bathroom door still had a hole in the center where Michael tried to punch through it to get me. There was nothing precious or off-limits in our home, and when Jimmy and I had the brilliant idea to cut a hole in the downstairs bedroom wall to create a secret passage into the adjacent storage room, all Mom said was, "Aren't you both so creative! What made you think of it?"

Our only real family rule was instated after I showed up to breakfast once in my underwear. "Kathy!" Mom exclaimed when she saw me. "Where are your clothes?"

"The boys always come to the table in their underwear," I said with eight-year-old sincerity. "Why can't I?" Which prompted Mom's one and only firm rule: No one can come to the table in their underwear.

When I was about fourteen, I took to joyriding in my mom's maroon Caprice Classic station wagon whenever my parents weren't home. Once I took the Caprice to pick up Johnny from a friend's, and as we pulled back onto Mason

Avenue, I saw Dad's car parked in front of our house. My parents had come home early.

"Shit!" I yelled to Johnny as he tried to jump out of the car before I'd stopped. "You are not abandoning me! You're the whole reason I'm in trouble!" I was so panicked that I couldn't properly park the car, and I left the back end sticking way out in the street. Johnny and I walked into the house and met our parents at the top of the stairs.

"You'll have to repark the car," I said sheepishly, hanging my head as I handed the keys over to my father.

"Both of you go to your room," Mom said. "Dad and I need to talk about this before we talk to you." As I said, they always spoke with one voice when it came to parenting, and for years I tried to employ this strategy with my own kids. That night, I couldn't fathom the punishment ahead of us.

"Kathy," my mother called to me after what felt like an eternity. I walked into the living room, shooting Johnny a scared glance as I passed his room. "Your dad and I want you to understand what you did. You have no idea how scared we were. You could have hurt someone, and you could have hurt yourself and your brother. If anything had happened, Dad and I could have lost everything. What you've done is so big, it is beyond punishment." I tried hard not to smile, because in that moment, I knew that I wasn't grounded and that my parents weren't angry with me. It would take raising my own girls for me to realize how remarkable my parents were. I didn't come from a climate of anger; I came from empathy and understanding.

•   •   •

My life on the South Side was tightly circumscribed, small and stable. And it wasn't until I was accepted to a competitive academic high school on the west side that I had my first glimpse of life beyond my neighborhood. St. Ignatius College Prep was one of the oldest schools in the city, a large, imposing brick building that dates to before the Chicago Fire of 1871.

Getting accepted to St. Ignatius was a competitive process, and hundreds of kids didn't make the cut, but for some reason, I did. I met kids there who came from every corner of the city. Kids who lived in wildly elegant apartments and kids from subsidized housing. Kids who acted in plays and kids who had intractable opinions about world affairs. I devoured the newness of it all, but it was also the first time in my life that I felt behind, as though someone had forgotten to give me the operating instructions to this new, worldly life.

On my first day, I asked my mother to walk in with me. "No, Kathy," she said to me as we pulled up in her station wagon. "You can do it." I slid out of her car in my new black corduroys and pink sweater, feeling incredibly self-conscious.

Every class was seated in alphabetical order, so I was up front: Kathy Buhle. In all but one class, Deirdre Close sat behind me. "It's *Deir*dre," she told me at the start of that first day. "The *r* comes before the *d*." At lunch I didn't know where to sit, so I stood staring at the candy bars behind the glass of the vending machine until a breathless Deirdre came up behind me, grabbed me by the arm, and whispered, "Did you see that guy? He's so cute! Come sit with me."

At Ignatius, I wanted to become a quiet and serious student, because I admired my classmates' intellect and drive. I vowed that I would shed my lazy grammar school persona and become an academic. My effort may have lasted a few months, but by senior year I was a regular in detention for talking too much, and I graduated with a 2.4 GPA. I did try in my classes. But only just enough. In the end, the greatest gift I received from St. Ignatius was a glimpse of the world beyond my block. That first, frightening step outside my comfort zone gave me the courage to keep pushing. When I look back to pivotal moments in my life, Ignatius was the first and most consequential.

Despite my poor academic record, I was accepted at the half dozen small liberal arts schools I applied to. I didn't visit any of them, and my final decision was based on who else was going there. St. Mary's in Winona, Minnesota, was popular with kids from Chicago, and while it was a five-hour drive from home, in many ways it felt a lot like my South Side neighborhood.

Patty, my friend since first grade who lived two blocks away and knew me as well as anyone, joined me at St. Mary's, along with a large group of kids from Chicago. For the first time, I started to take my studies seriously and think about what kind of life I wanted to live as an adult. Always in my mind was the idea of community service. As a psychology major, I wrote my thesis on what motivates people to volunteer. I wanted to do something meaningful.

After I graduated from college, I went back to St. Ignatius and talked to Father Thul, a Jesuit priest who had taken me under his wing while I was in high school. When I'd find myself in detention, Father Thul would pull me out to help him with his newsletter, which focused on his mission work in Peru. To me, the work he was doing in Peru seemed noble and important. I wanted to do something to help people too. Father Thul told me about the Jesuit Volunteer Corps, a domestic service program with a one-year commitment. It would prove to be the entryway to my entirely surprising life.

THREE

WILL YOU MARRY ME?

In the spring of my JVC year, 1993, Hunter and I flew from Oregon to Chicago for a friend's wedding, and we got to meet each other's parents. We'd already told both our families that we were in love and that someday we wanted to get married. I'd gone as far as to call my mom at two in the morning after that first kiss to tell her that Hunter felt different. It was the first and only time I ever called my mother in the middle of the night.

Hunter and I landed at O'Hare and found my parents waiting at the curb in my dad's blue Ford Five Hundred sedan. They looked so excited and happy. We drove to our house on Mason Avenue, where Hunter met Grandpa Dutch and Johnny, my only brother still living at home. Hunter was relaxed, engaged, and sweet. I felt proud to be showing him off. Grandpa Dutch, however, had some doubts. "What does he want from us?" Maybe he didn't trust the way Hunter shook his hand. There was not a lot of handshaking going on in our house, and Hunter's outstretched hand may have been just a little too polished for Grandpa.

That first night, we went to a bar where Hunter received a very Chicagoesque welcome from my friends. "Buddy, you better not consider running for office in Chicago," my friend Marty said. "No one named Hunter will ever win an election here." Hunter laughed, completely at ease.

The next day he and I drove downtown to meet his parents at the Park Hyatt on Michigan Avenue. Whether by coincidence or design, they were in Chicago as well. I was as nervous as I'd ever been before. I'd never met a U.S. senator.

Hunter parked my mom's Honda Accord and we got out, holding hands as we walked toward the hotel. Turning the corner, Hunter spotted his dad and called out to him.

Joe looked up, smiled, and ran across the street toward us. I stood next to Hunter on the sidewalk while Joe gave Hunter a kiss and a bear hug. Turning to me, Joe put his hands on my cheeks and looked me in the eyes, his nose almost touching my own.

"Honey," he said, "my boy tells me he loves you, so that means I love you too. Understand? I love you." He said this with the greatest earnestness. My parents didn't talk to me like this. No one did. I honestly didn't know what to do with it.

"Thank you," I said awkwardly and looked to Hunter, who smiled back at me as his dad put his arms around both of us. We headed into the hotel and up to their suite. In the elevator, Joe wanted to know everything about me, and as he asked question after question, I felt the same mixture of shock and pleasure I had felt during our initial meeting on the street.

When we got to their room and I saw Jill for the first time, shyness came over me. I don't know if I'd ever seen anyone so stunningly beautiful. Even up close, she didn't have a hair out of place. I'd never worn makeup, and I felt unkempt next to her. No one in our Portland house shaved their armpits or legs. That day I was wearing a long flowered dress my mother had bought me, which now felt like a burlap sack next to Jill's fitted knit suit and heels.

I was nervous as we all took the elevator down to meet my parents in the hotel restaurant for lunch. I spotted my mom and dad across the lobby, smiling and holding hands, and I wondered what they were thinking. As many boyfriends and girlfriends as my brothers and I had had, my parents had never met any of their parents, let alone gone to a fancy lunch with them. But Joe and Jill were lovely and attentive to me and my parents, and my mom and dad seemed to hold their own.

Jill and my mom were both educators, and they found common ground quickly, while my dad put his arm around me at the table and launched into a story. "Kathy ran track in high school," he said. "You should have seen this race. I never laughed so hard in my life."

Oh, God, I thought, *why is he telling this story?* Dad just smiled and kept going: "Kathy was running hurdles, and she went to jump the first hurdle and knocked it over. While all the other runners kept running past her, she went back and picked up the hurdle she'd knocked down. Now she was at least half a lap behind the rest, and her girlfriends were cheering her on, running beside the track, loudly humming the song from *Chariots of Fire*. You'd think Kathy was running in the Olympics the way they cheered. She came in dead last, and when she found me after, she was crying. She said, 'Dad, I thought if you knocked over the hurdle, you had to go back and pick it up.' I told her, 'Don't worry about the race. You have some great friends here today that love you!' "

The next story Dad told was how I'd changed a letter grade in my sixth grade teacher's gradebook. "Kathy didn't think the grade she had been given was fair," Dad laughed. This was my family. We laughed at one another.

Joe and Dad went on talking nonstop, telling family stories. Dad told how I fought head to head with my brothers, and how I always looked miserable when I worked at Comiskey Park serving hot dogs. When lunch finally ended and Hunter and I were alone outside the hotel, I leaned into his chest.

"How do you think that went?" I asked him. "Do you think your parents like me? I'm afraid your mom thinks I'm a derelict who doesn't know how to run a race and cheats in school."

"You're crazy," he said. "They love you. Mom already told me how sweet you seemed. She's just different from my dad. She's quiet. Do not worry. Everyone loves you."

A few weeks after we returned to Portland, my mom called to say that my oldest friend Patty's father was dying back in Chicago. Hunter and I got on another city bus and rushed to the airport again. We'd already mapped out our future by now: We'd get married and go wherever he was accepted to law school. We couldn't wait to start our lives together. *When will we be engaged?* I asked again and again. All spring he'd been coy. *Just wait,* he'd say whenever I brought it up.

Sitting in the back of the bus that day, with my head on his shoulder, I dreamed of our future. As the bus neared the airport, I turned to him with a smile. "Hunter, will you marry me?"

He laughed. "Yes, Kathleen." Then he kissed my head. "We are going to be married."

"It's official!" I said, settling back in the seat with a sly smile. "We're engaged!"

"Kathleen," he said, laughing, "stop. This is not official. You are so impatient."

"Aw, honey," I said, putting my arm around his shoulder. "You just got engaged."

My parents picked me up from the airport and took me straight to Patty's brick bungalow. Patty and I had become friends in first grade, walking the mile to school together once I'd graduated from walking with my brothers. She lived with her parents, three brothers, and one sister in a little brick house with a giant picture window, a St. Mary's statue tucked in the front bush, and one bathroom for all seven O'Neills. Her dad was an ironworker who liked to hold court from his recliner in the family room after his long day. He called me Fridge because the first thing I did whenever I walked into their house was open their refrigerator in search of food. Patty's mom was the head of nursing at Mercy Hospital and worked long hours, so Patty was staying at home now to take care of her father whose cancer had rapidly progressed. She hadn't known that I was coming, and when she saw me on her stoop, she pulled me into a tight hug. Then she led me to her father, who lay in a hospital bed in the family room, right in the place where his recliner had always been. When I leaned down to give him a kiss, he opened his eyes. "Hi, Fridge," he said softly.

Mr. O'Neill died that night, and the next morning Patty and I sat on her front stoop as relatives arrived. One after another, friends and family pulled up in their cars, crying. We greeted them with a sad smile. "In other news," I said to Patty as she sat smoking a Marlboro Light, leaning against the brick wall of her house, "I'm getting married. I asked Hunter on the way to the airport, and he said yes."

"Sounds like you," she said, smiling. "Did you give him a ring?"

I stayed with her through the three-day wake and the funeral. On my last afternoon we were out in her backyard when she looked at me and said, "Your boobs are giant."

"Hmm," I said, looking down at my chest. "I think I must be getting my period." But my mind started working back through the calendar. When *did* I last have my period? I felt a trickle of fear as my heart started beating faster. "I can't remember when I had my period. Shit. I'm terrible at keeping track." We were sitting across from each other on lawn chairs as I looked at Patty with panic. "I can't remember. Oh, God. Shit. Shit."

"You're not pregnant, Kathy," Patty said. "Go to Walgreens and take a test so you feel better."

Back at my parents' house, I sat on the toilet and stared at the test stick. It took only a second before the plus sign materialized. My only thought was to call Hunter.

"I'm pregnant," I blurted as soon as he answered. I had nothing else to say after that. No idea what to do next.

"It'll be okay," he told me, without a hint of fear. He was his calm, comforting self. "I love you. You love me. This is a good thing. A great thing," he said, sounding so certain. "I'll pick you up at the airport tomorrow." But I could hear the effort in his voice as he comforted me. "I love you," he said again, and it was what I most needed to hear.

When I flew back to Portland, Hunter was waiting for me at the gate with an earnest look on his face, a bouquet of flowers in one hand, and a stack of pregnancy books in the other. He handed me my gifts and put his arms around me. "I promise everything is going to be okay," he whispered in my ear.

Sitting in the front seat of his beat-up sedan, the flowers and books stacked on my lap, I felt numb. We went back to his house and I crawled into his bed. He sat next to me, reading the pregnancy books out loud, trying hard to make me feel better, but I was twenty-four, pregnant, and unmarried. We'd been hoping to have a family, of course. We'd already talked about our children's names. We just hadn't planned to start it yet. From the very beginning of our relationship, Hunter had put me to sleep by rubbing my back. His physical touch always calmed me. That night he rubbed my back until I felt myself calming down and drifting off.

The next day we sat in my office in the Episcopal church and called our parents to tell them we were having a baby. The conversations were not long. Each of our parents showed us nothing but love and support. If they were shocked or upset, not one of them expressed it.

The following morning my mom flew out and brought the

book *What to Expect When You're Expecting*. Craving her comfort, I stayed in the hotel room with her. Pregnancy was not kind to my emotional state. My mom tried to get me to accept the reality that I was having a baby. But I kept holding firm to the plans Hunter and I had made before I'd become pregnant. We'd finish our JVC program, Hunter would start law school, and I'd look for a graduate program. We'd get married the following summer just as we'd decided.

"You can do whatever you want to do," my mom said as she pushed my hair back from my face as I lay in the hotel bed. "I just—want you to think it through."

After she left, I went back to my routine, though now in a fog, and struggled to accept that my life was forever changed. On a rainy spring night a few weeks later, Hunter joined me at work in the church, as he often did, and we served dinner to the clients and played board games in the multipurpose room. Hunter was a regular by now, and everyone there knew and loved him. Before we started cleaning up the kitchen, he asked me if we could step outside together for a minute. I followed him out the side door and watched as he nervously pulled a box from his pocket. Standing close to me on the stairway under a drizzling Portland rain, Hunter touched my face gently and said, "Kathleen, will you marry me?"

A few weeks later, I left Portland and flew back to Chicago to plan our wedding. In the end, we'd decided to get married that summer before he started law school, but every choice about the event overwhelmed me. Until then, the extent of my family's entertaining had been casual gatherings in our basement.

But Mom did understand how to complete a checklist, so we just kept crossing things off on a poster board she'd taped to the kitchen wall to keep us organized.

I sat in the passenger seat of my mom's car as she drove me around the city, picking out my wedding dress at the first store we visited, then booking the least expensive hotel ballroom we could find. Hunter and I talked on the phone several times a day, and he seemed genuinely worried about me. Reassuring him, though, felt beyond me. I still wanted to be married to him; I just didn't want all the other stuff that seemed required in order to get there. My wedding felt less like something to celebrate than like something to endure.

Not long before the actual date, I flew to his family home in Greenville, Delaware, for an engagement party. Most of my Chicago family joined me, and when we drove up the long, tree-lined driveway of the Bidens' house, my grandpa Dutch, sitting in the backseat of our rental car, asked, "Who's buried *here*?" The lush green grounds and expansive lawns looked more like a cemetery to him than a home.

My family and I had never seen a house like Hunter's before. A stone wall ran along the front of the house, separating the lawn from a vast field. The front door opened into a foyer with a marble floor and double staircase. The library was adorned with wood carvings of nymphs and opened onto an actual ballroom. Hunter had described his home, but seeing it in person was overwhelming.

Greenville is known as Château Country because of its sprawling estates and winding, tree-lined drives, and everyone there seemed to have stepped out of a Fitzgerald novel. Hunter's friends all had good teeth, nice cars, and a swagger I hadn't encountered before. At first I recoiled from it all. How had I ever imagined I could belong here?

Beau came bounding out to meet me. He had brown hair, blue eyes, an elegantly straight nose, and a chiseled jaw. Just like his dad, Beau came straight over to me and took me in a hug. Hunter had talked more about Beau than anyone else, so I felt I already knew him.

Ashley, Hunter's younger sister, was shy but sweet and polite, with a poise far beyond her twelve years. I met every single member of Hunter's extended family that weekend, and they were all genuinely warm, yet I felt so homesick. One person I instantly felt comforted by was Joe's mom, whom everyone called Mom Mom. She had a stoic, wry Irish way about her that reminded me of Grandma Ann. I stayed close to her throughout the weekend, and when I couldn't decide what to wear one night, I asked her to come up to my room with me. "I feel fat and ugly," I told her as she sat on my bed. "Honey," she said, "the white dress looks great. Put it on and let's go." She wasn't going to let me feel sorry for myself.

The night before our engagement party, I went to the movies with Ashley and Beau's girlfriend at the time, another heir to a prominent family, and as we left the theater, we ran into some women who were part of Beau and Hunter's circle of friends, all looking perfectly chic in their jeans, cashmere sweaters, and gold jewelry. I had on another loose flowered dress (this one I'd bought in the parking lot of a Grateful Dead show), and as I watched them size me up—all the way down to my toes poking out from my Birkenstocks—my pregnancy left me feeling like a whale. A new insecurity found space in my head that day, lodging itself in tight, and it never really let me go.

In Chicago, I'd always been able to find common ground with people—by way of school, or our shared park district, or the parish. Here in Delaware, I couldn't land shared experiences. Those late nights in Portland that Hunter and I had spent talking about our similar backgrounds now seemed ridiculous to me. His home, family, and friends didn't look or sound anything like mine. While Hunter was growing up among winding country roads and compounds with long driveways, I was playing in the alley and along railroad tracks.

I didn't know who I was yet, but I felt certain I didn't fit in here. Shackled by a new insecurity that I barely understood, I was intent on keeping my past hidden. If only his family knew where I grew up. If only they saw the Archer Avenue bus I used to take for an hour to get to high school every day. They all lived in big, beautiful homes and drove fancy cars. Surely they would think less of me if they knew where I came from. Hunter's family and friends showed me nothing but affection and acceptance, but whether because of my pregnancy, my upbringing, or both, I felt a strong sense of not belonging.

I'd already tried to reinvent myself many times: in high school, at the JVC in Oregon, and now as Hunter's fiancée. I'd played at being the shy girl, the mysterious girl, the intellect, the social activist, but I could never make it past lunch without blurting out some wild story and blowing my cover. In the end, I was still the outspoken one, always silly and self-effacing. And as much as I'd tried to downplay my life growing up under the rumble of freight trains and the hum of

planes coming in and out of Midway Airport, I was still the
only daughter of Jim and Roberta, a mediocre student and
subpar athlete. My grandparents were a bookie, an assembly
line worker, a secretary, and a railroad boss. But in Delaware I
began leaving those parts out. I was now simply Kathleen
from Chicago.

In Chicago, my engagement and my pregnancy had been announced together and equally celebrated, and my burgeoning
boobs were a great source of jokes among my family and
friends. In Delaware, no one mentioned the pregnancy before
we were married. I knew Hunter had told his parents and his
brother, but I didn't know who else was aware. And so I
couldn't overcome my deep fear that the Bidens' friends and
family would think Hunter and I had only gotten married because I was pregnant. I felt I couldn't tell anyone the truth, so
I hid the pregnancy in Delaware until after I was married.

After our wedding on July 2, 1993, our families joined us
at the Knickerbocker Hotel in downtown Chicago. Our two
families shared the dance floor, but anyone could have separated the South Siders from the East Coasters. At one point,
my dad's cousin and my namesake, Aunt Kathy, climbed onto
a chair to sing her signature song, "Flaming Mamie," her dyed
black hair and bright red lipstick on full display. Normally,
everyone throws coins at her after she sings. As she started her
deep-throated rendition—"They call her Flaming Mamie,
she's the hottest thing in town"—my family started throwing
dollar bills rolled into balls. "This party is too fancy for
coins," my cousin Pat yelled out, a dinner napkin on top of his

head. Hunter's family laughed along with mine, but I worried that they thought we were crazy.

A few weeks after our wedding, Hunter and I drove to the homes of all his family in Delaware to share our "big pregnancy news," as if it had just happened, as if I wasn't standing before them five months pregnant. Each time we announced the baby, everyone feigned surprise. The whole charade felt degrading and humiliating.

I often wonder what would have happened if I'd felt more comfortable in my skin then—as comfortable as Hunter seemed in his. What if I'd just said to everyone, "I'm pregnant and we're in love, and that's the way it is." I remember crying at the Bidens' house the night after first sharing our announcement. Jill found me in the hallway and put her arms around me. She asked who'd made me feel so bad. She could have no way of understanding my pain, though, because I saw no way to tell her.

I missed my mother so much that night. But for the first time in my life, I couldn't turn to her. Right before the wedding she'd told me, "Be careful what you tell your father and me about Hunter. You'll forgive him, but it will be harder for us." Her warning stuck with me throughout my marriage.

FOUR

IT'S A GIRL

Within a matter of months, we left Portland, got married, and moved to D.C. I worked at an office job that I hated, while Hunter was at Georgetown University Law School. We moved into a little garden apartment on Capitol Hill. When I was home, I kept the shades drawn and spent most of my time in bed.

My life had changed so quickly and so dramatically; nothing seemed to be in my control anymore. My year in Portland had been the most important and meaningful time of my life, and then it ended abruptly. Suddenly I felt I didn't have any choices. I was married. I was going to be a mother. I loved Hunter, but our life no longer resembled a romantic movie. And I missed my parents. I could see the concern in Hunter's eyes as he tried to make me feel better, but I remained closed off. I couldn't really understand how I felt myself, let alone explain it to Hunter, so we lived in a state of limbo.

My mother worried that I wasn't facing the fact that I'd

soon have a real-life baby to take care of. She asked me to talk to Dr. Levy, the psychiatrist everyone in our family had seen at one time or another. When my brother Jimmy was very young and refused to go to school, staying up all night crying, my mom looked for guidance. Talking to a psychiatrist helped my parents understand Jimmy's anxiety over school. From that moment on, our family would lean on therapy when we needed it. So I called Dr. Levy from our little apartment, sitting nine months pregnant on the couch. I told him I didn't want to be a stay-at-home mother and that I planned to go back to graduate school. He said I didn't have to be a full-time mother to be a good mother, and his words were a great relief to me. But, he said firmly, I did still need to buy diapers!

As fall turned colder and the days became shorter, I felt stuck in our little apartment. The place upstairs from us had been broken into and a cabdriver was shot on our corner, so we spent most of our nights at home. No longer plotting our future over Hefeweizen, we were just waiting, unsure what our lives would look like with a child. We chose not to find out the baby's gender, but I clung to the hope that I'd have a girl.

"Looks like you're having a boy" was the prediction from almost everyone I encountered. Apparently I carried my pregnancy "like a basketball," which somehow meant a boy. My emotions were upended by pregnancy, but my only physical complaint was a constant pain under my rib cage. When I mentioned the pain to my doctor, he dismissed my concern with "You're pregnant. It's going to be uncomfortable." He'd look past me in the little examining room and ask Hunter with a warm smile, "How are your classes going?"

A few weeks later, when my pain continued, the doctor checked the baby's position and discovered she was breech. "You'll have to undergo a C-section," he announced casually. "The pregnancy is too far along to try to move the baby." After weeks of Lamaze classes, I cried at the thought of surgery.

When the day arrived and I was being prepped, I asked the nurse if there was a mirror so I could watch the birth, and she looked at me, perplexed. "No," she said. "Not that I know of. I've never been asked that before. I guess I could find one if you truly want to watch?" She acted as if I was crazy, but I just wanted to see my baby come into the world.

"Hunt," I said. "Is it weird that I want to see?" He smiled and shook his head.

I asked if I could use a phone, and I called my cousin Amy at work. Amy was born a month before me, to my mom's sister Noreen, and she and I were raised together. She was tall and slim, with thick red hair and a beautiful cherubic face, and I always wanted to look like her. She'd graduated from the Art Institute and had the best taste, so I always looked to her for advice. Plus, she gave me a definitive answer to any question I asked.

"Do you think it's strange that I want to see the baby being born?" I asked her now.

"No. There's nothing strange about it." She was firm. "Ask for a mirror."

"Okay," I told her. "I'll call you again when we have a baby."

I hung up and said to the nurse, "Excuse me, but I'd like you to find that mirror if you could, please."

When they finally wheeled me into the operating room, the

anesthesiologist gave me an epidural. The whole process took much longer than expected, and by the time they brought Hunter into the room, he looked as though he might faint. But he stood by my side, with his hand on my head, while a sheet separated us from my giant belly. The nurse tried to adjust the mirror for me to see, while Hunter's eyes stayed focused only on me.

"Here we go," the nurse said, and raised the mirror. I watched as my baby was lifted out of my body and into the air, still attached by the umbilical cord.

"It's a girl!" the doctor announced, and I burst into tears.

"I *wanted* a girl!" I sobbed.

Hunter laughed. "We all know you wanted a girl." He leaned down and kissed me gently on the lips. When the doctor handed me our perfect little baby, I felt a flood of pure joy.

"I love this baby," I said to Hunter, while he kept kissing my face. The birth of Naomi King Biden brought a spontaneous, all-consuming love that I had never felt before.

While I was in post-surgery, my doctor came in to see me, or so I thought. "I have a letter here for your father-in-law," he told me. "Could you please make sure he gets it?" Then he tucked an envelope onto my gurney. *Sure,* I thought. *I'll get right on that.*

When the attendant came and wheeled me into a giant private room, I asked him to stop. "Wait—this isn't the room we were shown on our tour of the hospital," I said. "We can't afford a private room." I made him leave me in the hallway while he went to figure out what to do with us. When he returned and said the private room was a gift from the hospital, I didn't believe him.

"Are you sure we're not going to be billed?" I asked.

"I'm sure," he answered with a smile.

As I sat in my beautiful private room, the doctor's letter to Joe lying on the bedside table, I was beginning to see what it meant to be married to Hunter. But when the nurse put Naomi back in my arms, everything fell away. That little baby took over my heart. I didn't want anyone to take her from me, even for a minute. Hunter climbed into the bed and held both of us, and I felt forever changed. The purpose of my life was to care for this child.

For three days, I sat in that hospital bed with Hunter, staring at her. To feel this happy after nine months in a haze of depression felt almost jarring. "I can't believe how much I love this baby," I kept saying. Alone with Naomi, Hunter and I were closer than ever.

Three days later, on Christmas Eve, Hunter, my mother, and I, still sore from surgery, drove two hours north to the Bidens' home in Delaware. When we got to the house, Jill showed me to the guest bedroom, with its own sitting room and bath. My mother was given Ashley's bedroom across the hall.

As soon as we got there, I missed the sweet bubble of our hospital stay. I could tell that my mom and I felt equally out of place, and I could feel the enormous effort she was putting into this visit. She kept washing the dishes and wiping the counters.

"Mom, please stop wiping the counters and sit down," I told her. Hunter walked over and put his arm around her.

"Leave your mother alone," Hunter said, "she can wipe as many counters as she wants."

"Thank you, Hunter," she said, giving me a sly smile as she spun the dishrag. Hunter would soon become another son to her, and he'd laugh at her many stories and quirky ways. But that version of Roberta, the laughing storyteller, wasn't with us that Christmas at the Bidens'. She was a more subdued version of herself. Maybe it was the formality of this house that Mom and I weren't accustomed to. Hunter's family went all out for Christmas, and the house was filled with garlands, ribbons, and lights. I wanted so much for them to like me and to see that I would be a good wife, a good mother, a good daughter-in-law. I desperately wanted their approval.

The day after Christmas, I came downstairs and couldn't find my mom anywhere in the house and couldn't imagine where she'd gone. I found Jill making coffee in the kitchen and asked if she had seen her. Jill said Mom had tripped in the night and hurt her foot, so Joe had driven her to the emergency room to have it X-rayed. My initial reaction was deep embarrassment. We were now causing people to take care of us. I didn't want that attention.

An hour later, Mom walked into the kitchen on crutches with a boot on her broken foot. It turned out that she'd tripped on a step in the hallway right before bed and had woken up in the middle of the night in excruciating pain. Not wanting to bother any of us, she'd slid downstairs on her butt and waited for someone to wake up. Joe happened to be the first one who came into the kitchen, and she'd asked him if he'd mind taking her to a doctor.

"I'm sorry," she said to me now, looking exhausted.

"You have nothing to be sorry about, Roberta," Joe said, putting his arm around her. Then he smiled at me. "Your mother's tough. I know she is in a lot of pain."

I smiled back weakly. "I'm sorry, Mom." Now we were both patients.

When the day finally ended, I made my way upstairs and found Mom and Jill talking in the sitting room outside my bedroom. Mom was slumped on the couch and Jill had her legs crossed elegantly in a side chair. Mom's hair looked like she had just woken from a sweaty dream, and worse, she'd put her shirt on inside out *and* backward. The shirt's tag hung from the front collar while her shoulder pads sat atop her shoulders like little foam saucers. I wanted to throw a blanket over her. Jill looked beautiful and relaxed and made no mention of Roberta's shirt. But when Jill finally left to go to bed, I turned to Mom and said, "Your shirt is inside out and backward."

"I'm too tired to care," she answered, leaning back on the couch with her broken foot propped up on the coffee table. I laid my head in her lap, Naomi asleep in my arms, and closed my eyes.

FIVE

BELONGING

Born with a Buddha's disposition, Naomi slept through the night, woke with a coo, and could be passed from person to person with a look of total contentment. In many ways, Naomi's birth was more of a seal on Hunter's and my love than our wedding ceremony. We had created our own little family: father, mother, and child.

Hunter and I both took unwarranted credit for this perfect baby of ours. Want to know how to get your infant to sleep through the night? Ask us! The answer? Put her to bed, give her a kiss, and close the door. Works every time. I was proud of our little family, even if I knew people looked at our young faces and thought we were teen parents.

And I now had an identity that felt wholly my own: mother. I'd wanted graduate school and a career, but I reasoned that that could wait. Still, I was afraid to say how much I loved being with Naomi for fear of sounding as though I didn't have any ambition.

When Hunter transferred to Yale for his second year of law school, we rented an apartment in a New Haven brownstone on a narrow street off a park, where I took the strongest, straightest branches I could find to use as rods and sewed white gauze curtains for our bedroom. Hunter and I spent weekends driving Naomi around Connecticut in our blue Jetta, scouring antiques stores. We found a little drop-leaf table that we squeezed our new friends around for dinner and cards. We went to the Italian market and Sally's Pizza so often they knew us by name. Hunter and I would make dinner together, and we took turns waking up with Naomi. If one of us wanted to sleep in and skip our turn, we had to make it up the next day. We were equal partners in parenting.

Once a week we'd each get a night to ourselves. On my night, I'd go to an Indian restaurant on Chapel Street, a few blocks away. The restaurant was in a 1955 prefabricated chrome diner where I'd sit in a booth, my book propped up on the table while I ate. On Hunter's night, he'd take a book and his journal to the Anchor Spa, a bar that had opened in the 1930s and where little seemed to have changed since. Hunter and I liked each other's company, but we liked our alone time too.

"We'll move to Chicago, right?" I would often ask him back then, bringing up the promise he'd made to me back in Portland.

"Yes, Kathleen," he'd say, with equal parts fondness and exasperation, but I could already feel the strong gravitational pull on him of the East Coast. Still I held tightly to his promise.

In the winter of 1995, during a visit to Wilmington, Hunter met with someone to get career advice. I was in the kitchen with Naomi, fixing her lunch of cut-up broccoli and chicken, when Hunter walked in, looking stunned.

"You won't believe what just happened." He shook his head. "I was offered a *job* at MBNA bank." My body stiffened. A job with MBNA meant working in Delaware, and Delaware had never been part of our plan. We were supposed to be finding a way to move back to Chicago.

Hunter slid a small piece of paper toward me on the table. I picked it up and saw a dollar amount greater than anything I'd ever imagined someone our age earning.

"No," I answered immediately. "I don't care how much money you'll make. I don't want to live here."

By "here" I meant Delaware, certainly, or anywhere on the East Coast. I felt a sinking feeling in my stomach. "You promised we'd live in Chicago," I pleaded. "I don't *want* to live in Delaware. I don't belong here."

Hunter was unwavering, though, certain that this bank job was the best move for us. But having spent the last few years trying to fit into his world, all I wanted was to get back home. If we could get ourselves to Chicago, I felt sure we could shape our little family on our own terms. And maybe I could find myself again. That girl who had had such purpose out in Oregon. That girl who trusted herself.

Hunter couldn't convince me that I'd be happy living in his Delaware. But it didn't matter. He won the argument. Somehow taking this job was about what was best for our family, while my ardent wish to move to Chicago was only about what was right for me. It was then I could feel the balance of power shifting in our marriage. I told myself that Hunter was the one financially supporting us. And it really was a great job, with potential to move up in the company. But in the end, it was his decision, his choice. For six months after he took the bank job, my anger seemed to seep into almost every conversation we had, but he remained measured, never raising his voice. The fight didn't so much resolve as fade away, and maybe some part of my own inner resolve faded with it.

Before Hunter was to begin his position at the bank, we both had plans to work on Joe's Senate reelection campaign starting in August 1996. We rented a little row house in Wilmington, Delaware, not far from the campaign headquarters. Hunter was named co-chair of the campaign with Joe's sister, Valerie. Val had been managing every one of Joe's campaigns for years. She was Joe's best friend and a fierce defender of all things Biden.

It was my first political campaign, and public life did not come naturally to me. Early in the campaign, a family photo shoot confounded me. I seemed to be the only one who didn't know how to hold her arms correctly for the camera. The photographer kept trying to adjust me, while the rest of Hunter's family leaned casually on the post-and-rail fence like pros.

Any pretense of equality in our marriage took another hit when I walked into campaign headquarters for the first time with Naomi on my hip and saw Hunter sitting across from his aunt at a desk in their shared office. My campaign job, I learned, was to travel to senior centers to pass out cookies and literature. Back in Portland, I'd organized the programming and scheduling for the nonprofit where I worked and spoken to church and business groups throughout the city. I'd developed an entire fundraising campaign. I'd written grants. My work back then had felt as important as Hunter's.

"It feels kind of bizarre to be working for you," I said to him when we were alone in his office.

"Kathleen, you *don't* work for me," he said, and he kept repeating that I'd enjoy the work I was going to be doing. I'd have the freedom to come and go as I liked, while he'd have to be in the campaign office every day. He always hated conflict. But I was a fighter. He couldn't stand to see me mad at him, but I wore my emotions on my face. One of my teachers in Catholic grammar school once told my mother, "If looks could kill, I'd be a dead nun."

"Trust me," he said now. "You'll have far more fun than me." Standing in his blue blazer and button-down shirt, he carried himself so comfortably in this leadership role. I knew relatively nothing about the political world he'd been immersed in since birth. I'd also spent hardly any time in the state of Delaware. But I wasn't thinking rationally at that moment; I simply didn't like the imbalance of power I felt between us. And I don't know if it was irritation, a lack of ambition, or fear, but I simply didn't push myself during the campaign. Naomi and I mostly visited senior centers all over the state with Hunter's grandmother Mom Mom, where she chatted with the seniors as if they were all old friends.

Living in Delaware, I began to spend more time with Beau and Ashley. Ashley was a teenager, so I felt like a big sister to her, and from the beginning, we were close. Having grown up with three rough brothers, I loved the sweet relationship Ashley and I quickly formed. She always wanted to be with us, holding Naomi in her arms.

Beau was a different story. Before me, it had always been just Hunter and Beau. And although Beau was kind and charming from the minute I met him, it took us a while to figure out how I was going to fit into their friendship.

Many of Hunter and Beau's friends joined the campaign, and most nights our back porch became the place for drinks and downloading the day's events; we were the only ones with our own home and the only ones with a baby, giving us the feeling of being "true grown-ups." I liked hosting everyone and started to feel myself slowly accepting this new life in Delaware. I was still unhappy about staying out east, but I didn't do anything to try to change the course of my life. What if I'd gone out to Chicago and tried to find a job for myself there? I could have made the argument that with Hunter's résumé, he'd have an easy time finding his own good job in Chicago. If I didn't like his plans for us, I should have offered up an alternative. But that thought never occurred to me. In the end, I chose to make the most of living in Delaware because it was easier than pushing myself to find a different way.

THAT GIRL WITH
HER TRUMPET

When the campaign ended, Hunter and I started looking around for a house to buy in Delaware. Hunter's new job came with a signing bonus in addition to his considerable salary. I wanted to talk to a financial adviser so we'd know what we could afford. Hunter didn't think we needed financial guidance, but my entire family had all used the same adviser. On her suggestion, my brother Johnny and his future wife, Michele, bought their home before they were even married and started a college fund the minute their first baby was born.

I made the appointment myself and filled out pages upon pages about our expenses: how much we spent on groceries, and on movies, and on travel. We went to the adviser's office and sat across the desk from a clean-cut, efficient-looking man barely older than us.

"How many children do you plan to have?" he asked pointedly. "And when will you have them?" Hunter and I looked at each other and raised our eyebrows.

"We don't know," we answered, sheepishly. Our family of three was working well, and I think both of us were reluctant to disrupt a good thing.

"Well, if you're thinking about having another baby, let's go ahead and plan for two," the adviser said. Then he talked about retirement, college savings, and an emergency fund. "You should always have enough money to live for six months in case something happens with your job."

I nodded and took copious notes. Hunter and I had never discussed any of these things before. Retirement? We weren't even thirty yet. College? Naomi hadn't started kindergarten.

"You have to get in the habit of putting money away," the adviser told us, and then gave us a number to aim for when looking at houses. "You should be spending between $150,000 and $170,000." We smiled at him and left with our folder of information and our marching orders. A few weeks later, we bought a house for $310,000 and never saw the adviser again.

There are times in this story when I find myself pointing to a moment, a clue, that marks when I lost control of my life. The big house we bought on Centre Road is a very telling one.

The house was an old estate, parts of which dated back to before the Revolutionary War. "We'll just look at it for fun," Hunter had said, giving me an affectionate nudge in the car. We found it while driving through his parents' neighborhood. It was set back from the road by a long, U-shaped drive behind a high hemlock hedge. The wide front steps led to a deep porch and giant front door. As we got out of the car, I felt overwhelmed by the scale of the place. I couldn't imagine owning a house this big. It also seemed abandoned, with a pool table sitting in the middle of the living room. Apparently, the family that owned it had let their twentysomething son live there with his friends, and it showed. But looking beyond the disarray, I could tell it was a stunning house, unlike any I'd ever seen before.

When we peered through the windows at the high ceilings, plaster crown moldings, and impressive marble mantelpieces, the rooms looked like a movie set. "Let's have the realtor show us the inside," Hunter said with his infectious grin.

Later that same day, we walked through the ten-thousand-square-foot house with its six fireplaces, and Hunter pointed out which bedroom would be ours. There was that certainty again. He wasn't nervous about the price. Just excited. We could definitely afford it, he told me. The financial adviser was being overly conservative. Standing on the porch, I wanted to comfort myself with Hunter's certainty. Why should I be worried about the money if he wasn't?

The biggest selling point for me, though, was that the house was big enough for my cousin Amy to move in with us. When we were little, Amy and I had always dreamed of living together, and now maybe it could actually happen. I could easily set aside all my other worries if it meant I could have her here with me. Amy and I had grown up like sisters. To this day, we can still do a mean rendition of our childhood talent show performance of "Me and My Shadow." As much as I looked up to her, I knew she looked up to me too. Our strengths and weaknesses complemented each other's. Amy was thoughtful, methodical, artistic, and wry. She was also shy and nonconfrontational, so from the time we were kids, I was her protector.

Amy had just broken up with her boyfriend of many years and was looking for a change. She'd been out to visit us regularly since we'd married, and she already knew Hunter's family and friends almost as well as I did. When I pitched her the idea of moving in, she barely took a day to say yes. She was working as an interior designer for hotels across the country, so she could work from anywhere. I promised her not only the adjoining guest cottage but an office on the third floor of the house. The thought of having Amy with me made everything better.

Hunter and I bought the house on Centre Road and lived out of boxes while plaster dust coated everything. I learned how to rewire light fixtures and replace broken ones, and Hunter laid tile on the bathroom floor and walls. Every room had something that needed to be fixed, and I'd drag Naomi around the house with me, moving from one project to another. A few months in, Joe discovered me crying in the laundry room as I tried to paint the ceiling. Every time I moved my roller, plaster chips rained down on my head. Naomi sat at my feet picking up the plaster pieces and playing with them.

"*Please* don't put those in your mouth," I said. She was still covered in paint from yesterday's porch project. Hunter's dad stepped into the room and surveyed the two of us. He took the roller out of my hand and leaned it against the wall. Taking me by the hand, he walked Naomi and me outside to the front steps.

"I'm going to get you a flight to see your family tomorrow morning," he said. "Pack a bag for you and Naomi. I'll take care of this." It wasn't the first, or the last, time Joe stepped in to help.

Naomi and I flew to Chicago the next day. Being back home with my family always made me feel better. My mom and I went out with her sisters and my girl cousins, talking nonstop and passing Naomi from one person to another. While I was gone, Hunter, Beau, and Joe finished our bathroom and closets and put away all of our clothes. Soon Beau moved into the third floor while Amy and our friend David moved into the attached two-bedroom coach house. David was one of Hunter's and Beau's oldest friends, having grown up with them in Wilmington. He had a quick wit and a dry sense of humor. Amy and I both thought of David as part of the Biden family and loved his company.

My life with Hunter had gone from our quiet family of three to nightly dinners that felt like a party. Naomi had all of us at her beck and call and acted as the house mascot. Amy became my co-parent, cooking pasta feasts and setting the long oval dining table to squeeze in as many friends as possible. When we celebrated Naomi's fourth birthday, she sat at the head of the table surrounded by our friends, all wearing paper crowns.

Most weekends, the house was filled with friends who often slept over. We'd crowd into the room where we kept the stereo and dance late into the night, Naomi in the center of things, dancing away. I'd often wake in the morning to find bodies sleeping under coats on the couch and curled on the Adirondack chairs outside. Life in Delaware was often one big party, but it never felt out of control, and I loved those weekends. It was my house. My new extended family. And I wore my new nickname proudly: Mama Bear.

This time, when Hunter and I decided we wanted to have another baby, the pregnancy didn't sideline me. I had Amy with me this time around, and we became partners in all things. I'd act as her assistant when she was putting together design proposals, and she'd help me with Naomi and the house. Amy, Naomi, and I spent hours every day gardening and working on the house, me in a giant sun hat and bikini, my pregnant belly popping. One night in September 1998, while we all sat around the living room after dinner, I felt my first contraction. With a mixture of excitement and trepidation, I sat on the couch holding Amy's hand while Hunter started timing the pains.

Look at me, I thought, *I'm killing it. The pain isn't so bad at all. I won't even need any drugs.* When the contractions started coming closer together, we drove to the hospital, where the doctor delicately told us I was still a long way off. "Go home and get some sleep," he said.

A few hours later, when a contraction really hit, I sat in bed crying and rocking my body until it passed. I took off all my clothes and paced the room. When the sun finally came up, we headed back to the hospital. Finnegan James Biden was born with Amy holding one of my legs and Hunter hold-ing the other.

Unlike the quiet home that we had brought newborn Naomi back to, Finnegan had five adults in the house, and often more, to pass her around. Music was always playing, and friends came in and out of the unlocked front door. Finnegan also had a four-year-old sister who thought she was the perfect toy. While Amy and I gardened and worked on the yard, Naomi would sit on a blanket with Finnegan, playing with her as if she were a little doll.

Romance was in the air at our house on Centre Road. Amy had begun dating one of Beau's and Hunter's closest friends, Chris, and after a year, he asked her to marry him. Chris had grown up on Long Island, New York, and had the quintessen-tial accent along with an irreverent sense of humor. With a slight frame, curly blond hair, and a St. Christopher's medal always hanging around his neck, he seemed more like the kids we grew up with than the rest of the East Coast crew. Eventu-ally, Beau would go on to marry his girlfriend, Hallie, whom he'd begun dating while we lived on Centre Road, and David would marry his girlfriend at the time as well.

Living in Delaware allowed me to spend time with Hun-ter's family in an entirely new way, and now Joe and I talked about the work we were doing on our respective houses. I often wore my tool belt from morning until night. Joe and I spent equal time at Home Depot, and we had a shared work ethic.

With Jill, I was finally able to be the host instead of the nervous guest. And when we held a Christmas party the first year on Centre Road, I felt a whole new sense of satisfaction when all the Bidens arrived as guests in our home.

Slowly I stopped feeling like an outsider. I was Kathleen Biden, Hunter's wife and the mother of Naomi and Finnegan Biden. I'd let go of my anger about our living on the East Coast and was consumed with taking care of the girls. I no longer made excuses about not working outside the home. I was finally feeling that I had a real identity. The problem was that that identity was becoming more and more linked to who I was married to and less about me.

Hunter and I often told each other "I love you" a dozen times a day. When I was growing up, my family didn't say that to one another very often. I felt completely loved as a child, we just weren't effusive. As I started picking up the manners of the Bidens, I began to notice the difference. When I'd tell my mom I loved her, she'd answer, "I know you do." I asked her why she always said that back to me, and she told me that when her own mother had died, she worried that her mother might not have known how much she loved her. My mom wanted to assure me that she knew about my love, that she knew what she meant to me. When my own girls were old enough to be ornery, I would pass along the same sentiment: "I know you still love me."

With Hunter, I heard it every day and with flourish. *I love you more than anything. I can't live without you. You are the most important person in my life.* I'd never felt loved like that before. I'd never felt needed like that by anyone. Hunter's love gave me power.

I look back at it now and wonder about this love of ours—

built partly on the premise that we, and we alone, uniquely *needed* each other. From the beginning, needing each other became part of the language of our love, and soon my sense of value and self-worth came almost entirely from that need.

Despite my deep belief in our love, after Finnegan was born, I didn't turn to Hunter in the same way that I did with Naomi. He was working full-time, leaving the house in the early morning and not returning until dinner or later. Parenting became my full responsibility. When he was home, he was very much a part of our life, but I no longer depended on his help in the same way.

I also quickly learned that I wasn't as wonderful a parent as I had thought. This new baby didn't possess Naomi's easy disposition. Finnegan didn't nurse as easily. And the only way to get her to sleep during her first six months was in a car seat on the floor next to our bed. Lying on my stomach, I'd reach my hand out to rock her. Around this time, Naomi stopped sleeping through the night as well and began coming into our room.

While I adjusted to having two kids, I still wanted to be a good wife, which felt as important to me as being a good mother. Growing up, I'd watched my own mother take care of my father. Even after she went back to graduate school and began her own career, she did his laundry, cleaned the house, fried his eggs, and buttered his toast. I always sensed she was happy to do it. I wanted to take care of Hunter the way I'd seen my mom take care of my dad.

I also abdicated financial responsibility to Hunter, who was much more ambitious and interested in it than I was. I kept my responsibilities squarely in the domestic arena, not wanting to carry the burden of keeping a budget. For the next fifteen years, I'd leave every financial decision to Hunter, trusting his judgment and in many cases ignoring warning signs that we were in over our heads.

By the spring of 1999, Hunter had decided that he didn't want to stay at the bank. He wanted to go to D.C. and work at the Department of Commerce. I jumped at the idea. Amy was moving to New York City with Chris, and I was ready to be back in a city. We ended our time on Centre Road by hosting Amy and Chris's wedding, which felt like the perfect send-off. Weeks later, our group would disband and say goodbye to the nightly parties and start being official grown-ups. But the night of Amy and Chris's wedding, we danced on the front lawn until dawn.

When the band played "My Kind of Town," Amy and I draped our arms around each other and belted out "Chicago is my kind of town!" The idea that she was marrying one of Hunter's best friends felt like a dream come true.

At one point, I ran into the house and grabbed the trumpet case I hadn't opened since 1987. I returned to the tent and asked the band if they knew "The Rose," the only song I could remember how to play. Then I stood onstage and poured my heart into my old trumpet.

Mom later told me that while everyone stood watching my trumpet playing, Beau leaned over to her. "Does she ever scare you?" he said. "She scares *me*." I can imagine his body tensing as he saw me climb onto the stage. He'd never do something so silly—nor would his brother. But that was the real me on-stage, the one who wanted to play the trumpet in my brides-maid's dress until dawn. I think I've been searching for her on and off my whole life, that girl who doesn't care what people think. That girl with her trumpet, at home in her own skin.

SEVEN

NEED

I n the summer of 1999, Hunter got the job in the Department of Commerce, and after three years of a full house, I was ready for a quieter life. We found a little place in northwest D.C., in a neighborhood filled with young families.

Naomi started kindergarten at Sidwell Friends School in the fall, which proved to be another introduction into a world I didn't know. Early on, while we were standing and watching a school recital, a woman knocked me back down into my seat as she pushed by me to get to my father-in-law. I laughed as I heard her call out to him, "Joe, it's me," as if they were old friends. When she realized that Joe was with me, she looked at me with a smile. *Lady,* I thought, *you literally just knocked me over.* Later that day, I received an email invitation for a party at her house. This was Washington, D.C., networking, and the Sidwell Friends community was fully wired.

That Christmas, as we did every year, we took the girls to my parents' lake house in Indiana. Owning a second home was not common in our Chicago neighborhood, but my parents had always been frugal with their money and they considered the lake house an investment as much as a vacation home. When I was growing up, this house is where we spent every holiday. Not once did my parents take all four of us on a plane or even on a road trip. This house was always the destination.

My parents' cottage was the heart of my family, with cousins and aunts and uncles and grandparents coming and going. The house sits at the top of a narrow road on a shallow half lot, with barely space to park a car, so you have to be careful not to dent the house's painted-blue aluminum siding or run over the gutter hose that drains into the street.

Built in the twenties, it has an off-kilter charm. The wooden floors creak, and none of the doors close properly. If there's a theme to the house, it would be hooks, which my mother puts everywhere. Hooks for beach hats, beach towels, bath towels, clothes, flyswatters, necklaces, and toothbrushes (twenty of those). Taped in the bathroom next to the toothbrush hooks is a handwritten index card matching every family member to their brush. I'm #13.

The kitchen is itty-bitty but open all hours of the day and filled with notes taped to the fridge, walls, and cabinets. Most of the messages are about waffles, because waffles are my mom's specialty, and they are often written by the grandchildren: "Dearest Grandma, we know how hard you work, but if you are able to make waffles, we would be so grateful." There's a small pantry with a second fridge that has a different note on it: "Do not drink Grandma's last Diet Coke." Between me and my three brothers, there are eleven grandchil-

dren, so when we're all together at the lake house, it's a cacophony of noise, and with as many as twenty of us jammed
in, the dishes never stop.

Sleeping arrangements sometimes required detailed charts,
and regardless of the plan, a kid or two always ended up
asleep on the couch. Most everyone slept in the loft, accessed
through a narrow stairway off the dining room. It had a
pitched ceiling, and seven beds and a few cribs were tucked
under the eaves. Only in the center of the room could you
stand straight up. Many a morning a groan has been heard as
someone gets out of bed and forgets that the ceiling is just a
few feet above their bed. Hunter and I secured the back room
of the attic early on, by growing our family faster than my
brothers.

When my brothers, cousins, and I started having our own
families, we chose Christmas at the lake as the time for us to
be together. As the years went on and our families grew, we'd
continue to squeeze into my parents' little lake house. During
Christmas of 1999, with about thirty people spread throughout the living and dining rooms, Hunter and I slipped into the
bathroom together. I'd asked him to sneak out to the drug-
store earlier for a pregnancy test. By this point, I recognized
the changes in my body and felt certain I was expecting.

Now Hunter sat on the edge of the tub as we both stared
at the positive stick. We could hear Finnegan, just over a year
old, yelling in the next room. I felt overwhelmed. "Hunter,
Finnegan is still in diapers."

"It's going to be great. You're a great mother," he said,
rubbing my leg.

People kept knocking on the door, and I yelled, "I'm still in here. Stop knocking and go downstairs." When we finally walked out of the bathroom, all eyes were on us. "No," I wanted to say, "we were not having sex." I wasn't ready to tell the kids yet, so instead, I spelled "I'm P-R-E-G-N-A-N-T" in a stage whisper. I watched Hunter wrap his arm around my mom's shoulder as they both started laughing. They knew pregnant Kathy wasn't always easy to deal with.

I went into the kitchen and dialed Amy on the landline. She had moved to New York and hadn't made it home this Christmas because she was pregnant and due in a month. "I'm pregnant again," I said when she answered. "I just took the test. I'm in shock."

"Kathy!" Amy yelled. "That is the best news! Our babies are going to grow up together!"

"It has to be another girl," I told her. I loved my mother's tight relationship with her two sisters, and I wanted that for my daughters. "Oh my God. I'm going to have three kids."

That next morning, I sat in the kitchen watching the little cousins sitting on the floor patiently waiting for waffles. One by one, Mom handed them a plate to take into the dining room. My sister-in-law Michele came in and joined me at the enamel table that sat underneath the kitchen windows. She and my brother Johnny had started dating in high school, so she felt like a sister to me. She had two babies under two and knew what was in store for me. "Naomi is never going to be on time for school once this baby is born," I told her. "I'm already dropping her off late all the time."

"Listen, Kathleen," Michele laughed, "you're lucky you had one easy baby with Naomi. Brendan and Ryan are both up at the crack of dawn. Once the baby comes, you'll just find a way." Michele never seemed rattled or overwhelmed. She came from a big Irish family and, like me, had three brothers. I've always thought that if you are the only girl, you are either the princess or the housekeeper. Michele and I both came out of the housekeeper mold. Our mothers depended on us more than on our brothers and it left us both with a hardworking, practical outlook. Of course I'd be fine with three kids. I knew that. But sitting in the kitchen, staring at Finnegan sticking her finger in her cousin's ear, I just saw years of poopy diapers and sticky hands ahead of me.

We'd only just moved to D.C. a few months earlier and I was still trying to get my footing with Naomi in school. I hadn't made any friends of my own yet, and the Sidwell parent community was intimidating. With a third baby, I imagined it would be even more difficult. How would I do it all?

In August 2000, nine months pregnant and feeling like a whale, I went in for a checkup and was gently told by the doctor that the baby was a long way from being born. "I'm carrying this baby between my knees," I said. "Seriously, I feel like the baby is going to slip out. Please don't tell me that I'm not even close."

"Well," he said, "honestly, your baby is really big. I suggest we schedule a C-section. Regardless of your vaginal birth with Finnegan, there's a risk if the baby is too big." I hadn't wanted another C-section, but I also wanted this baby born. "When could you do it?" I asked.

"As early as tomorrow," he answered.

"Yes!" I screamed. "Yes, please! Tomorrow. We'll have the

baby tomorrow!" I decided that maybe if I had another C-section in the very same hospital where I'd had the C-section for Naomi, this new baby would have her disposition, too.

Hunter and I were so excited that when we left the doctor's office that day, we got on the beltway heading in the wrong direction before making it home. It was perfect timing, because Amy, her new baby, Celia, and Amy's mother, Noreen, were visiting that week. Amy had been at Finnegan's birth, and now she'd be here for this new baby. I'd been with her for Celia's birth as well.

I barely slept that night, and when I woke up, Amy set my hair in rollers. I was going to celebrate this birth with my hair done right. With a headful of curls, I headed to the hospital, holding Hunter's hand.

When the doctor handed us our third daughter, I felt the same overwhelming joy as when Naomi and Finnegan were put in my arms. Three daughters. Just like my mom and her sisters. We named her Roberta Mabel Biden—Roberta after my mother, and Mabel after Jill's grandmother. I wanted to call her Birdie for short, but Jill asked if she could call her Maisy, and after a few weeks of confused Birdies and Maisies, Maisy was what stuck.

Once she was born, parenting felt more all-consuming than ever. But now I felt comfortable in my role as a full-time mother. Surely three young girls needed my full attention, and I wanted to get it right.

For two weeks after Maisy was born, I sat in an oversized green velvet chair and held her. Because of my C-section, I had to restrict my movements, and I wanted to be sure Maisy latched on and that I could nurse. But at her first pediatrician visit, the doctor told me that she'd lost weight. "You either have to supplement with formula or try pumping. She can't afford to lose any more weight," he'd said, and I'd cried.

"I'll get a pump. She'll gain weight. I promise." For the next month, you couldn't talk to me about anything other than nursing. I nursed and pumped continuously until Maisy's weight looked good and my milk supply was strong. She would be my last child and I wanted to get it right. After Maisy's C-section, I'd had my tubes tied.

For his job at the Department of Commerce, Hunter was traveling all over the world. When he was away, he'd call and say how much he missed us. I think he felt guilty leaving and I missed him, but I liked my life. I liked taking care of the house, the kids, and Hunter. Like my mom, I was always moving, and I felt better when I was productive. I also looked to my mom's late-in-life career and felt that I had time too. She had received her doctorate at fifty. In my mind, there was another chapter for me after I got my three girls through high school and launched to college. But first, eighteen years of parenting lay ahead for me.

My dad had worked seven days a week, and in some ways, he wasn't really present when we were young. So I didn't see anything unusual about Hunter's absence. In fact, he was more involved than my dad had been when I was little. When Hunter was home, the kids hung on him and wanted his constant attention, which he gave in a way that I wasn't able to do. I couldn't sit still, while he could let the girls paint his toenails and put a dozen barrettes in his hair.

The dependency we developed over time—this very specific part of our love story—was a need that ended up carry-

ing a very different meaning for each of us. Hunter's need was
emotional. He told me he needed me to be happy. My need
was emotional but also literal. I needed him to support me.
Hunter often said, *I can't live without you* and *I don't want to
be away from you*. When he said these things, I believed him.
I believed we needed each other in order to be happy. What I
never acknowledged then was that I also believed I needed
him to survive.

EIGHT

QUITTING

During a visit to Delaware in the fall of 2001, Hunter and I left the girls with his parents one night and drove through the lush countryside around their house. We could have been in the south of France, the way that the roads curved and the hills undulated past the sprawling estates, all bordered by beautiful old stone walls. Hunter had just left the Department of Commerce and had taken a job as a partner at a lobbying firm. He was working long hours and traveling as he built his business, so time alone together was rare. Our home life felt completely child-focused, so by the time we got them to bed, we were often exhausted.

Driving through Delaware that day, Hunter and I talked about the strain his family was feeling. At the time, Hunter's paternal grandfather was dying, and Mom Mom was struggling to take care of him on her own. Joe was also running for reelection to the Senate. But, most important, Beau had just returned ill from Kosovo, where he had been working for the

Department of Justice. Beau was in constant, mysterious pain. He could barely walk and was seeing doctors everywhere to figure out what was happening.

"I feel helpless," Hunter said as we drove that day. "I wish we lived closer so I could be there for Beau."

"Let's do it," I said. "Let's move back." It was a rash decision, but it came easily. I hadn't made any close friends in D.C. yet, and Delaware had come to feel like home to me too. After eight years of marriage, Hunter's family was my family. Hunter took my hand and kissed it. "Just think of the house we could afford here," he said, smiling.

We found an old stone Tudor just down the road from his parents, and bought it on the spot. By the time we settled into our new house, Beau had made a full recovery and was excited to get back to work and a normal life. He'd been treated for what was believed to be an infection. He'd been dating Hallie now since 1997, and over Thanksgiving of 2001, on the island of Nantucket, he asked her to marry him. A year later, they'd marry on Nantucket in a little Catholic church.

Hallie had grown up in Wilmington and had known Beau and Hunter her entire life. She and I had very different personalities, but we made an effort to be close. She was strong-willed and opinionated, and I admired her ability to get what she wanted. As the years went by, she would become a trusted friend, someone I turned to often when I worried about Hunter.

When we made the decision to move, we didn't consider what the commute to Washington would be like for Hunter. His dad had been doing it for thirty years. But once we moved, I felt Hunter's absence deeply. Though we were surrounded by family in Delaware, I felt lonely. Except for Mom Mom, everyone worked, and I missed being able to walk to the park with the kids. Now my days were spent shuttling Naomi to Wilmington Friends and sitting in Mom Mom's sunroom with the girls.

Working two hours away in D.C., Hunter either spent the night there or came home late. In the past, Hunter and I had talked on the phone throughout the day. Now whole days could go by without my talking to him. It felt as though we were living two very different lives. But more upsetting, I recognized for the first time that Hunter's drinking could be a problem.

Before this time, I'd never noticed him drinking more than any of his friends. I didn't see him drunk. Now I watched his drinking spiral from social to problematic. One Saturday morning when we had friends visiting for the weekend, Hunter walked into the kitchen looking as if he hadn't gone to sleep. I was making pancakes as I watched him pull a bottle of Jack Daniel's out of the cabinet. "Hunter! What are you doing?" I said. "It's ten A.M.!" I don't think he knew what time it was, and he still seemed drunk. He laughed and put the bottle back. We all stared, speechless and uncomfortable, as he walked out of the room.

"Pancakes are ready," I announced.

In fact, I don't know if his drinking had steadily increased or if it just stood in stark contrast to our home life now. Back when we lived on Centre Road, our house was the party house; now we were living a quiet life, just the five of us. Watching how much he could consume scared me. I'd never focused on his drinking before. Now I'd see him refill his Jack and Coke over and over again.

I had the impression that Hunter's drinking worried Beau too, but we didn't talk about it, maybe because neither of us wanted to admit what was happening. I always felt better when Hunter was with Beau because I believed Beau kept him in check. But when Hunter stayed over in D.C., he was almost certain to come back to Delaware exhausted and hung over.

I resigned myself to the fact that this might now simply be the reality of our marriage. My childhood friend Patty's dad, Mr. O'Neill, used to drink continuously when he came home, often passing out in his recliner, and Patty's mom patiently tolerated it. He was loved by his whole family; he just wasn't as present. I wondered if I would simply have to tolerate that kind of marriage too.

One Saturday in the spring of 2002, I went to New York City to see *The Producers* with Amy. After the show we walked to one of our favorite restaurants, Balthazar. We sat at the bar of the crowded restaurant and ordered drinks, dressed head to toe in black, trying our best to seem hip. Amy had her elbow on the bar as she sipped her martini. "Stay over," she said. "We'll wake up and go to the flea market. Stay!" Time together kept us sane, as we were both spending most of our days chasing kids. "That is a brilliant idea," I said, and pulled out my phone and called Hunter to ask him.

"Sure," he answered. "Fine with me."

I gave Amy the thumbs-up and told Hunter that Naomi needed to get to Sunday school by nine the next morning.

"No," he said, less defiant than simply stating a fact. "I'm not going to do that, Kathleen. I'm not getting up and taking her to Sunday school." It was a declaration.

Amy sat next to me at the bar, still smiling. "Hunter, she can't miss," I said, with a sinking feeling. I didn't know what else to say.

"I'm not going to do it," he answered calmly.

I hung up and looked at Amy, smiling. "Let's have dinner. I'll figure out what to do when we get to your apartment." I tried to push away the nervous feeling in my stomach. Could I actually not count on my husband to do this simple thing?

I didn't tell Amy what Hunter had said. I didn't want her to think badly of him. But I felt a deep sadness as I sat next to Amy, my excitement about staying with her gone.

When we got to the apartment, we stayed up late talking, and around midnight, I told her I'd actually feel better if I went home. She didn't push me or ask me why. Penn Station was empty when I boarded the 3:00 A.M. train back to Wilmington and took a taxi home.

I found the entire house lit up, and when I opened the front door, I saw Hunter sitting in front of our fireplace with a group of friends. They were shocked to see me. It was five o'clock by now, and they were all drunk.

I headed straight upstairs, and Hunter followed me to our bedroom, while the rest of the men continued to sit in front of the fire, drinking and smoking.

"What are you doing? Why did you come home?" he asked.

"You told me you wouldn't take Naomi to Sunday school. She can't miss," I said. "Where are the girls?"

"They're at my parents'. Kathleen, I would have taken her. I was just kidding. I can't believe you took the train home in the middle of the night." He was kneeling by the bed, stroking my head, but I could smell the alcohol and cigarettes on him. I wanted him out of the room. "Let me sleep," I said, not hiding my irritation. "I have to get up in a few hours."

When I went to bed that night, I knew I couldn't ignore Hunter's drinking. He was a grown man with three children and yet he stayed up all night drinking.

But for some reason, I didn't say anything to him then. I simply rolled over and closed my eyes. A few hours later, I woke to Hunter asleep next to me as I climbed out of bed to take Naomi to Sunday school.

For the first time, I didn't trust my husband. I didn't believe he had to stay over in D.C. as often as he did, and his constant late-night meetings made me suspicious. He'd often blame his sour mood on work, but to me it looked more like a hangover. There was a dark cloud over our marriage, and yet neither of us was addressing it, although we were both feeling it.

Finally, in the winter of 2003, when we'd been in Delaware barely a year, I spoke up. "Hunter, I'm not happy," I said out of the blue. His response surprised me. "I thought I'd be able to commute, but it's harder than I thought," he said. He didn't mention the drinking, but, I thought, if we could move back to D.C., maybe things could return to the way they were.

"I think we should move back to D.C.," I said with conviction. Hunter agreed, but I knew the logistics of the move would fall on me. As long as he was okay with our moving back, I set myself firmly on course to make it happen.

Throughout the spring, I worked to sell the house we'd just fixed up and enroll the girls in school back in D.C., working with a dogged sense of purpose. This move felt like a reclaiming of the life we had before. But as the summer approached, Hunter's drinking was an open strain on him that he could no longer hide. He'd gone on a business trip to New York City, and I'd received a worried call from a friend of his. Hunter had gone on a bender and someone needed to pick him up and bring him home. When he arrived, he looked as if he hadn't slept in days. "Hunter," I said, "what are we going to do?" He walked past me silently and went up to bed. I don't think he was sober enough to have a conversation.

Right before the girls and I left to spend the summer in Indiana as we always did, Hunter came to me with an earnest look on his face. "I'm going to stop drinking," he said. "I know it's become a problem and I'm going to fix it. I promise." He didn't say he was an alcoholic or that any particular thing had happened to make him quit. But I felt a flood of relief.

"I'm proud of you," I said, putting my arms around him. Finally, the unspoken weight of his drinking was lifted. He, not I, was bringing the problem out of the dark and into the light. Looking back, I wonder how long it would have taken for me to say something. We didn't talk about what led him to quit or how it was affecting our family, and I'm not sure why. Maybe my relief at his quitting left me wary of dredging up the bad stuff. If he was going to stop, what was the point of telling him how hard it had been for me? Now I could just be hopeful about our future. His father had never taken a drink. Both of his paternal uncles had quit, and Beau had stopped drinking after we decamped from Centre Road, so it made sense that Hunter could stop too, if he wanted to.

NINE

AND DID YOU GET
WHAT YOU WANTED FROM
THIS LIFE, EVEN SO?

When I arrived in Indiana for the summer, my brother Jimmy was already there with his wife and two daughters. He was a competitive triathlete who was in constant training mode, often doing fifty-mile bike rides around the lake, swims that went on for miles, and epic runs along the wooded roads.

A few days after I arrived, he and I walked our five girls the two miles down the road to a little zoo that sat high on a series of sand dunes. The girls squealed as they stuck their hands through the wooden fence to pet the goats. As we began our walk home, Jimmy said to everyone, "Come on, let's jog the rest of the way!" I hadn't so much as done a jumping jack in years, and I knew I wouldn't get far running and pushing Maisy in her stroller, but I started jogging behind him, looking out for cars on the narrow road. After a few minutes of huffing and puffing, I stopped and told Jimmy to go ahead with the kids. He seemed genuinely surprised. "You look fit, but you're in terrible shape," my painfully honest brother said with a laugh.

"Thanks, Jimmy. So kind," I said. "Maisy and I will see you back at the house." When I walked into the house later carrying Maisy, Jimmy came at me before the door closed behind my back. "Let me take you back outside for a run. I want to see what your heart rate looks like," he said, holding the belt he wore to track his runs.

"Okay. I will give you five minutes," I said, indulging him, if only to shut him up.

During that last year and a half in Delaware, I'd felt a daily exhaustion that flattened me. Between caring for the three girls and worrying about Hunter's drinking, I was barely holding on until I could climb into bed at night. But as I put on an old pair of sneakers I found in a closet, I thought, *Who knows, maybe I could be a runner.* Jimmy put the monitor on his wrist and told me to put the band around my chest, near the center of my rib cage. Standing on Lake Shore Drive, he peered at the little monitor that looked like a watch.

"Okay, I've got your resting heart rate now. Start running slowly." I began moving, my feet feeling clumsy and my body awkward. Within minutes, I felt a sharp pain just under my ribs. I stopped and showed Jimmy where I was feeling pain.

"You just have to build up the muscle and get your heart in shape. The pain will go away. I promise. Once you move past the cramping, it gets easier. We need to get you to three miles."

"It will never happen," I panted. The sun was warmer now, and I was hot and achy. I stared at other runners as they passed by me and studied their gait. Jimmy jogged so easily beside me, as if he were walking.

"Wow, Kathy, you really are in bad shape," Jimmy said, staring at his wristband. "But you're going to start feeling the endorphins, and then you'll be hooked. There's no going back once you're hooked." I stared at him as if he'd lost his mind. But after that first afternoon, Jimmy and I began to hit Lake Shore Drive every day. And Jimmy was right—the pain eventually went away. As my runs grew longer, I started to actually sweat, and I realized that I'd never sweated during a workout before. I felt proud that my shirt was soaked through.

I felt physically strong for the first time in my life. I'd stay in my running clothes for hours after, walking around the house talking about my heart rate ad nauseam. Now, when I drove the girls to the summer camp down the road, I slowed to watch other runners and studied the ones that moved like gazelles. I wanted to be a gazelle too.

In the years to come, running would often be the only thing that allowed me to feel confident at all. It gave me some small reprieve. Over time, my body grew fitter and stronger, as if it understood something that my mind was unwilling to see: that soon I'd need all the strength I could muster and more.

Hunter was commuting between the lake and work in D.C. that summer. When I saw him, he seemed withdrawn. He said he was sober, but I had no real understanding of how hard it would be for him. In fact, I imagined he'd quit as easily as my dad had.

Growing up, I always knew my father didn't drink, and when I was much older I learned that he had woken up with a bad hangover one morning and decided to quit forever. His abstinence was simply how he lived, and we never talked about it. I imagined Hunter would do the same, and I took his new sobriety as fact. When we were all on the beach with the kids, he took them into the water and played with them for hours. I could see our life slowly returning to normal.

Then one weekend he and I drove to Chicago for a high school friend's backyard wedding. Hunter went to the bar and came back with a drink that looked like Coke. Since he'd announced he'd quit, we hadn't done anything social. As I watched him take a drink, something about his behavior made me suspicious, and I reached for the glass. "Can I have a sip?" The minute the liquid hit my tongue, I could taste the whiskey. "Hunter, this has alcohol in it," I said with a stone in the pit of my stomach.

"Kathleen, I asked for a Coke." He looked irritated at me. "Everyone here is drinking, and I'm sure the bartender just assumed I wanted a drink too. Obviously I didn't *order* it." He took the glass back and angrily went to the bar.

I didn't say another word to him about it. I don't even know what caused me to take the drink out of his hand in the first place, but my action seemed to cross a line. Yet once again something kept me from talking to him about it. We didn't discuss things that bothered us about each other.

From the very beginning of our marriage, we had set up a structure that allowed both of us to do what we wanted to do. When we lived in New Haven, I read my book at the Indian restaurant while he went to the bar and wrote. My parents had lived their lives together respecting each other's independence, and I followed their lead. But how could Hunter and I possibly be as close as I imagined and not talk openly about this massive problem that had developed in our lives?

In my lonely moments, I still worried that I might end up like Patty's mother. Mrs. O'Neill had soldiered on, carrying her husband's alcoholism quietly, never pushing back. Hunter might not have been drinking six-packs in a recliner, but I knew something was wrong.

And yet I kept my worries buried, not wanting to disrupt the narrative of our love story. He and I still savored telling people how we'd met for the first time in the Jesuit Volunteer Corps and fallen in love. We were the first of our friends to start a family, and people seemed to look to us for a road map, which gave me a sense of purpose. Given all this, I didn't want to admit that something was wrong.

Our tenth wedding anniversary fell a few days later. We'd decided to stay at the lake and go out to dinner with Amy and Chris. I walked down to the beach to find Hunter facing the water reading. He always had a book in his hand. It was one of the things we had in common when we first met. But now the books often felt like a shield.

I'd bought him a stack of poetry books for this anniversary, and I'd inscribed one of them with a line from the Raymond Carver poem we both loved.

> And did you get what you wanted
> from this life, even so?

There was so much left unsaid as we sat next to each other, the books piled between us in the sand. He wanted to know what was wrong, and to me it was painfully obvious. I wanted my husband back. Yet we sat there silently, my gifts to him not having the impact I'd hoped for. When I started to cry, he was surprised by my emotion.

"I love you, Kathleen," he said. "What's wrong?"

"I'm just emotional remembering when we used to read poetry to each other," I said, still crying, not mentioning my true worries. When we lived in Portland, we'd read Raymond Carver's poems, and those of his wife, Tess Gallagher, aloud to each other.

"That's all," I added, not wanting to say I felt lonely. Not wanting to say I was scared.

TEN

CROSSROADS

When we left the lake that summer, we moved into a rental house in D.C. and enrolled all three girls in school. I wanted D.C. to become a place about which the kids could say "I grew up there," just as the South Side of Chicago was for me. Over the last four years, we'd lived in three different homes. I had such a strong sense of being grounded in a place from my childhood, and I knew Hunter did too. I wanted that for our girls. I wanted them to feel that sense of security.

The house we rented was a center-hall colonial that sat up on a little hill on the corner of a block filled with young families. I envisioned this new chapter as building a life in which Hunter and I had a routine with dinners together every night, followed by family walks. But days after we'd moved into the new house, Hunter's façade of sobriety fell away.

I woke up early and realized Hunter hadn't come to bed at

all. He'd gone to the movies the night before with a friend. As I got out of bed, I could hear him in the kitchen.

I walked downstairs, the pale early light coming through the picture window in the living room. Stacks of unpacked boxes stood next to the couch. The house had a small kitchen in the back with a linoleum floor and Formica counter. I could hear Hunter moving around in there. Turning in to the doorway, I found him leaning against the counter, drunk.

Hunter had held firm to the claim that he hadn't been drinking all summer, despite the drink I'd found him with at my friend's wedding, and we carried on as if his sobriety wasn't in question. Now I stood in our kitchen doorway, watching him sway back and forth. His bloodshot eyes indicated he'd been up all night, and he looked disheveled in jeans and a T-shirt. I could no longer hold back.

"I can't take it anymore," I said. I didn't know what I wanted from him in that moment. I just knew that I was too tired to keep up the charade. "You have to stop." I expected an explosion from him, but he just looked defeated. "I need help," he said, with drunken earnestness. "I know I have to stop drinking. I'm sorry, Kathleen." I had a shaky feeling, seeing my husband look so vulnerable. I'd never seen this side of him before. The confidence and certainty that he always carried were gone.

I heard fear in his voice. Standing in our kitchen that morning, I began to understand the power alcohol had over him and that he was scared. I was scared too. The girls were still asleep upstairs as we stood staring at each other, not knowing what to do.

"I think I need to go to rehab," Hunter told me. "I'm going

to call Beau and figure it out. I promise, I want to get better. I want to be here for you and the girls." Hunter came over and put his arms around me. I held him tightly. I'd never seen him so exposed before, and it was obvious we were both scared.

"Call Beau," I said as I pulled away and stroked his cheek. "We'll figure something out."

Hunter went out to the screened-in porch off the living room to make the call. We were entering uncharted territory, but bringing Beau in meant I didn't have to figure it out.

As Hunter talked to Beau on the porch, I went upstairs to collect the laundry. I'd learned that from my mother: When in crisis, clean.

Beau came down to D.C. from Wilmington right away to help, and Hunter left that morning for a center called Crossroads, all the way in Antigua. I knew Hunter felt great shame and guilt that morning, but I wasn't angry with him. I was just fearful and tired. Very tired.

After he left, I went straight to work unpacking boxes. I didn't know what the next twenty-eight days would look like without Hunter, but I knew how to keep busy. I put on my Home Depot tool belt. There were a few weeks left before the girls started school, and I wanted the house "finished" by then.

When I'd emptied all the boxes, I set about hanging our artworks. We didn't own anything of real monetary value. Hunter and I liked to buy street art whenever we traveled. My favorite was a little painting that he'd bought me for my birthday the first year we were married: a man and a woman in a close embrace, rendered in bright colors with heavy acrylic brushstrokes.

The minute I started hammering nails into the walls, down came the girls, hungry for breakfast. Finnegan was smiling, with a mischievous look on her face, and wearing a nightgown so short it looked like a T-shirt. Finnegan's laughter came easily and frequently, often at the expense of her sisters. Maisy was right behind her, holding on to the giant stuffed neon fish she'd named Arnold. As they walked into the living room, Finnegan gave Maisy a nudge. Maisy took Arnold and hit Finnegan over the head, causing both girls to burst into laughter.

"Mom, did you buy cereal?" Finnegan asked.

Naomi was the last one down, in her oversized T-shirt, still half asleep, She gave me a pained look.

"Did you really need to start hammering this early? Seriously, Mom! You couldn't wait to hang the pictures?" She walked past me with an eye roll and went into the kitchen. She was going into fourth grade, and the age difference between her and her younger sisters seemed vast.

I smiled at the girls as they settled down at the dining table. "You're all going to help me unpack today, okay?" I told them. "After that we can do something fun in the afternoon." Then I set three bowls of cereal on the kitchen table.

Within seconds I heard Naomi say, "Maisy!" with revulsion. "Seriously! Can you please chew with your mouth closed?" This only caused Maisy to chew louder and laugh as milk spilled out of her mouth. Naomi took her bowl and moved to the other end of the table. I sat down next to her and put my arms around her. Her thick brown hair was falling out of her ponytail and covering her face. Her thick hair was our nemesis. It could take me an hour to blow-dry and straighten it, which we rarely did.

Hunter wasn't an early riser, so his absence that morning wasn't unusual. The girls were also accustomed to their dad being gone for work, but not for twenty-eight days. I told the girls their dad was traveling on business, and for twenty-eight days I maintained that lie to them.

When Hunter left that fall of 2003, he missed Maisy's third birthday and Finnegan's fifth birthday. He missed everyone's first day of school. My heart broke that he wasn't there, as much for him as for the girls. He was allowed to call home once a week, and each time he'd tell me what he was doing. He sounded engaged and committed to the program.

"Hunter!" I'd say excitedly, whenever he called. "We miss you so much! How are you? Tell me everything. What's it like?"

"I miss you and the girls so much," he said. I heard the earnestness in his voice. "It feels indulgent to be here, but I promise I am working hard. I'm waking up at five A.M. and working out every day. I know how difficult it's been for you, but I promise this is going to work. I can't wait to come home. I miss putting the girls to bed." I always tried to assuage his guilt. And I knew he was lonely, just like me.

"Please send letters," he said. "I wait for the mail every day."

I'd written him only once by then, and I felt guilty for not writing more. "I'm sorry. I'm just busy with the girls and the house. I promise I'll write more. I promise." But I didn't. While he was gone, I sent only a few letters, pushing thoughts of Hunter's rehab out of my mind during the day. I'd become adept at compartmentalizing.

Beau called me almost daily that month and was always optimistic about Hunter's recovery. This was a turning point in my relationship with Beau. I knew there was nothing I could say about Hunter to Beau that would make him love his brother less. Beau's empathy for Hunter was boundless, and I think it had everything to do with their having lost their mother and their sister when they were so young. In some crucial way, they were each other's partner. Of course, they had Joe and Jill, and Ashley, and many other loving and supportive Bidens, but at its essence, Hunter's soulmate was Beau, and Beau's was Hunter. Telling Beau how Hunter's drinking impacted our life didn't make him think less of his brother, and I felt enormous relief in being able to share those stories with someone.

To Beau I confided my fears about Hunter's business, started just a little over a year ago. How could his new lobbying work survive a twenty-eight-day absence? "Won't his clients be upset?" I asked, genuinely concerned.

"No. It's all good. Eric and I are making sure that business keeps moving. Do not worry. Eric is returning everyone's calls and emails." Eric had worked with Hunter at the Department of Commerce and they'd gone into business together. Eric was a great comfort to me, a steady, reliable, and trustworthy friend.

Halfway through the twenty-eight days, the girls started school. Naomi was going back to Sidwell and looking forward to seeing the friends she'd left when we moved to Delaware. Finnegan and Maisy were off to their very first day at preschool and were excited. This marked a milestone, and I felt sad that Hunter was missing it: the first day in ten years that all three girls were in school at the same time.

When I got home from dropping them off, the house was completely quiet. I hadn't been alone since before I could remember. As I put on my running shoes, I thought about Jimmy telling me that I'd get hooked. He was right. I put some headphones on, grabbed an old iPod of Hunter's, and started up Massachusetts Avenue.

The first song was Johnny Cash's "The Man Comes Around." Hunter loved Johnny Cash, and I had come to love him too. Then came Springsteen and Huffamoose. When "Distance" by Cake came on, I lengthened my strides and ran in rhythm with the lyrics: "He's going the distance, he's going for speed." Hunter was on my mind, and as I ran, memories of dancing in our Centre Road house, and images of Beau and Amy hovering over the CD player, fighting over which song to cue next, flooded my mind. The memory of Hunter doing his karate kick dance moves made me laugh out loud as I ran.

I thought about how Hunter was going to be okay, how our marriage was going to be okay. How my girls would get their father back and I would get my husband back. This became my mantra: "Hunter is going to be okay." I accepted it as truth.

ELEVEN

YOU CANNOT TELL ANYONE

O ther than Beau, I didn't talk to anyone about Hunter's going to Crossroads. When Hunter's parents called to check in, I never brought it up and neither did they. The same went for my parents. The hardest person to hide it from was Amy. It was easy enough for me to explain Hunter's absence at school events with excuses about work, but Amy was another story. She and I talked almost daily, but the conversations usually revolved around our kids. Somehow I was able to hold on to the secret that Hunter was in rehab for three weeks—until she and Chris came down with their kids to stay with us for Finnegan's birthday. She had only to look at my face to know something was wrong.

When the front door opened, her daughters, Celia and Clare, came running into the house in search of their cousins. Within minutes, the house was a cacophony of noise. Amy, pregnant with their third child, came in holding a portable crib. Her thick red hair was up in a knot, and she laughed when she saw me in my running clothes. "Look at you, you little runner!" she said as she dropped the crib and took me in a tight embrace.

Chris was behind her, holding a plastic laundry basket of children's clothes and toys. He was wearing a tracksuit, his gold St. Christopher medal around his neck. He could have passed for a twenty-year-old with his slim build. He dropped the basket with a flourish and opened his arms to me with a wide smile.

I hadn't prepared either Amy or Chris for the fact that Hunter wasn't home. "Where's Hunter?" Chris asked. They were both looking at me. I scrunched my nose and puckered my face as I stared back at them.

Amy is my fiercest defender, just as Beau was Hunter's. There's nothing I can't tell her. Amy's father died from AIDS when she was twenty-two, and for the two years leading up to his death she lived with him and took care of him—bathing him and administering his meds. He was diagnosed in 1982 and died in 1991. He was the head of human resources for a big international company, and his illness would remain a secret until his death. I saw how painful it had been for her to carry that secret, feeling shame when there was absolutely no reason for it. I know Amy always thought of me as stronger than she was, but to me, she was the strong one. I'd kept Hunter's secret from her because I didn't want to show a crack in my marriage, even to the person I'd shared every detail of my life with for decades. But I knew I could trust her; she understood the pain and shame of carrying hidden truths.

Chris and Amy followed me into the kitchen. Now I stood staring at them. "Hunter's gone to a twenty-eight-day rehab,"

I said quickly, wanting the news out. "You cannot tell any-one." By now, this caveat of mine automatically came after anything having to do with the Bidens. *You cannot tell any-one.* It was a refrain that would follow me for the next four-teen years. This refrain wasn't expressed to me by the Bidens. I recognized early on their protective approach to family and wanted to show my willingness to do the same.

"He's going to be okay, Kath," Chris said then, giving me a hug.

Amy came over and put her arms around me too. "We're here for you."

The three of us stood with our arms around one another, rocking back and forth. "I love you," I said to them. I felt ut-terly safe in that circle. They didn't show surprise or ask for details. They took my lead and just showed me support.

Amy went out and bought balloons for Finnegan's birth-day that she tied to the dining chairs at our old pine table. Amy could always make a room look beautiful. Celia and Clare came running in with Finnegan and Maisy chasing after them. They ran circles around the table as Naomi quietly walked in and slipped under Amy's arm, resting her head on Amy's shoulder. I looked at my family and felt hopeful.

That night, we sat around the table and toasted Hunter. "To Dad," I said, raising my glass. "We love you." "To Dad," the girls screamed as they knocked their glasses together. "To Uncle Hunter," Celia and Clare chimed in. Yes, I believed in my heart we were going to be okay.

When his twenty-eight days ended, a tan and fit Hunter showed up at our front door. Beau had picked him up from the airport and stood just behind him on the stoop, smiling. *My God, how I love him,* I thought as we held each other tightly.

"I missed you so much," he said into my ear.

I'd missed him while he'd been gone. But really I'd been missing him for a lot longer than twenty-eight days. The man holding me now was the man I thought I might have lost forever. Those nights in Delaware when he'd call to say he wasn't able to make it home, I'd crawl into bed and feel so alone, would lie there staring at the empty space where I wanted my husband to be. Those mornings when I'd wake up knowing that I didn't have a partner to help me get the girls up and ready for their day. Now I saw someone I thought would be there with me, next to me at night and there when I opened my eyes in the morning.

As the girls fought to get his attention, I put my arm around Beau and we both smiled broadly, taking in this sober and healthy version of Hunter. He could barely set his bag down and walk into the dining room with all three girls holding on to him.

Before his arrival, I worked to make the house look cozy. Fresh flowers centered on the dining table. Lighted candles. Dinner warming on the stove. I wanted everything in place. I wanted him to know how good his life was here at home, the life he'd been missing.

Now the girls fought over who got to sit next to him at the table. He put Maisy on his lap while Finnegan and Naomi pulled their chairs to either side of him. Beau turned to me and whispered in my ear, "He's back. Everything is going to be okay now. Everything is going to be great."

Hunter seemed more at peace that night than he'd ever been, and the girls never stopped talking to him while we ate. Hunter nodded and listened to each of them. Really listened. I kept staring at him, he looked so handsome. At times I caught myself holding my breath. This all seemed better than I could have hoped.

Hunter began to rebuild his life with a vengeance. He created a structure and routine for himself that I'd never seen before. He worked out every day, and he approached his business with focus and drive. Previously, he had talked about his work as a job. Now he talked about building his business with a new passion and purpose.

He went to his first AA meeting the night he returned, along with Beau. Soon Hunter ran the Sunday night AA meeting and started inviting some of his AA friends to the house for barbecues. He woke up early every morning with me and knew the girls' school schedule as well as I did. At night, he sat patiently with Naomi and helped her with her schoolwork.

Our marriage felt stronger than ever too, his affection and attention returning with a new sense of gratitude. It had been a long time since he'd shown his appreciation for me. Now he commented on everything. "Your mom is a great cook," he'd say to the girls when we sat down to dinner. "Kathleen, the house looks great," he'd say when he came home. His hands always found mine when we walked or sat watching TV.

Hunter was healthy and in control, so I didn't see the need

to understand anything more about his recovery. All I needed to know was that it involved daily workouts and AA meetings. I didn't need to go to Al-Anon. I didn't want to talk about the impact his drinking had had on me and our family. That was all in the past. Now that he was sober, we didn't have to revisit what we'd gone through. I didn't see the point in telling him how disengaged he had seemed when we lived in Delaware, because now he was here with us. I had the gift of a short memory, and I could push away the sadness of the past few years.

A few weeks after Hunter got back, he sat me down and told me we owed a significant amount of money in taxes. He said he wasn't worried, and neither should I be. By this point in our marriage, I knew almost nothing about our finances. As our family grew and our expenses increased, I had dug my head further into the sand. I liked simply asking Hunter for money rather than discussing where it was coming from. So I took the tax news without question. If Hunter said we were okay, that was good enough for me. He would figure out our finances while I continued that willful ignorance I first adopted when we bought the house on Centre Road. In this way Hunter had all the pressure, with no partner, when it came to financially supporting our family. I know now what a burden that must have been for him.

He also became my partner at school events. The D.C. world of hyperfocused parenting still felt foreign to me, and he saw my worry about doing the right thing for our girls. He didn't carry those same worries. "Kathleen, just say we're happy with the work the girls are doing and that we'll support it at home," he'd tell me before we went to teacher conferences. He'd take my hand as we walked into school and say, "Our girls are great. Just smile and say thank you to the teachers."

Once, when a teacher said that she was worried about Maisy's chewing on her shirt during class, Hunter gently asked her whether any of the boys were doing the same thing.

"Um, some of them," the teacher said, and nodded.

"Well," Hunter said, smiling, "I think you have your answer."

While I took every comment about our girls as a sign of my flawed parenting, Hunter always said, "They're fine. Do not get worked up about the little things." My parents had been hands-off and had never once known a single grade that I'd gotten in school. Maybe because Hunter had gone to a school like Sidwell, he wasn't rattled at all by the attention our kids got now.

That spring, Beau and Hunter decided to train for a sprint triathlon in Rehoboth Beach, Delaware, excited to be doing it together. Hunter had been born with a lanky and lean frame, and I'd never known him to exercise until he got sober, but now he was as fit as he'd ever been in his life. We all drove down the night before and stayed in a high-rise hotel on the beach. The next morning was gray and cold, as the whole Biden clan stood shivering on the beach. Joe, Jill, Ashley, and Hallie stood with me and the girls as we waited for the swimming portion of the event to begin. Every few minutes, someone stopped by to say hello to Joe, and he greeted everyone with a wide smile. He looked proud to be watching his boys in the race.

The ocean looked daunting, with huge gray waves break-ing at the shoreline. When the racers entered the water, many of them struggled to swim against the incoming tide. I stood on the shoreline, nervous, straining to find Hunter in the crowd, and when I finally saw him running out of the water, I actually cried. He waved at us and got on his bike and rode off for the bike loop, and the girls and I made our way slowly to the finish line.

No one in the family openly talked about Hunter's rehab or what this race really meant to all of us, but the subtext was there. At least for me. I assumed Hunter's parents knew he'd gone to rehab, but it was never discussed. All we talked about now was how great he was doing. How proud we all were that he and Beau were doing a triathlon. Joe positively beamed as Hunter ran across the finish line, smiling as he looked over at us with a wave. I never could have imagined this for him just a year ago.

"Hunter!" I said, hugging him. "I can't believe you made it through the swim! I could see everyone getting pulled by the tide!"

"I swam out against it and circled the buoy wide." He smiled. "I knew the tide was pulling hard." I'd watched the tide pull racers inside the buoy, disqualifying them from the race. The ocean had looked as rough and menacing as I'd ever seen it.

I took a picture of him with the girls at the finish line: Maisy on his shoulders, Naomi and Finnegan leaning into his side. We looked like a family again. A better family than be-fore. Our marriage was stronger too. Hunter was sober, and I'd never have to worry about his drinking again.

TWELVE

QUEST FOR FRIENDS

When I returned to the Sidwell carpool line, I was determined to make friends, even if I may have been intimidated by these parents. I hadn't really made any friends of my own since I'd married. Except for Amy, all of our friends out east came through Hunter. Now that our life was settling down and all three girls were starting school, I felt a real longing for girlfriends.

The move back to D.C. had empowered me. I handled selling the Delaware house and enrolling the girls in school in D.C. I took control in a way I hadn't since we'd married. We were back in the community that I wanted for our family and I was feeling more confident because of it, more certain about how I wanted to live.

Before Hunter returned from Crossroads, I'd spotted a woman in the carpool line who'd always given me a friendly smile during our earlier stint at Sidwell. Tall and slender, with a wholesome beauty and a casual ease, she leaned against her beat-up black minivan while her youngest son sat on the ground next to her.

"Bettina, right?" I said, walking up to her. Finnegan and Maisy were running along the fence line surrounding the school's field. "We just moved back here. Can you come over for coffee tomorrow and maybe be my friend?" I said, smiling. "I'm looking to make some friends."

She laughed. "Sure," she said. "I'll come over after my therapist appointment." With that admission, I knew I'd like this woman.

Karen was another mom in the carpool line who had a friendly face, a quick laugh, thick blond hair, and sweet dimples when she smiled. "Hey, want to join our foursome for the golf fundraiser?" she asked one day early in the school year as we stood in the school's playground, watching our kids run in circles.

"I wish I could! Except I don't golf," I said, smiling.

"Oh, that doesn't matter," she said. "It's just for fun. I'm no good either."

The weekend before the golf outing, Hunter and I were in Delaware with the girls visiting his family, and I mentioned my golf date to my father-in-law.

"Honey," he said, looking serious, "you can't golf if you've never played before." We were standing in the kitchen, and he looked at me with a furrowed brow. He seemed genuinely concerned. I laughed and hugged him. "It's okay, Pop. Karen told me it didn't matter. It's a fundraiser for the school and it's just for fun."

Joe walked out of the room and returned minutes later. "Honey," he told me, "you have a golf lesson tomorrow morning." He put his arm around me and kissed my head. I took the lesson, trying my hardest to concentrate on hitting the ball. When my hour was up, the instructor told me to use a seven iron the whole time and wished me luck.

When Karen picked me up later that week, I was standing on my front porch holding a seven iron. "Where are your clubs?" she asked.

"Oh, I'm just going to carry this one. I don't need the whole bag." She burst out laughing, and we spent the day drinking warm beer and making up a golf score that seemed halfway presentable.

Karen and Bettina were my first grown-up friends, and I was in awe of them, because they seemed fearless to me in every way. Their parenting also aligned with mine. Our kids were the ones with skinned knees and messy hair, often forgetting their homework in the car. Both of them were also home with their kids. Within a few weeks, we started meeting every morning at Karen's house, heading out for runs on the wooded trails that spread throughout the city.

The three of us laughed through a lot, but we also confided in one another, and I found comfort in their friendship. They shared stories about struggles in their families, and there were runs when we stopped in the middle of the woods to hold one another. Slowly I started to share some of my own secrets, but always with the caveat: *You cannot tell anyone.*

"My God, Kathleen, you don't have to say that every time! We know!" they'd say, exasperated with me.

I told them Hunter didn't drink, but I left out the rehab and what our life had been like in the lead-up to it. My stories always held back anything that showed a crack in my marriage.

Both of these new friends had such confidence, which I desperately wanted to rub off on me—and some of it did. By 2007 they had me training for my first triathlon, although the first time I clipped into a racing bike with them, I struggled not to tip over.

On the day before our race, we arrived at our hotel in Columbia, Maryland. After we checked in, we walked around the sea of racers buying swag and equipment in the parking lot. I took my bike to a tent that checked our tires for air pressure. A young guy with a white mohawk hung my bike up on a hook to check the tires. "Question," I said to him as he spun the tires, "which gear should I use to go uphill?" He turned to look at me to see if I was joking. I was not. I can imagine him wondering what I was doing at a triathlon if I didn't know how my bike worked, but I simply stood smiling at him. He took out a Sharpie and wrote on my handlebars: "Up" on the left, and "Down" on the right.

"Got it," I said to him with what I hoped was a confident nod.

Bettina ended up skipping the race, so it was just Karen and me nervously getting ready the next morning. If Karen was nervous, that didn't bode well for me. The first part was a one-mile swim, followed by a twenty-five-mile bike ride and then a six-mile run. As Karen and I made our way to the lake, we were both shivering in the early morning mist. The lake was black-bottomed and it didn't appear to me like anyone should ever actually be in that water. I had on my wetsuit and a hot pink swimming cap I'd been given to denote my age group. As the age 45–50 women began to gather in a sea of pink heads, I heard my name being called somewhere behind me: "Kathleen! Kathleen!"

Running toward the shoreline was my mother-in-law, carrying a giant sign that read WE LOVE YOU, KATHLEEN! Jill was followed by Hunter, and our three girls, and Beau and his family. I felt moved that they were here but also scared. Now I had to actually finish the race. I walked toward them with a nervous smile, gave them all a quick hug, and headed back toward the lake.

When the whistle blew, I secured my goggles and slipped into the lake. Right away someone kicked me, and my goggles dislodged. I tried to tread water and adjust them, but dozens of women were now swimming over me, knocking me around like a pinball. After six months of swim class, I decided to just do the dog paddle with my eyes closed. I'd lift my head to get my bearings every now and then, and zigzag some more around the lake. Every time I looked up, I could see that I had swum toward shore again, so I'd reset my course back to the route. At one point a lifeguard in a rowboat asked me if I was okay.

"Not really," I responded. Had he told me I needed to get in the boat right then, I would have been gleeful. But he just laughed. I couldn't quit. Hunter and his family had driven two hours at dawn to watch me race.

By the time I finished the swim, I was depleted, and as I walked toward shore, my calf muscles went into spasms. Everyone around me ran toward the transition area, unzipping their wetsuits as they went. I walked slowly, so relieved to be on solid ground that I could have curled up and kissed the dirt if not for the people that surely would have run right over me. I still had twenty-five miles to bike and six to run.

Under my wetsuit, I had on the biking shorts that made my legs feel liked cased sausages. I put on the biking shoes that caused me to walk like a penguin and strapped on my helmet. When I saw the hill up ahead, I looked down at my gears and reminded myself which one I'd need. As I started the ascent, I began frantically pressing the gear marked "up." The bike lurched as I tried to keep pedaling. Suddenly I felt I was moving backward. I looked down and saw the chain hanging off. With all my might, I twisted my foot off the pedal and dragged the bike to the side of the road.

I was kneeling by my bike when Karen, who'd started her swim later than me, went sailing by with a wave and a smile. I flipped my bike over and draped the chain back on, turning the pedals until it latched. Then I climbed back on, trying to catch up to Karen. I felt like I was pumping as hard as I possibly could, yet everyone kept passing me. By the time I headed back into the transition area, my butt was on fire. I took the awkward biking shoes off and put on my sneakers. Now things were as they should be.

Catching Karen was my driving force, and three hours after she'd passed me, with just a few minutes to the finish line, I spotted her blond ponytail bobbing up ahead. I felt such joy catching her, I'd forgotten about my irritation at the delight she was taking in the race. When we approached the finish line, we held hands and raised them above our heads.

Afterward, everyone ran over to congratulate us. I'd never felt more physically exhausted in my life. "I am so proud of you," Hunter said, putting his arms around me. "I can't believe what you just did." Then he kissed me. "*I* can't believe what I just did," I replied, meaning it.

Standing with my medal around my neck, I was in awe that I'd finished. But I couldn't get over how scared I'd been, especially during the swim. I'd trained so hard over the last six months, and I didn't want that to be my takeaway. As Karen and I packed up our things, I said to her, "We need to do another one. I didn't do all that training to feel that scared."

"Sure!" Karen answered with enthusiasm. "Let's do the Nation's Triathlon in the fall!" Sure enough, that fall, Karen, Bettina, and I stood along the bank of the Potomac, waiting for our race to begin.

When my turn came to enter the water, I slipped in slowly and found a spot on the outside of the group. As I swam, a woman kept knocking into me.

"I'm sorry," she said as we bobbed along, "this is my first race."

"No worries," I called out to her, my head above water. "You can follow me. My name's Kathleen."

As I crossed the finish line hours later, Hunter and the girls came running up to hug me. This time I wasn't depleted, I was surprisingly energized. I'd done it.

"You know," Hunter said to the girls, "your mom just finished an Olympic-distance triathlon. My race was nowhere near this long. I'd never be able to do what your mom just did." He was proud of me, and I felt it. And for the first time in our marriage, I accepted that I might be better than Hunter at something.

THIRTEEN

A SILLY GIRL
FROM CHICAGO

n 2006, Hunter and I bought our own place in D.C., another center-hall colonial with a sprawling backyard. I was
excited to buy the house and ignored the way we pulled it
off with a mortgage and a home equity loan, purchasing it
with basically no money down. I wanted a house, and I wasn't
going to go searching for reasons why we should wait.

We were living in one of the most affluent parts of the
country and our kids went to one of the most exclusive
schools. In my mind, I understood that the families around us
weren't living paycheck to paycheck, but I pushed away any
misgivings about spending above our means. Hunter never
showed me any concern over our finances, and I certainly
wasn't asking.

I took on leadership roles at school and kept watch over
the girls in a way my parents never did with me. Every day I'd
pick them up from school and drive from sports practice to
tutors to piano lessons. I was fully enmeshed in every aspect

of their lives. In our new house, I'd make dinners and push the whole family to take nightly walks. My parenting was by no means better than my parents'; it was simply more controlling. In the end, I'm left to wonder if having a life and career of my own might not have been equally, if not more, impactful for my three daughters.

Hunter seemed comfortable in his sobriety. He never announced it; he'd just say, "No, thanks" when offered a drink. He never expressed any struggle. He became friendly with the husbands of my new friends while also maintaining close relationships with the men from his AA program.

By the time Finnegan and Maisy joined Naomi at Sidwell, new parents were coming to me for advice. This community was far from my South Side roots, but I held my own in this world of East Coast elites. I took on the role of co-chair of the Middle School Parents Association, and at Back-to-School Night I stood with pride on the stage in front of politicians and entrepreneurs, CEOs and heads of international nonprofits, and smiled. Did I think they were all smarter than me? For the most part, yes. Did I care? No.

I did joke that someone needed to be mediocre, and I was okay playing that part. I always liked making people laugh. But being self-deprecating wasn't just a shtick for me, it was a defense. *Don't have high expectations for me, I'm just a silly girl from Chicago*. I figured, if you aren't trying, you can't fail.

I wonder if, in the end, our life was too quiet for Hunter. Maybe he needed more. Joe and Beau both experienced success in a very public way, and they spoke often about the passion they felt for their work. They considered work a type of service, a civic duty. I never saw Hunter show anything but pride toward his father and brother for their incredible accomplishments, but I wondered if their success took a toll on him.

I think being a son and a brother were as important to him as being a husband and a father, and I knew how much his father and brother valued him. But I worried that it was hard for him and his own sense of worth to be the supporting act. Still, he carved his own path. He was the reader in the family, the intellectual, devouring everything from Allen Ginsberg's poetry to Stieg Larsson's crime novels. He seemed to retain every little bit of information that he encountered. I loved this about him.

But all three of them did have something in common: ambition. From early in our marriage, according to Hunter, the "big breaks" were always just on the horizon, and every new partnership held enormous opportunity. I supported all of Hunter's ideas, but I wasn't exactly tracking them. I assumed that this was how success worked: You kept trying out "big ideas" until one hit.

And where was my own professional ambition back then? I'm not sure, but one thing I believed to be true was that no matter what I tried to do, I could never reach the same level of success as Hunter. Maybe that kept my ambition at bay. The memory of walking into the campaign office all those years earlier, seeing Hunter in a leadership role and myself at the bottom of the ladder, had stuck with me. Maybe my ego, something I'd never once considered having, kept me from seeking work outside the home. Maybe I was afraid of failing.

Hunter didn't fear failure. Some of his ideas worked, some of them didn't, and he just rolled with it. I admired that about him. He started many ventures, exploring partnerships with class action attorneys, co-founding a broker-dealer business and a real estate investment fund and then a technology company. I didn't understand any of it, or what pieces of his businesses actually generated income for us.

I worried that we lived above our means, but I did nothing to change it. I didn't manage a budget for myself, and the way that Hunter and I handled money was that whenever I needed any, I called Hunter. More than once my debit card was declined at a store. I'd have to call Hunter to transfer money into my account. My parents earned far less than we did, and they had never had a card declined or an account go below zero. Hunter and I drove nice cars and had a beautiful home, but we were running fast on that hamster wheel and barely staying on.

Before I got married, the nicest hotel I'd ever stayed in was a Holiday Inn. Now Hunter and I stayed at the Four Seasons. I liked my house growing up. I loved having my grandparents upstairs. But I liked my big house in D.C. more. I liked the luxury that came with Hunter's salary.

I'd hustled to earn money since I was twelve years old, when I got a job filling the giant ketchup and mustard jars at Comiskey Park. Hunter and I had that in common. He'd hustled too and worked through high school and college. The difference was that everyone I knew had always worked that hard, while Hunter and Beau were an anomaly among their friends. The Biden brothers lived on a beautiful estate and traveled in a circle of wealthy friends, but they needed to work for their spending money. They may have lived in a mansion, but Hunter's family maintained a tight budget.

And while Hunter appeared to grow up with privilege, he was not spoiled by his parents. They had a beautiful home, but it was often behind on its upkeep, and whole sections were closed up to save on heating costs. His family had scraped by financially at times, and his dad often talked about how he sold parcels of the property to put his kids through college. Hunter straddled these two worlds: his upper-class "old money" neighbors and his father's middle-class ideals and experience.

But Hunter had instant entry into the world of power because he had something better than money: an actual U.S. senator as a father. Hunter also wanted to write noir novels and wear cowboy boots. And this was the contradiction in my husband: He listened to Johnny Cash's working-class ballads but drove a Porsche.

Nonetheless, Hunter had grown up in a world of affluence beyond my understanding. He'd talk of those with "new money" and those with "old money," with a disdain for the showiness of new money. Floodlights illuminating your big house? New money. An old home discreetly hidden behind a high hedge? Old money. Was it discretion that made the distinction? A type of modesty? The reasoning behind this made little sense to me.

Slowly I began to see that old money didn't actually talk about money. To discuss your personal finances was crude. The working-class people I'd grown up with talked openly about money. And I felt no embarrassment over the nice things we bought. Being successful, making money, these were good things. When Hunter bought me a Mercedes station wagon, I called Amy excitedly. I had nothing to hide and felt only pride. Later I would carry shame over not being financially responsible, but at the time, I was living the working-class dream.

I didn't grow up spoiled, so now I liked being taken care of. My brothers and I rarely asked our parents for anything. If we wanted something, we saved for it. When Amy and I were teenagers, we'd meet at Marshall Field on State Street in downtown Chicago and spend hours walking around the store, trying things on, and then carefully returning them to their hangers. We'd try on makeup at the cosmetics counter and gaze at ourselves in the mirrors. Whole days could pass like that for us, never buying anything. It didn't take me long to learn to thoroughly enjoy going into a department store and buying whatever I wanted.

Early in 2006, Hunter acquired a stake in a hedge fund in New York City, and it seemed to mark a change in our lives. Hunter was commuting, spending a few days a week away from home. His routine fell away and his daily AA meetings were hard for him to keep up. I also started to notice a level of stress. While I barely understood this new business venture, I could see the strain it put on Hunter. This marked the beginning of my true disengagement from Hunter's work. When he eventually moved on to different ventures, they remained vague and complicated to me. I was busy with my own life. My position as co-chair of the Middle School Parents Association felt like a part-time job. I should have tried to understand what Hunter was going through professionally, but I didn't. I let him carry that burden alone.

· · ·

In the summer and fall of 2007, Hunter joined his dad in Iowa to campaign for the Democratic presidential nomination. There had been many family conversations about whether Joe should run, and everyone was supportive. For me, the idea of Joe's becoming president seemed beyond my imagination, but I too was excited for him. Hunter didn't have an official role in the campaign, but I know his presence helped his dad feel calm and grounded.

Beau had become the attorney general of Delaware in January 2007 and was back home, unable to be with his dad as much as Hunter. While Barack and Hillary covered the state in huge caravans, Joe traveled in our old Suburban with just a handful of staff, his son by his side.

The day after the Iowa results came in, with Joe receiving less than a single percentage point, he conceded with all of us standing behind him. It was a brutal loss, but we were proud of him. Just a few days after Joe pulled out of the race, he sent me an article on adolescence he thought I might find interesting. He wasn't defeated, he simply pivoted. He was back to being a senator and an attentive full-time grandfather.

FOURTEEN

A NEW REALITY

After our usual summer at the lake in 2008, Hunter and I were back in D.C., getting ready to take the girls to Colorado for the Democratic National Convention. While I stood in our bathroom packing up toiletries for the trip, Hunter walked in and closed the door. "Barack just asked Dad to be his VP," he said with a smile. My eyes widened and my jaw dropped.

We'd known Joe was a contender and had spent hours going over articles and editorials about Barack's choice for vice president. One day we'd think it might happen, the next it seemed beyond reach. As we stood in our bathroom that day, holding each other, some part of me knew, in that moment, that our lives were going to change beyond recognition, and nothing would ever be the same again.

November in Chicago could be brutally cold, but Election Day 2008 was beautiful. We arrived in Chicago on a campaign plane that morning and made our way to the hotel in a motorcade. Since the convention back in August, our lives had become surreal. Suddenly our every movement was choreographed, and we were constantly surrounded by Secret Service and campaign staff. The idea that people were working non-stop on the logistics of our every move was completely unreal to me. The smallest question or request could send staffers running to find answers. There seemed to be nothing they couldn't solve.

We got out of the motorcade beneath the hotel. "Kathleen, here is the key to your hotel room," a young staffer quietly said, handing the keycard to me. "This way." It felt like an entire soccer team of highly competent staff were now managing my little family. We were led toward the loading dock and into the large service elevator.

The Hyatt Regency sat on East Wacker Drive, in the heart of Chicago. I'd walked by the building hundreds of times when I worked downtown as a college student, never really taking notice of the thirty-three-story Chicago skyscraper. Now I was here as the daughter-in-law of the vice presidential candidate of the Democratic Party. This was beyond any of my adolescent fantasies, which never stretched beyond renting a cool apartment and throwing grown-up dinner parties.

Standing at the picture window of our hotel room, I looked out over Lake Michigan. I couldn't sit still, and my mind raced as I tried to unpack and organize our things. I had too much adrenaline coursing through me and needed to move.

Hunter sat at the desk, his laptop open in front of him. "Hunk, do you think it's okay if I sneak out for a run?" I asked, using the nickname I teased him with. "I think it will calm me." I leaned over his shoulder to see his computer screen. "What is the press saying?"

"It's all good," he said, turning toward me in his chair. I sat on his lap and put my arms around him. "I'm so nervous," I said, laying my head on his chest. "Please go for a run," he said with a laugh. I gave him a squeeze and got up to change. "How are you so relaxed?" I asked.

"My nerves just look different from yours. You can never sit still. Go!"

I called Hallie in her room and asked her to join me. Running was one of the things that bonded us. When we were together as a family, Hallie and I would take long runs. The lobby was packed, so she and I sneaked out the front door wearing baseball hats and sunglasses, keeping our heads down, trying to avoid conversations with the hordes of family and friends filling the hotel. We ran out toward the lake. The streets around Grant Park were already closed, and crowds of people holding Obama-Biden signs had begun gathering. The sun was out, and everyone was smiling. "Look at all these people!" I said to her.

If you had told me back when I was selling hot dogs at Comiskey Park that I would be in town to watch my father-in-law accept the vice presidency, I would have laughed at the absurdity of it. Life didn't work that way. I had spent the first eighteen years of my life in Chicago, but this city didn't feel like the city of my past now. Today it felt like a magical place.

"Hallie," I said as we ran along the trail in front of the lake, "I hung out down here when I was in high school. I cannot believe I'm back here like this." Hallie was here without Beau, who was with his National Guard unit at Fort Bliss, preparing for a deployment to Iraq. Hallie had the added responsibility of being a single parent on election night. Everyone in the family was proud of Beau's service, but his absence was felt by us all. He'd be in Iraq for a year while Hallie stayed home, working full-time, with their two young children. "I wish Beau were here with us," she said as we ran along the lake.

When we got back, she and I showered and put on big white terry cloth hotel robes. While we lay on the bed, drinking wine and watching the news, Hunter was down the hall with his dad. Our kids were in the next room jumping on the beds, and soon enough we'd have to start getting everyone ready. I'd worried so much about doing everything right during the campaign. Hunter never seemed rattled, but I obsessed over every little detail about getting the girls dressed and to campaign events on time.

I savored that quiet lull watching the news with Hallie on the bed. We listened as every commentator talked about the "historical significance" of this night. Even though Hallie was there with two small kids and no husband, she seemed far more relaxed than me. I tried to mirror her calmness while also trying to soak up every detail of this experience.

Hallie and I got ready together. "Do you think the necklace is too much?" she asked. She had a simple but elegant style and had chosen a black shift dress with a multistrand yellow necklace. No matter what Hallie wore, she always looked great.

"You should definitely wear the necklace. It's super stylish."

I had bought a burgundy chiffon dress with a ruffle detail, brown suede heels, and chandelier earrings that matched my dress. I'd already ironed the girls' clothes and now waited until the very last minute to get them ready. The campaign outfits had been a constant battle, and so was my attempt to keep them clean. Once, during the Democratic convention in Denver, as we were about to go onstage, I turned to see Maisy eating strawberries. With every bite she took, red strawberry juice dripped down her white shirt. In a panic, I'd tried to get rid of the stain, but nothing worked. I took her shirt off and put it on her backward to hide it. "Mom! This feels so weird," she complained. I told her she was fine and to leave it. As we walked out onstage, I turned to see Maisy, her shirt turned back around with the stain in full view, as she looked back at me with her dimpled smile.

After we were done changing, Hunter came back, and we took the service elevator down to the parking garage. He and I stood against the back wall of the elevator, holding hands. We were excited but also somber, feeling the weight of the day. We walked to the parking garage where staff and Secret Service stood waiting to usher us into a slew of armored vehicles. "Hunter and Kathleen, you and the girls are in this car," one of the staffers said to us.

"Thanks, buddy," Hunter said, as the girls climbed in back.

As soon as we got in our seats, he and I held hands again. "I love you," he said, and leaned over to kiss me.

"I love you too."

I looked out the window as we drove down an empty Lake Shore Drive toward Grant Park. Thousands of people lined the street, shouting, "We love you, Barack!" Somehow I was in a motorcade with the future president of the United States. The first Black president. And my father-in-law was going to be the vice president.

When we arrived at Grant Park, we were taken backstage to a maze of tents and trailers and then led to a simple room with white walls and a couch. A TV played on a small table, and we could see Barack walking to the podium. I stood against the far wall of that room, next to Michelle Obama, the future First Lady. She was quiet, with an intense look on her face as she watched her husband. I felt in some ways like a voyeur, seeing Michelle during this incredibly personal moment. I could not imagine the weight of her emotions, the enormity of what was happening to her family.

Although we hadn't yet spent any intimate time together, I felt an instant connection to her. Like me, she came from a working-class family on the South Side of Chicago. In all my years of living in D.C., I had never met anyone else who came from a background like mine. Whenever someone said they were from Chicago, I'd learn they were actually from a suburb like Evanston, which is about as different from the South Side as Texas is. But Michelle knew where I came from. She understood. Over time, she would become an invaluable friend and inspiration, helping me to own my past and my choices with honesty. But on election night, we still hardly knew each other.

I could hear Barack's voice over the cheering crowd, and my excitement now was the heart-racing kind. It felt like pure joy, and it pushed every other thought out of my mind. When our turn came to join the Obamas and Joe and Jill onstage, Hunter and I walked out, each of us holding hands with Mom

Mom, and I could feel her tiny frame between us. Looking out past the stage, the crowd seemed to go on forever. There was a soft breeze blowing and a sky full of stars as we all knocked around up there, hugging one another, not sure where to stand.

I held on to Hunter's arm as we all waved to the crowd. I could see my parents and my brothers and their families down in the front, along with all my cousins and Patty. Everyone was smiling and waving up to us. "Hi, Mo!" Finnegan called out to our cousin, who stood waving from the crowd. The night truly felt blessed.

I watched Hunter hug his father, first kissing him on the cheek. I knew how happy he was for his dad, and it made me happy too. After the humiliating defeat in the Iowa caucus, this was redemption. I hugged Joe and Jill, and when they told me they loved me, I felt it. I also felt Joe's pride in his family, and that pride was something I cherished.

When we finally left the stage, I walked off with Hallie, our arms around each other. This was a happiness unlike any other I'd felt before. A surreal, shared celebration. A true collective joy.

When we returned to the hotel, I felt a mix of exhaustion and nervous energy. "Hunt," I said as I changed out of my dress, "I don't know if I'll ever be able to fall asleep."

"I bet you will," he laughed. "I'll rub your back." Still in his suit, he lay down next to me on the bed. I knew he wouldn't be going to sleep for hours. He'd always stay up after I went to bed, reading his book and watching his shows. As soon as I felt his hand on my back, I knew I'd be asleep in minutes.

FIFTEEN

BIDEN BLOOD

Joe introduced me as his daughter everywhere we went. "This is my daughter Kathleen. Well, actually she's my daughter-in-law, but she's a daughter to me," he'd say, while I beamed next to him. Joe made me feel special with his attention. With every compliment he gave me, my self-esteem grew. "Honey, your daughters are amazing. You are a wonderful mother," he'd tell me often. I loved his approval and his praise. Being considered a daughter to Joe and Jill never felt like a betrayal of my own parents. My parents offered me comfort in other ways, in the form of their laughter, the smell of my mother's cooking, the feel of my mom's hand in mine. With them I always felt like my truest self. But from the beginning of my marriage, my parents had always encouraged my relationship with Hunter's family. Because our families were so different, my relationship with Joe and Jill never felt like a slight to them.

While Joe seemed to be the sun around which we all revolved, Jill always maintained her own identity and her own life. She modeled a sense of independence that I admired. Jill didn't live by Joe's schedule. She taught me how to entertain and how to make the simplest dinners feel cozy and elegant. She also showed me how to prioritize my health and wellness, which was something I didn't learn growing up. She always encouraged me to take my runs and spend time on making myself feel good.

I liked people seeing how close I was to Hunter's family. My marriage was at the core of my identity now, and our being close to both sets of parents seemed to make our bond stronger. Any feelings of being an outsider had long vanished.

There was just one frequent reminder that I wasn't in fact a true member of the Biden family. Shortly before Inauguration Day in January 2009, a Secret Service agent came to the house to talk to us about our family's coverage. Mike, about my age, dark-haired and fit, looked like someone from my old neighborhood. He had that clean-cut, deferential working-class air about him. He sat down with us at our kitchen banquette and opened a big black binder to begin our initiation into the Secret Service world.

"Hunter and the girls will all have a detail assigned to them," he said. "Two agents with them twenty-four hours a day." Mike looked at me and said, "Kathleen, of course if there is any type of emergency, you will also be picked up and included in any plan."

Suddenly I felt embarrassed. I knew the Secret Service would be a part of this new life, but I didn't know how. Did this mean I was less important than my husband and my kids? What I heard in his words: I was not truly a Biden.

Being excluded triggered an old memory from early in our marriage. We were taking family photos and Hunter's aunt was running the show. "Okay, how about one with just Joe and Jill," she'd said. We all stood around as she directed different iterations of us to be photographed. At one point she announced, "Now let's do Biden blood only." I stepped out of the picture and off to the side, next to Hunter's grandmother, Mom Mom.

"Let's ask them to take a picture of the two of us next," she'd said, putting her arm around me, and I knew that she understood my embarrassment. My daughter and my husband were in the picture, but somehow I wasn't included.

That day when the Secret Service agent left, I felt like I was fighting for my place. "Can you decline coverage?" I asked Hunter, but he was unwavering. He was not going to forgo Secret Service protection. "Kathleen, this is how it has always been. It isn't personal. In-laws have never had protection," he said.

I backed down, ultimately understanding that it wasn't personal, but it remained a sore point for me. He didn't stick up for me, or at least that's how I felt. Whenever Hunter and I walked anywhere—through an airport or a city—I'd have to remind him not to walk in front of me, which caused the agents to also walk in front of me to keep up with him and made me feel I was following his entourage.

But for me it was another reminder that I was not "family," an echo of the call to have me step out of the picture. *Biden blood only.* Maybe some part of me knew that soon I was going to have to fight as hard as I ever had just to stay in my marriage.

PART II

DURING

SIXTEEN

THE BEGINNING OF
WHAT'S NEXT

n the spring of 2010, Hunter and I went to a wedding at a swanky resort in the Dominican Republic. The groom was a new business partner of Hunter's, and the wedding party seemed about a decade younger than us and mostly lived in New York City.

On our first night there, as we got dressed for a cocktail reception, I asked Hunter about the bride and groom. "He's a good guy," Hunter said. "His wife is very sweet. You'll like them." He said this standing in the bathroom, straightening his tie. He wore a suit the way most people wore sweatpants— all the time and appearing utterly comfortable.

We headed to the cocktail party in a golf cart and walked into the crowd, holding hands. I was proud to walk into a room with Hunter. To me, he was always the most handsome man in any group, and he carried himself with an air of confidence, even among everyone at this party who were gliding around in Gucci suits and couture dresses looking as though they'd stepped straight out of *Vogue*.

"Hunter!" the groom called out when he saw us. Lorenzo was born in New York and had grown up in Venezuela. He had a handsome face and a broad smile.

"I want you to meet some friends," he said as he brought us over to the bar. I wasn't surprised by his attention toward Hunter. Since Joe had become vice president, Hunter was treated with deference by most people.

From the moment Joe was announced as Barack's running mate, people started treating us differently. When Joe was a senator, people had taken an interest in us, but now we were on a whole new level. Hunter had become something of a celebrity in D.C., and people now seemed appreciative of our attendance at any event, as they did at this wedding, as though our time had somehow become more precious.

After we met some of the guests, Hunter was introduced to more men, and I drifted away. The room looked like a photo shoot with beautiful women in gauzy floral gowns that fluttered in the breeze.

I settled on a seat in the corner of the room with Eric, Hunter's business partner. By now Eric managed almost every aspect of our financial life, so our relationship was an odd one. Born of mutual need, perhaps. But I trusted him. Now we sat on the fringe of the cocktail party, staring at the scene as if it were a movie. "Who *are* these people?" I asked him. "And why is everyone here so good-looking?"

"Lorenzo is a good guy," Eric said, laughing. "He's good for our business."

I'd given the cocktail party a good hour and wanted to get

back to my hotel room and read my book in bed. I found Hunter holding court at a high-top cocktail table near an outdoor bar strung with white lights. Soft music was playing, and waiters walked around with trays full of colorful cocktails and hors d'oeuvres. I put my hand on his arm to get his attention. "Hunter, I'm tired. I'm going back to our cottage."

"I'll be there in a little bit," he said as he leaned over to give me a kiss.

I was a little surprised that he wanted to stay at the bar. In D.C., he was always the one wanting to leave the party early. I didn't think much of it, though. Maybe he stayed because it could help his business. That night and the next two, I went to bed alone. I was accustomed to going to bed before Hunter. He was a night owl, while I loved the early mornings. And I was happy to have my book, a beautiful bed, and nothing but the sun to wake up to in the morning.

On the final night, the wedding was held at an old church on a hilltop at the corner of the property. As we took our seats, I felt the side of my dress pulling open, my bare skin exposed. I looked down and saw the zipper had separated. "Hunter!" I said as the music began, and everyone turned to watch the wedding party walk in. "The entire side of my dress just unzipped! I'm literally naked on my left side!"

"Honey," he told me, "as soon as the service is over, I'll take you back to our room and you can change. You can't see it. You look beautiful."

"I look crazy. And naked." I tried to hold it closed.

"Here." He took off his jacket and wrapped it around my shoulders.

When the service was over, we followed the crowd to dinner. "The minute dinner is cleared, I'm sneaking out," I told him and kept my hand on my hip, holding my dress closed in a death grip. When I finally found my chance to slip away, Hunter walked me to the golf cart.

"Sorry, Hunk, you're going to have to find your own way back," I said with a smirk as I handed him his jacket. I couldn't wait to get the dress off and put on my robe.

When I got back to our room, I called my dad. He was in D.C. with the girls, and when he was with them, I never worried. I'd given him the big white binder that contained all their school and sports schedules, contact information, and maps to their games and activities. He was diligent about his chauffeur duties, driving to the various locations while the girls were in school to make sure he knew how to get there.

I listened to his updates while I got ready for bed. Tossing a tissue into the waste bin, something caught my eye. A little blue glass vodka bottle sat at the bottom of the otherwise empty basket.

"Dad," I interrupted him. "I have to call you back."

I bent down and picked the bottle up and stared at it. My first thought was someone had broken into our room. My jewelry still lay on the bathroom counter, untouched. But someone had come in and taken the bottle out of our mini fridge and drunk it. And that scared me.

When Hunter came back to our room much later, I was still up, reading in bed. "Hunter!" I said, picking up the empty bottle I'd set on my bedside table. "You won't believe this. I think housekeeping drank one of the bottles from our mini fridge!"

Hunter looked at the bottle, and then at me. "Who knows,

Kathleen?" he said, with little curiosity. "Maybe the bottle was there the whole time, and we didn't notice it. It's not a big deal. Don't worry about it."

I didn't question him. Maybe I was unwilling to even entertain the possibility that he'd drunk the vodka, because to imagine that was to invite a cascade of doubt and fear. He'd been sober for seven years at this point. Sitting in bed, listening to my husband, I had no reason to doubt him. I trusted him completely.

I put the vodka bottle back in the wastebasket and went to bed, still wondering who could have possibly drunk it. Because Hunter didn't drink.

SEVENTEEN

MY FAVORITE PERSON

During Joe's time in the White House, I traveled to Europe, Asia, Africa, and South America multiple times. I went to Ghana, Ethiopia, and South Africa. Poland, Romania, the Czech Republic, Belgium, France, Germany, England, Switzerland, Italy, and Spain. China, Japan, Mongolia, and the United Arab Emirates. Costa Rica, Mexico, and Argentina. Some of those trips I took with Joe and my girls. Some were just me and Hunter. Naomi and I walked along the Great Wall of China; the whole family visited the national parks and everything in between. Some trips were official business, some were vacations, but they were all first times for me. I'd hardly ever traveled, and now I was on a plane every month.

Suddenly my wardrobe went from a few dresses to dozens, and I found myself on private jets alongside political and business leaders. I soaked it all up, the amazing absurdity that

Kathy Buhle had this life. And how had this happened? The answer was clear: my husband.

The girls and I were always coming or going. They'd do their homework on Air Force Two's pullout bed in Joe's cabin, quickly adapting to their strange new world. Hunter and I were always passing each other, always unpacking and packing again. It was an exciting time, but we were always in transit. Never grounded. Structure and stability were losing out to travel and adventure. I didn't want to miss any of it, but eventually that came at a cost.

Everyone wanted to know about Hunter's family, from my own relatives to the dry cleaners who'd raise their eyes when I said, "Pickup for Biden." I had plenty of charming anecdotes about the Biden family, and I'd tell them with a flourish.

"Joe and Jill don't miss anything for the girls. They are there for the Halloween parades and soccer games," I'd say with pride, adding, "Joe walks along the field, yelling coaching advice to the girls throughout the game." I cherished my role as a family representative.

In August 2011, Naomi and I went with Joe on a trip to Asia and sat under an open tent in a pasture at the foot of the Khentii Mountains separating Mongolia from Russia. The president of Mongolia sat at the head of the table, beaming at the VICE PRESIDENT OF THE UNITED STATES baseball cap that Joe had given him. Our hosts had prepared a long presentation of traditional Mongolian sports and arts. There were young boys riding bareback on horses galloping from the mountains toward us, giant Mongolian wrestlers wearing nothing but sashes wrapped around their middle, and women

dressed in bright, colorful costumes contorting their bodies
into pretzels while balancing plates on sticks. Naomi and I
were in awe. "Mom! A camel!" she said at one point that night.
"Can you take my picture with the camel?" She sounded like
a little kid instead of the seventeen-year-old that she was.

Naomi and I had left for this trip from our summer at the
lake. The day before she and I had left, Hunter and I noticed
the For Sale sign on a raised ranch house three doors down
from my parents' lake house.

"Hunt," I'd told him, "go look at the house while I'm gone.
You have my permission to buy it!" I'd said it half jokingly. For
years we'd looked at houses for sale at the lake. We'd always
dreamed of buying a second home, but we'd never talked
about it seriously. With a double mortgage on our D.C. home
and three kids at Sidwell, our cost of living was extraordi-
narily high. By 2011, the housing market had corrected, so to
buy a home you needed a substantial down payment. As far as
I knew, we were not putting money away. We were spending
every cent Hunter made.

Naomi and I landed in China with Joe. We were told to
leave our cellphones turned off on the plane. After dinner, as
we walked along a hallway with Joe and Vice President Xi, a
staffer approached me and handed me his phone. "Hunter
needs to talk to you," he said quietly.

I took the phone and slowed down. "Is everything okay?" I
asked Hunter nervously.

"Kathleen!" he yelled. "I've been trying to reach you. I
hope you were serious about buying that house because that's
what I did! It's the house three doors down from your par-

ents'!" Standing amid dozens of staffers and security, I could barely process this news. Hunter had bought the house.

"Hunt, are you kidding me?" I whispered into the phone. My excitement about buying a home close to my family pushed aside the rational questions I should have been asking, namely, how could we possibly afford it?

"Kathleen," he said, laughing, "you and I will have our own bedroom *and* bathroom. I can't wait for you to see it."

I didn't ask any details. I never did. My life was moving so quickly, and I didn't want to stop and worry. I refused to think about how we could afford it. If Hunter said we were good, we were good.

When Naomi and I returned to the lake from our trip to Asia with Joe, Hunter was giddy.

"Kath, you're going to love it. It's perfect. It has a cool seventies vibe to it. The owners said we can have everything—all the furniture, dishes, all of it! I can't wait to show you." He was more excited about this house than any house we'd ever lived in, and Finnegan and Maisy were beside themselves, jumping up and down.

"Mom! It is so cool!" Finny said. "It has a tiki bar in the basement. And built-in speakers in the living room!"

A few months after we got the keys, Hunter and I went back by ourselves and explored the house. We walked through all the rooms while I wrote things down in a little notebook I carried around with me.

That night, we lay on the carpet in front of a fire in the living room, listening to the jazz albums that the former owners had left. "Let's do this every fall," Hunter said. "Let's make sure we come here, just the two of us." He kissed me as he put his arms around me. "I love how quiet it is."

We hadn't gotten those early years alone together that some couples get, because we'd become parents so quickly. But now it was just the two of us. As I looked into his eyes, I couldn't imagine any place I'd rather be than with him, curled on the floor with his arms around me, the fire warming us as we listened to the music.

The next morning, we bundled up, went down to the beach, and walked along the waterfront, holding hands. "I'm so happy," I said to him, snuggling in close while we walked along the lake on that cold October day. He squeezed me back. "You are my favorite person," I said.

EIGHTEEN

SOMETHING SHATTERED

By 2011, with all of our kids finally settled in school, my friends Bettina and Karen started exploring work outside the home. Bettina and a friend of hers created a pop-up shop that eventually became a hugely successful vegetarian taco restaurant called Chaia. Karen, who was a lawyer, co-founded the DC Volunteer Lawyers Project, offering pro bono representation to women escaping domestic abuse. Karen and her co-founder's idea was that by joining forces with DCVLP, several lawyers could work together under the umbrella of one malpractice insurance policy, making the cost of the policy more affordable. The response to their concept was overwhelming. Many women with deep job experience who'd taken time off to raise their kids were looking for a way to return to work. I was so impressed watching my friend turn a thought into action that when the time came to have a fundraiser for DCVLP, I knew I'd found a way to help.

It felt good to finally have somewhere to direct my passion for social service, a place to lend my voice and my energy. At first, we all started out volunteering at DCVLP. I asked my in-laws if they would come to our first fundraiser at Karen's house, and without hesitation, they said yes. They were always supportive of me, and I knew the mission spoke to both of them.

When the night of that very first fundraiser came, about three dozen people squeezed into Karen's family room while Joe leaned against the lectern and spoke passionately about the importance of fighting against domestic violence. I felt proud of this little organization and my role in it.

As DCVLP grew to include more volunteer attorneys, Karen needed to raise money more consistently. So I joined the Advisory Board and began advocating in a professional way. I had not worked outside of the home in many years, and it felt great to wake up that part of my brain. Plus, the program's business model was as impressive as the services it provided. Using volunteer attorneys allowed us to keep our staffing small and thus our budget low. Wherever I went in D.C., I shared the work of this tiny but mighty program.

Joe recognized my passion and invited me to every White House event on domestic violence. In the fall of 2012, at a daylong program on domestic violence, I spotted Lynn, the White House advisor on violence against women, and went over to sit next to her. I was beginning to learn the importance of making contacts. While previously I'd been a bit allergic to the type of networking I'd seen in D.C., now I developed a new appreciation for connecting with people. I'd never look over anyone's shoulder to scan a room for VIPs, but I did begin to track people who might be able to help my nonprofit. Lynn already knew about DCVLP because I'd cornered her at a previous event. When I sat down, she turned to me with a smile. "Kathleen," she whispered, "can you speak in an hour at one of the breakout groups about your program? I love the model and think it's important to share with others."

"Of course," I answered, and promptly panicked. I had nothing prepared. I didn't have any of our literature with me and couldn't remember any of our talking points. What was the percentage of cases that we won? Ninety-five, right? And what were the exact budget numbers? I could barely concentrate on the speakers while I tried to work out what I would say.

When the speeches ended, Lynn told me the room number where I would speak. "Great," I said. "I'm just going to run to the bathroom first." I went straight to the last stall, sat on the toilet seat, and called the office. "Numbers," I whispered into my phone. "I need numbers. How many women do we serve? How many volunteer attorneys do we have? How long does a case take? And what's the cost?" I scribbled it all down on a piece of scrap paper.

I found my assigned room, where a dozen people stood around a large conference table talking. We all had name tags on, and mine said KATHLEEN BIDEN, DC VOLUNTEER LAWYERS PROJECT. I think people were far more interested in my name than in my organization, but I didn't care. After a few minutes, Lynn walked in with Eric Holder, the attorney general. What was I doing here? These people all ran giant nonprofits. Eric Holder was literally the head of the Justice Department. Me? I was there representing a legal program, but I was not even an attorney. I was still learning how simple civil protective orders worked.

Lynn made introductions around the table and then turned and introduced me. Thankfully, I'd been talking about DCVLP like a proud parent, so suddenly my nerves disappeared and the information I thought I'd forgotten came back to me. Without looking at my notes, I explained our mission. We protected and represented survivors of domestic violence because, as a country, it is our responsibility to protect people against violence. When I got to the numbers, I checked my notes. Yes, we won over 95 percent of our cases. And yes, within a two-week commitment, a volunteer attorney could change the trajectory of a victim's life. It was easy to sell this program because I believed in it. I stood at the table, confident and comfortable, feeling a new sense of pride growing.

We drove Naomi to college in August 2012. For eighteen years, she'd been part of my every day. Watching her pack up her room brought tears streaming down my face. The University of Pennsylvania was two hours away and still it felt as if she were leaving the continent. I'd worn her in a sling against my chest for months after she was born, and I'd come of age while I raised her. For many years, being her mother was my entire role. So I cried at her leave-taking. Even at the time, I thought my tears were a bit much, and I wonder now what else I was really crying about. What did I fear about my life after she was gone?

Hunter and I stood with her outside her dorm and took her between us in a hug, Finnegan and Maisy joining in. As we walked away, I started to cry again, and Hunter put his arm around me. "We're going to see her in a few weeks," he said, placing a little kiss on my cheek.

"I know. I know. It isn't that. I know we'll see her. It's just the end of a chapter." I tried to stop crying. "She's been my little partner and now that part of our life is over. I don't think I'm actually sad. I'm just emotional." He nodded, smiling, tears in his eyes now too.

The next morning before we drove home, we all met Naomi for one more goodbye at the coffee shop. This time Hunter and I both cried. "Mom! Dad!" Naomi said, standing up from the little table in the corner of the café. "Seriously. You two *have* to stop." She looked around the coffee shop, making sure our scene wasn't being watched by anyone.

Naomi hugged us all and stepped away. She wanted to get on with her day and her life. We all left the café, watching as she strode off in the opposite direction, waving casually. I turned to Hunter and wrapped my arms around him as we stood on the sidewalk. "Thank God we like each other," I told him. "Because, before we know it, it's just going to be the two of us."

But back in D.C., Hunter wasn't himself. He was late, forgetful, and short-tempered. He'd started scheduling meetings in the evenings instead of at breakfast. Normally he always picked up my phone calls. But now, some days he was impossible to reach. And sometimes his eyes would close while we sat talking at the dinner table. I tried to push away my worries, but finally I reached out to Beau. Had he seen anything?

Was he worried? He gave me the comfort that I needed and let me know that he'd be there for me and for Hunter. But he didn't say I was wrong or that Hunter was fine. He said that he'd talk to him and that together we'd figure out what to do.

I felt relief sharing my secret, but now I also had to face it. Bringing Beau in meant that it was real and that our life, our family, was fragile. I felt a pit in my stomach at the thought of going back to a life with Hunter drinking. And as my suspicion grew, so did Hunter's defensiveness. I began to see the quick anger I hadn't seen since he'd gotten sober. But then he'd stride up to the soccer field in his suit, looking handsome and put together. Maybe I'm wrong, I'd think. Was I losing my mind?

Soon I began seeing painful signs from our past consistently. He was short with me. He wasn't picking up my calls. He produced defensive excuses for his tiredness and his absence. He was "working late" and often traveling, often gone from us. And now, when he was with us, it felt as if he wasn't really there.

"Are you okay?" I asked him again and again at dinner when he seemed spacey. Each time I asked, I felt more worried.

"What are you talking about, Kathleen?" he'd answer with aggravation. "I'm tired. Why can't you understand that? Why are you making me feel like I've done something wrong?"

I'd feel rebuked. Maybe I was wrong. Maybe it was nothing. Maybe he really was just tired. Still, I was sure that something was off with him. That something wasn't right. He made me think that I must be crazy, when what I wanted from him was honesty. But I didn't know how to ask for it.

·   ·   ·

When we all flew back to Chicago for the reelection, the weather was gray and cold. There would be no outside celebration in Grant Park. The festivities took place at McCormick Place Convention Center in a giant, cavernous hall. Before we went to the hall, we waited in Joe and Jill's hotel suite for Mitt Romney to concede. This was a far calmer and more somber election night than four years earlier. This time the excitement and butterflies had all gone.

We sat in the living room of their suite, and everyone seemed exhausted, but Hunter couldn't sit still. A creeping sense of dread came over me as my husband paced back and forth across the room. He seemed almost manic.

A few days later, he was accepted into the Navy Reserve. He'd serve one weekend a month and a few weeks a year with the Navy. For years Hunter had discussed the idea of joining the military, but he'd never acted on it. Now, with Beau's encouragement, he'd gone through the process of getting a waiver for his age and for a previous arrest for cocaine possession when he was a teenager. He'd told me about the arrest when we'd first started dating and I'd filed it away as teenage experimenting. I believed that Beau thought the Navy could help keep Hunter healthy and on track. It could also offer Hunter a sense of pride. But now I had a deep, gnawing fear that he wasn't sober, so I couldn't talk about the Navy to him as if everything was okay.

As I watched Hunter walking back and forth across the room, I leaned my head on Beau's shoulder.

"Everything's going to be great, Kath," Beau said, putting his arm around me. I could feel him willing it to be true. Did he think Hunter was acting strange? There was no chance for us to talk about it in private, and I doubt we would have anyway—not on election night.

No one else in the room seemed to notice anything. Hunter wasn't ranting and raving. He wasn't making a scene. His changes were minute and subtle. But not to me. I watched him closely, and I saw the difference in his eyes.

NINETEEN

ARE YOU OKAY?

Hunter had a drawer full of prescription pills in the bathroom that I'd never really examined, but after election night I took pictures of everything and sent the photos to Beau. Hunter had always leaned on medicine when he didn't feel well, while I was raised to drink a glass of water and lie down. Hunter would often say to me, "You know there's a cure for your headache?" From the beginning, our medicine cabinet was filled with pills for allergies, and sinus, and stomach, and so much more. Now I pored over everything. I never found anything other than prescription pills for Hunter and I never threw anything away, I just examined all of it.

But neither Beau nor I ever asked Hunter directly if he was drinking or using drugs. I think we both knew he'd deny it. I know that we also held out hope that we were wrong and that Hunter was sober. Beau never doubted or questioned my suspicion, however. He trusted me and knew how much I loved

Hunter. I never came to Beau with anger, because I wasn't angry. I was scared.

I'd never talked to his parents or mine about Hunter's sobriety because I didn't want anyone but Beau to know that I was worried. Plus, if I acknowledged it, I'd have to do something about it. I wanted to protect Hunter, but I also I wanted to protect our marriage. A "special" marriage like ours didn't involve a relapse. A "special" marriage didn't involve lies.

I felt guilty for putting it all on Beau. He had a big job and two small children, and yet he was the one who fully understood Hunter. Beau and I were in sync on so many things. We both had definite visions of how we wanted things done. We were the ones who always came up with the route for the family's Thanksgiving Day ten-miler. "Why do you two always have to make it so complicated?" Hunter and Hallie would complain about the run. They just wanted to get it over with, but Beau and I wanted to map out the best trails.

Beau also possessed an unfailing empathy for his brother, and he never showed judgment about Hunter's drinking or resentment that his brother was letting him down or tiring him out. Beau only offered reassurances that everything would work out. I so wanted to believe him.

"Are you okay?" I asked Hunter again, about a week after the election, when he'd just sat through dinner with the girls and me, barely speaking.

"Why do you keep asking me that? I'm tired because I'm working nonstop. You make me feel like I'm doing something wrong." No matter how I asked, he was defensive and irritated. There would be no real conversation around my worries or his anger.

A few weeks after the reelection, I held a DCVLP fundraiser. I'd spent months planning the event. I now had a mission and was dogged as I had never been before.

We had an impressive guest list—local leaders in business, politics, and the press—and I'd been clear to everyone helping me pull it off that there would be no mention of money. None. I called it a "friendraiser." The goal was to show the impact of our programming. Eventually every one of the guests would be solicited to donate, but the dinner itself was about building trust and support.

I'd reserved a table for eighteen in one of the private rooms at a local restaurant and went over my presentation again and again. We wanted to keep it brief so people could ask questions and feel engaged. Karen and I went to the restaurant early that night to set up.

We walked around the table, putting pens and little pads of paper we'd ordered with our logo by every setting. "The table looks beautiful," I said to Karen. "No matter what, this night is already a success."

"I know my face is going to turn red the minute I start speaking," she said, touching her cheeks. The truth was that neither of us would be able to relax until it was over. What I didn't want to think about that night was Hunter's sobriety.

When he arrived at the restaurant, he looked handsome in his navy suit. "Hey, honey!" he called out as he walked across the room. "Hey, Karen!" When he leaned in to give us both kisses on the cheek, I saw something in his eyes that told me he wasn't okay.

My entire body tensed. I could smell alcohol, and I felt my throat closing. There was no longer any question. He was drunk at my dinner. The night I'd worked so hard for. But I said nothing; I just needed to get through the night. I had a roomful of people to host. I moved from person to person, thanking them for coming. I smiled. I told stories. But in my mind, my life was imploding.

When Hunter came over and put his arm around me, I stiffened again. Normally I'd lean into him, but I couldn't do it this time.

Midway through the meal, I gave my brief talk. Next Karen spoke. But when we were finished, my usually reserved husband suddenly took over the conversation. "Hey, friends," he said, standing up. He looked handsome and relaxed, but I noticed his glassy eyes. "We all need to help this organization. Everyone here needs to give." I froze in my chair and stared at him from across the table. I tried to make him stop talking just by my sheer will. He wouldn't let up. "Stop!" I wanted to scream. Did anyone else notice? I looked around the room to smiling faces. It was just me, knowing that my life was now in chaos.

When the last guest left, I grabbed my bag and headed out. I needed to get home and try to make sense of what was happening.

"What's wrong with you?" he asked with a furrowed brow.

"I know you're drinking," I said, not turning to look at him. My heart raced. "I don't want to discuss it now."

"What the hell are you talking about?" There was a mixture of surprise and irritation on his face. We were walking through the front entrance of the restaurant, heading toward the valet. I clutched my bag to my chest. I knew he'd deny it. I knew he'd be angry, but now I was angry too.

"You ruined it all." I turned away from him. We stood in silence outside the restaurant and waited for his car. When his Porsche pulled up, the sight of it rankled me even more. He'd cycled through so many luxury cars over the last few years, and each one seemed like just another sign that he was making bad decisions.

Hunter drove home, and when we got to the house, I walked straight up to bed and called Beau, telling him what had happened. "I'm tired, Beau," I said at the end of the call. "I want to go to bed. Can we talk in the morning?"

"Kath," he said, "I love you. I'll be down tomorrow. Everything is going to be okay. Do you hear me? He's going to be okay." I wanted so badly to let Beau handle it. I was looking for someone to save me as well as my husband.

Hours after I'd gone to bed that night, I felt Hunter climb in next to me. I inched away from him. I didn't want him touching me.

In the morning, after I'd taken the girls to school, I stood in the kitchen and waited for him to wake up. When I heard him walking down the stairs, I braced myself against the counter by the sink. I didn't know what to expect. All I knew was that I wasn't going to let him tell me that I was crazy.

"You're drinking again," I said. "Please don't deny it. I could smell it on you."

"I'm not denying it." He leaned his hip against the kitchen island, looking defeated and tired in his T-shirt and sweatpants.

"What do we do now?" I was at a loss. I still knew nothing

about treatment. And what I really felt like doing was lying down on the kitchen floor and waiting for him to go away, fix it, and come back cured, like he did before. But I asked, "Should you go back to rehab?"

"I know. I know I have to stop. Okay? But I'm not going now. I won't miss Thanksgiving." He seemed defiant but also fragile, almost like a child.

It seemed absurd to me—the idea that we'd just pretend everything was okay so we could all go to Nantucket for Thanksgiving. My brain may have understood that it was the disease talking, but my heart hurt at that moment. I just wanted him gone.

"You can't wait," I said, girded for the fight I could tell was coming. I tried to speak calmly: "Go now, and you'll be back for Christmas. I already talked to Beau. He's on his way down."

At first, he fought to postpone his leave, but he didn't deny that he needed to go. When he looked at me, his normal confidence was gone and all I could see was his fragility.

TWENTY

SEEMS LONELIER THIS TIME

I remember every detail about Hunter's departure for Crossroads in 2003. His bloodshot eyes. My fear. My sadness. My long runs listening to Johnny Cash. But the second time he went to Crossroads, I don't remember how he got to the airport or what the girls were doing. I don't remember if I cried, but I bet I didn't. I do know that I felt a strange relief after he was gone. For the next twenty-eight days, I didn't have to worry about him.

This time the girls had lots of questions about where he was and why he was gone. I lied. I told them Hunter had gone away to a wellness retreat to prepare for the Navy because he wanted to be super fit for when he started. The lie came quickly because I never considered telling them the truth. As far as I knew, they didn't realize their father was drinking.

Later, when they struggled to understand why he'd missed Thanksgiving, I stuck to the story. Growing up, my family shared everything. We knew who was struggling and why. Without realizing it, I'd developed this new code of silence.

I became adept at hiding the truth, at lying. To the girls. To the outside world. To my friends and my family and to myself. When we went to Nantucket for Thanksgiving with the Bidens, I smiled and pretended everything was normal. No one mentioned the fact that Hunter wasn't with us, and I can't imagine how confusing that must have been for the girls.

It was the beginning of a retraction for me. I didn't tell anyone the full breadth of what Hunter and I were going through. My mother's early warning, days before my wedding, still played in my mind: "Be careful what you tell us about your husband. You will forgive him. It won't be as easy for us."

When Hunter had gone away the first time, I felt only love, fear, and a keen missing of him. But in 2012, mistrust had built up between us in a new way. When he came back from Crossroads the first time, trusting his sobriety had come easily. But his relapse left me wondering if I could ever truly trust him again.

When he first went away, the girls were little. Now we had two girls at Sidwell and one in college. Our life was busier and more complicated. The girls were watching us closely and we needed to set the right example for them. The stakes seemed higher now. I look back and realize I gave my daughters no room for sympathy and understanding toward their dad. What was I afraid of? Scaring the girls, or showing that we weren't perfect?

Another difference between 2003 and 2012 was the Internet. Now, instead of writing letters while Hunter was away, we sent emails.

The first time I heard from Hunter was in an email where he asked me to send him a shirt. This wasn't the remorse I was expecting:

I love you. When you get home, can you send me those Patagonia lightweight shirts—only have a few minutes on email—ILY ILY.

I wrote back, "ILY too. Funny that this is your first email. I'll send ASAP."

Both of those emails were colored by addiction. Hunter's brief email came just days after he'd arrived at rehab. He might not have had the energy or strength to write more. My brief email simmers with anger, an anger I refused to acknowledge or address. I wanted to hear that he was sorry, not that he needed his shirts. After he had been there a week, he was able to call home. I told him that I was sad and scared about our relationship. He emailed me shortly after our call.

Sorry—I only get about 5 minutes twice a week to email. What I wanted to say is that all I think about is you all day long and dream about you all night. I am working really hard down here. It made me really sad to know you were sad yesterday. I feel guilty being here not just because of all I've put you through, but also because it seems so indulgent. Know I am thinking about you every day and how I can be a better husband and friend. I'm practicing Yoga and running so we can run together, and if you want I'd like to go to Yoga together too. I'll be able to call you tomorrow between 9 and 11 if you can take the call. Kiss the girls for me. I love you.

Later, I wrote him:

Hunter, I can't fall asleep thinking that you don't realize how often I'm thinking about you. I spent the first two weeks waking up crying. I kept thinking that I was just tired and that I needed more sleep. I just miss you. I miss Hunter. The last few days I woke up feeling rested. I'm ready for you to come home. You are in my thoughts every day. One more week and you're back with us!! We can't wait. Your absence is profound. We love you. I love you . . . all day, every day, even while I sleep.

But what I didn't say was: *I'm mad at you. You lied to me. You made me feel I was crazy. You blamed me.* I didn't explain everything he'd put me through. In the end, it shouldn't be surprising that he never realized his addiction's impact on our family, because I never really told him.

On another phone call midway through his rehab, I finally told him I was scared and that he'd made me feel as if I was crazy. I told him how worried I was that our family life couldn't survive his drinking. When he emailed me afterward, I felt great relief and hope because his email sounded not just earnest but honest. I could hear the man I'd married. I printed it out and took it to bed with me, reading it over and over:

The truth is that now that I look back on it I lost my sobriety long before I picked up a drink. It started with NY and me going to less and less meetings and becoming obsessed with fixing the problems at work, not working out every day, not spending more time w/ you and the girls. It took years for me to actually pick up a drink after that, but all the same behavior started then.

You are my best friend in the world. I love every part of you. And I can't stand the fact that I have made you feel so alone in this relationship for the last few years. All I know now is that I can't ever let my guard down again. I can't miss a meeting, stop working out, allow myself to be alone for long stretches etc. . . . I just can't do this to myself or you or the girls again. I'm just scared to death I'll screw it up again and lose you. I love you. I'll call tomorrow—leave your phone on.

After that message, I could let go of my anxiety and just miss him, miss the Hunter I'd fallen in love with. Now my messages held out love. I wrote back: "I really miss you too. Seems lonelier this time. Loving you and missing you."

The first time he'd gone into rehab, he'd missed Finnegan's and Maisy's birthdays. He'd missed their first day of school. This time, he missed Thanksgiving. He missed my birthday. He missed Maisy's championship flag football game. I felt the weight of his absence, but I knew if he wasn't sober, he wouldn't really be there anyway.

When the twenty-eight days ended, I drove to Dulles Airport to pick him up. While I waited outside the doors to the international terminal, I felt a nervousness I barely understood.

When I finally saw Hunter walking toward me, my chest tightened. He'd cut his hair short, almost to the scalp. His buzz cut reminded me of an episode a few months earlier when, I knew now, he was secretly drinking. I'd woken up in the morning to find him with a shaved head.

That time he'd said he'd been trimming his sideburns and had tried to even them out and ended up shaving all his hair off. Now, even as Hunter held me in his arms, I felt a pervading sense of worry.

"You cut your hair again," I said to him as he held me.

"Yeah. Why?" he asked, pulling back and giving me a look of genuine confusion. "You don't like it?"

"Sure," I said, smiling, "it just surprised me." Shaving his head seemed like a warning. I wanted him to look like the sober version of my husband, and a shaved head didn't fit that picture.

I knew that he just wanted me to hold him and love him outside that terminal. I wanted that too. I desperately wanted to trust him again, but of course, that isn't how trust works.

When we got back from the airport that night, I could sense both of us holding back, perhaps from a weariness of battle.

We tried to restart our marriage, but it didn't come naturally. We weren't fighting, not in the beginning. We just seemed to be drifting. From the outside, everything was as it should be. The family trips, family dinners, and weekends of sports continued. But inside, at home, we weren't sharing. Hunter could be lying in bed next to me and he'd feel a world away. We went through the motions, and I tried to have hope. But he was guarded with me, while I was suspicious.

By spring I'd started seeing the warning signs again. Unlike the last time, my antennae were always up. But I didn't ask him if he was okay. I didn't question him about his behavior this time. I didn't have the energy. Or maybe I was scared to.

In June 2013, he reported for duty at the Norfolk navy base in Virginia for his first weekend of Navy service. When his weekend of service was over and he returned home, he didn't have much to say about it. I didn't push.

TWENTY-ONE

FLAGS

'd bought Hunter art supplies for Christmas, and that summer when he came to the lake, we set up a little studio for him in the corner of our garage. He hadn't painted since the early years when we lived on Centre Road, but now he'd sit on an old red vinyl swivel chair and paint every night. I'd go see him before I went to bed, and the garage would be filled with smoke, reeking of cigarettes.

The art supplies were a way to keep him healing, and yet the painting he was doing felt dark. He painted cryptic, abstract paintings, all in shadowy colors.

There were other worrying signs. During the day, when we were on the beach with my family, he'd sit off to the side, reading his book and sneaking cigarettes. Worry consumed me. He had already gone to Crossroads twice. Would he need to go back again? Would this cycle of relapse just keep happening? I hadn't said anything to Beau about it yet. I didn't want to set the wheels in motion again.

There was also a noticeable difference in the way Hunter looked that summer. He was as handsome as always—with his strong jawline and blue eyes—but there was a sloppiness to him now, as if he didn't care how he appeared. When he was sober, he cared. He exercised and dressed well. But that summer, he wore the same pair of oversized Levi's and an old shirt. His blue eyes looked tired.

He'd often say he was going to an AA meeting in nearby Michigan City, Indiana, but I didn't believe him. One day, I found out where the meetings were held and pulled my bike out of the garage. It was an impulsive move, and I was still wearing my bathing suit and a cover-up as I started pedaling. I didn't tell anyone I was leaving, and I rode toward town, feeling stupid. What was I doing? I had members of my family looking at me, worried, because I was distracted and on edge. But I said nothing and held the fear close to my chest. I still didn't trust myself enough to tell anyone. Not even Amy.

I hid along the side of a building in Michigan City with my bike, trying to see if our old Suburban was there among the half dozen cars parked next to a beat-up brick house a few doors off the corner. There was a picnic bench on the sidewalk filled with men smoking. I'd driven by that house hundreds, if not thousands, of times throughout my life and never given it any notice. Now I stared hard. The house was just a block from Franklin Street, the main drag in Michigan City. I stood there, holding on to my bike, willing the house to give me answers, desperately wanting to catch sight of Hunter's car. I had resorted to stalking my husband.

But his car wasn't there. Maybe he was at a different meeting? What if he drove by and saw me? What would I say? I would lie. Of course I would. "Oh, I was just out for a ride and was taking a break." How could I say *I don't believe you*?

I didn't trust my husband. And he didn't trust me, either, as if my own suspicion about him made me suspect. I wouldn't tell him about this secret bike ride and how his car wasn't at the AA meeting—I'd keep what I knew secret. Maybe, I thought, he'd work it out on his own.

And not every day was bad. One day I'd find him glassy-eyed in the garage, painting next to an ashtray full of cigarette stubs. The next day he'd be swimming in the lake with the girls and letting them climb all over him. Part of my reasoning went like this: *Maybe if I hold off confronting him about his lies, the good days will outnumber the scary ones.* Sometimes I even believed that it was my own skepticism about him that was the problem. Wasn't I being paranoid? Maybe he didn't go to the actual AA meetings, but he went somewhere to get coffee and be on his own. That was okay, right? The lake house was always full of people and so very loud. Maybe he just needed some peace and quiet.

That August of 2013, Beau and Hallie brought their two kids to Indiana for their annual visit. Hallie and Beau had been coming to the lake for so long by then that they were a part of the fabric of my family. Years before Hunter and I ever had our own house, they'd stayed with us at my parents' and squeezed into the sleeping loft with everyone else.

When Beau's family arrived, Natalie and little Hunter were the first through the door, their small wiry bodies running up the stairs to find their cousins. Finnegan and Maisy grabbed them midrun and spun them around, as the noise level throughout the house spiked. Hallie and Beau came in after them. Beau was wearing a blue polo shirt and khaki pants. Hallie was in a fitted shirt and jeans, and after hours of traveling with two small kids, they both still looked irritatingly beautiful. Even their canvas bags looked attractive. "Kath," Beau said, "want to take a run with me?" He knew I wouldn't.

"Nope," I said, "you're too fast, and I'm not going to keep asking you to slow down."

Beau headed out the door minutes after they'd arrived, while Hallie and I went out to the front porch and ran through weekend plans. We'd go to my aunt Noreen's for a chili dinner for twenty of us, and Hunt would try to join if he got back in time from a work trip. I didn't mention my fears about Hunter. I just wanted to sit on the porch in the sun and pretend everything was okay. I hoped he'd be on his best behavior now that his brother was there. Hunter's charade was much harder for him to pull off with Beau around.

About an hour after Beau left on his run, Hallie and I saw him heading back toward us from the road. The sun was beating down, but the temperature was in the seventies with a soft breeze. Perfect running weather. Beau came out to the porch drenched in sweat but grinning widely. He sat and leaned against the railing, stretching his legs out in front of him. I went into the house to bring him a glass of water. I liked taking care of him. I liked taking care of everyone. "Drink this," I said as he smiled up at me.

I turned to Hallie and said, "Let's start getting the kids going for dinner," and headed back into the house. I grabbed a few bottles of wine in the kitchen, and Beau appeared from his bedroom, transformed in khaki shorts and a polo shirt. We herded the kids into the old Suburban. I drove, with Hallie in the front seat. Beau sat in back, behind Hallie, surrounded by the kids.

"Will the D'Amatos be there?" Natalie asked me.

"Yep," I said.

"How about Dorothy and Emily?" she asked, referring to my brother Jimmy's daughters.

"They're coming over the weekend. Everyone is so excited to see all of you!" I said, and meant it. When we pulled in at Aunt Noreen's, the kids flew out of the car toward the house. I climbed out and waited for Beau and Hallie to come around the car. After a few minutes, I walked back to find out what was taking them so long and saw Hallie leaning into the backseat. Then she turned to me, looking terrified.

"Something's wrong," she said. "He can't get out. Something is really wrong."

"We'll take him back to the house," I told her, with no idea what was happening. "Let me tell my parents." I ran toward the house and opened the door and told my mom that Hallie needed to go back to the house to call her family. The lie came quickly to me. How could I tell them that something was wrong with Beau? I ran back to the car and Hallie climbed in back with Beau as I pulled out.

"Beau," I asked him. "Did you drink enough water after your run?" But he couldn't answer me. Hallie was holding his hand and rubbing his back. "I'm going to call his doctor," she said, but reception was bad at the lake, and she couldn't get through.

I drove as fast as I could back to the house. "Call Hunter,"

I told her. "He should be home soon." I didn't think about whether he would be sober or not. We needed him, and I knew he'd tell us what to do.

My hands were shaking as I pulled the car into our driveway. Beau started repeating the phrase "I'm fine" while Hallie and I helped him out of the car and walked with him downstairs to their room. Hallie called his doctor, who said he might be dehydrated and that we should give him some Gatorade.

"We don't have Gatorade. I'll run to the store and get some." I sped to the gas station a few blocks away, bought Gatorade, and rushed back home. We tried to get him to drink it, while we kept calling Hunter. *Hunter, please get home*, I prayed. He had told me once that his greatest fear his whole life was that something bad would happen to Beau.

But somehow, in the terror of that evening, I did not even think about the small stroke Beau had suffered a few years earlier. It had happened back in 2010, and he'd recovered so quickly that we'd hardly even called it a stroke—it was more like a small aberration. The only thing that had stayed with me from that strange time was the premonition Hunter had on the morning of Beau's stroke. Hunter had woken early, sensing that something was not right. There was always this connection between the brothers that seemed beyond the physical—this need to know that the other one was okay.

Now I heard the side door to the lake house open. "Hunter?" I called out. "We're down here!" He may have sensed the fear in my voice, but I think he also just knew something was wrong. I heard him drop his bag in the hall and run down the stairs, and I felt a quick burst of relief.

"Hey, buddy. What's going on?" he said as he sat down on Beau's bed. "It's going to be okay. Hear me? You're going to be okay. Let's take you to the hospital and get you checked out." He stroked his brother's face. I stood against the wall of the bedroom, frightened out of my mind.

"Let's go," Hunter said. Now that he was here, he'd be in charge. That was always the case.

The drive to St. Anthony's Hospital in Michigan City was only fifteen minutes, but it seemed to take forever. Beau was quickly admitted, and Hallie and I sat outside his room in hard plastic chairs. She started to cry softly, and I put my arms around her. A few hours earlier, we'd sat on the front porch looking out toward the lake. Now we sat in the antiseptic hallway of St. Anthony's.

"We're moving him to Northwestern by ambulance," Hunter said as he walked back down the hall toward us, staring at his phone while he talked. "Kathleen, you go back and stay with the kids. Hallie, you can drive with Beau, and I'll follow in my car." Now I look back and think about the weight Hunter must have felt. But I don't think Hunter ever thought of it as a responsibility. It was more than a sense of duty. Saving Beau was like saving himself.

By the time I got back to our house that night, everyone had returned from dinner, and my mom was in the kitchen, waiting for me. "Is everything okay?" she asked, looking worried.

"Hallie and Hunter took Beau to Northwestern," I said quietly, pulling her into the corner of the kitchen. "Mom, you cannot tell anyone. Okay? No one." After twenty years with the Bidens, I knew that everything in the family was meant to stay private. But this secret felt so big. Beau's very life was in peril.

The house was full of kids now, and we decided to tell them that Beau wasn't feeling well, and that out of an abundance of caution, he'd gone to see a doctor. Because I didn't look worried as I told them, the kids all took in the information without question.

Then I walked out to the front porch and sat down. The sun had set, and there was a cool breeze off the lake. I rubbed my thumbnail along my lip, a nervous habit I'd had since I was a child, and searched my mind for answers. Maybe tomorrow Hunter would call, just like in 2010, and tell me Beau was fine. For now, I'd cling to that hope. And tomorrow I'd take the kids to the beach and maybe to miniature golf. I'd keep them busy all day long. I was good at distraction.

TWENTY-TWO

NO COMFORT, NO CURE

went to bed that night but couldn't sleep. Sometime after midnight, I got up and quietly slipped out the side door and pulled my bike out of the garage. The night air felt cool as I rode down Lake Shore Drive in my cotton nightgown and helmet, pedaling as fast as I could. The road was empty, and the lights from my bike were the only illumination. I couldn't calm my mind, and I wanted so much to exhaust myself. Hunter and Beau both seemed so vulnerable to me. The two men I'd come to rely on more than any others both felt so far away, on the brink of some awful ending.

I biked to the end of the road and back, my nightgown plastered to my body with sweat. My legs felt tired, but my thoughts still wouldn't slow down. When I got back, I left my bike leaning against the side of the house and tiptoed back to bed, feeling that sleep would never come. I held the phone to my chest the whole night and woke to its ringing.

"Someone from the hospital leaked to the press," Hunter

said into the phone, sounding angry. "We're working out a statement." I didn't care about the press, I wanted to hear about Beau. I also didn't like that Hunter sounded angry. Angry wasn't good. Angry meant that Hunter might be struggling. Could my fear of his relapse be real?

"I'm arranging a flight to take Beau to Thomas Jefferson University Hospital in Philadelphia to see his doctors and get more tests done," he said. "We're still trying to understand what happened and put together a plan." I felt far away from him then, a distance that kept growing. "I want you to stay at the lake with the kids," he said.

Asking me to stay away made sense in a way, but we could have easily left the kids with my parents, too. I tried to push away this feeling that he didn't want me around him. We'd always gone through everything important together. He was with his brother in the hospital, and I was at the lake with the kids. I knew that Beau and Hunter were both in crisis. Hunter's addiction was invisible to almost everyone but me. I felt the weight of the situation, and yet I no longer had Beau to lean on.

I tried to keep up a façade that nothing was wrong. My whole body was shaky when I walked down to the beach the next day with Patty, Amy, and Michele, and I dropped a container of food into the sand. "Shit. Shit!" I said, as I knelt down and tried to salvage the sandwiches.

"What's going on?" Patty asked.

All three of these women had stood by me my whole life, but I couldn't let them in. The story hadn't come out yet. I still believed that keeping secrets showed my loyalty. My secret stayed mine alone.

Hunter called me that night. Beau had been examined at Jefferson Hospital in Philadelphia and a mass was found in his brain. He needed surgery. Hunter and his family were all flying to MD Anderson Cancer Center in Houston for the procedure.

"I'll fly and meet you," I told him, feeling such a strong pull to him. I wanted to be there. I thought he needed me as much as I needed him.

"There's no reason for you to come out," he said. "It's better if you stay with the kids. If you come, they're going to be scared that something is really wrong. I'm fine. I promise. I'll feel better knowing you are with them."

I struggled to accept this. How could I not be there?

Hallie felt differently and told me so. "I want you to be here," she said on the phone. "Please. Fly out and meet us. I need you." Hallie, far more than me, was comfortable asking for help.

While Hunter may not have wanted me there, I didn't want to let Hallie down. And I needed to be there for myself. I flew out to Houston and took a cab from the airport. Walking up to the front entrance of the hospital's hotel, I saw the telltale sign of my in-laws' presence: a man with a discreet earpiece standing off to the side of the door. I smiled as I walked up to him. "Can someone help me find the family?"

He turned slightly to talk into the microphone tucked into his shirt sleeve. A few minutes later, another agent arrived to bring me up. When I walked into Beau's hospital suite, I found him and Hunter sitting at a table near the window with their dad. The air in the room felt heavy. I'd called Hunter that morning and told him I was coming, and now I went over and

kissed him first before going and kissing the rest of the family.
Ashley and her husband, Howard, sat together with their
computers open in their laps. Jill sat over to the side, holding
a red pen in her hand as she graded her students' papers.
Hallie sat on the couch, a magazine open on her lap.

After a quiet dinner at a local restaurant, we all went back
to the hospital hotel and up to our own rooms. Ours had dark
wooden furniture and a stiff coverlet on the bed. I climbed
under the sheets while Hunter stood with his iPad by the bathroom door, the glow from the screen casting a blue light onto
his face. He looked exhausted, but I knew he wasn't coming to
bed. Beau's surgery was the following morning, and I knew
Hunter's head was filled with worry. He'd take his iPad downstairs and smoke somewhere outside the hotel.

"Hunt," I said to him, "will you lie down with me?"

Since arriving in Houston, I'd felt even more disconnected
from him. He was consumed with every detail of Beau's treatment, but he wasn't sharing any of it with me. I didn't know
how to reach him, my husband of twenty years. He climbed
into the bed and draped his arm around my waist. I held tight
to his arm.

"I love you," I said, feeling the rise and fall of his chest. "I
am here for you."

Even when I felt emotionally distanced from him like this,
I still craved his physical touch. I turned toward him and laid
my head against his chest. There was no conversation between
us—no discussion about what was going on. We seemed to
have no words for how worried we were about Beau. How
could I possibly bring up my fear about Hunter's drinking
now? A few minutes later, he slipped out of bed, and I felt that

tightening in my chest return. He picked up his iPad and phone from the dresser, and I knew in that moment that I wasn't enough. He needed to find comfort somewhere else. Or maybe "comfort" is the wrong word. That night, there could be no comfort. All I could think was, would Beau's illness make him stronger or crush him?

Within days, we learned that the growth in Beau's brain was a tumor, a glioblastoma. It was the worst possible outcome. An aggressive and quick-moving cancer. A disease with no cure. Hunter and I both said if anyone could survive, it had to be Beau. Yet we couldn't erase what we knew. The average survival period was twelve to eighteen months.

When Hunter and I returned to D.C. after Beau's surgery, our old lives felt like a distant memory. But I didn't allow myself to fully absorb the bad news of Beau's diagnosis, just as I hadn't really ever allowed myself to take in the full scope of Hunter's addiction. He stayed laser-focused on Beau, and I didn't know where Hunter's sobriety even fitted into the conversation anymore.

In September, my calendar said that Hunter was going away for two weeks of Navy training. But he'd been evasive about the Navy all summer, and I didn't push it. One day early in September, I asked about the upcoming trip while we were standing near our kitchen island, and he told me, with a solemn look on his face, that he'd failed the Navy's drug test back in June.

"What does that even mean? You're taking drugs? What drugs?"

"Of course not, Kathleen. I have no idea how the drugs got into my system. I'm fighting it. I have a lawyer and we are trying to figure out the best way to handle it."

"What drug?" I asked, pressing my hands on the countertop.

"Cocaine. But obviously I didn't take it. Why would I take cocaine knowing that I would be tested?"

"But *how* could you test positive for cocaine?"

He told me he'd gone to a bar down on K Street for a drink and asked someone for a cigarette. That's when he thought he'd inadvertently ingested cocaine. Someone had given him a cigarette with cocaine in it. His story was so hard to believe, but he was unwavering.

I didn't press him. Still, I was spinning with the news. Cocaine. It was a whole new frightening thing. And he'd gone to a bar for a drink? "Are you drinking now?" I asked, staring hard into his eyes, wondering then if he had a "tell."

My mother said she always knew when I was going to tell a lie, and she called it my "tell." If she ever asked me something and I answered, "What?," she knew the next thing I said wouldn't be true.

"Kathleen," he answered with conviction, "I'm not drinking now. I promise."

What was Hunter's tell? Anger? Denial? I still didn't really know after all these years.

As fall turned into winter, I continued to quietly worry about Hunter. He traveled for business and to be with Beau. I was busy with the girls and was spending more and more time on

DCVLP. But, when Hunter was home, I'd watch him closely. He seemed to bristle at my attention. If I asked him if he was okay, he'd answer, "Seriously? I'm working to pay for this life and taking care of my brother. No, I'm not okay." Then he'd walk away. It was true. This weight he carried of supporting our family and taking care of his brother was monumental.

When Hunter started coming home late, night after night, I stopped asking where he'd been. My mother always told me, don't ask a question to which you already know the answer. And yet he still had a softness and affection for the girls, and they wanted that affection badly. Maisy would sometimes wait until he came home to go to sleep. He'd lie in her bed, rubbing her back until her eyes closed. There were many mornings I'd find him asleep in his suit, lying next to her. His anger seemed reserved just for me. It wasn't a screaming anger; it was quiet and accusatory, as if every single thing I did irritated him.

TWENTY-THREE

DRUNK AT CHRISTMAS

We flew to the lake for Christmas, but nothing was as it should be. Hunter kept disappearing during family meals, and he'd spend what seemed like hours in the bathroom. We hosted all my cousins and their spouses for New Year's Eve dinner, and he seemed to be looking for a fight. When we went to the living room after dinner to play charades, his voice had an angry edge to it. He kept referring to obscure books that no one had heard of, taking pleasure in our not knowing.

"Hunt, please stop. Just use books and movies we'll all know," I said.

"Kathleen, I'm simply playing the game," he said with a sneer.

The next day, he announced he was painting our bedroom and went to the hardware store and bought paint and a sprayer. Back home, he closed the bedroom door and blasted the walls with the spray gun for hours. The light blue paint found its way onto the carpet and the furniture, and when I opened the bedroom door, I could smell the alcohol. But his angry stare kept me silent. I wasn't going to confront him there.

I deflected any family discussion of Hunter's behavior or Beau's illness. "How is Beau?" my mother asked me as we stood in the kitchen. "He's good," I said, walking away and shutting down further conversation. I didn't give any explanations or ask for support. I tried to pretend everything was okay, but I can't imagine anyone believed me. During that trip, I found beer cans and vodka bottles each day in the pockets of his coats, in the file cabinet, on the floor of the closet, and scattered throughout the garage. And each day Hunter's anger simmered, looking for an outlet. He practically seethed with it. I was now living in a state of constant apprehension. There was no question about Hunter's drinking, and yet we silently went through our days, avoiding each other as best we could. I didn't know how or when it would end.

When we returned to D.C. I called Beau. "Hunter is drinking again."

I began to lose faith that he could stop. He'd already gone away twice, yet his drinking seemed worse than ever. Now Beau and I tried to find another option, something he could do without going away. The Executive Addictive Disease Program (EADP) operated out of a row house on Wisconsin Avenue, just a few blocks from the girls' school. I'd driven by the nondescript brick building a million times. I didn't know how Beau got Hunter to admit he was drinking, much less agree to this program, but he did.

When Hunter and I arrived at EADP on a dreary January morning, we were met by Beau, who had driven down from Delaware. I rang the bell while Hunter stood quietly next to me on the stoop and Beau kept up a running commentary: "This place seems great. Hunt, you can stop here on your way to work." The city felt gray and cold that morning. I had on a long down coat that reached below my boots and I was still shivering, but mostly because of nerves.

The three of us were led by a counselor into a little sitting room with a beat-up plaid couch that looked like the one from my college apartment. I kept my coat zipped all the way up and sat on the couch between Beau and Hunter, feeling like a rag doll. I cried through the entire two-hour meeting, tears of both exhaustion and fear. I knew that I had not been facing the truth. But with Beau and Hunter on either side of me, I'd finally lost the energy to pretend.

Two people sat across from us: the program director and the woman who would be Hunter's counselor. Both of them were in recovery themselves and showed an earnest empathy as they asked Hunter questions. Beau never stopped campaigning on his brother's behalf during the whole intake session. "I know my brother can do it," he said, leaning forward, his elbows on his knees. He had on a beige sweater over a button-down shirt and the sincerest expression on his face. "This is the right time. He's worried about me but I'm good. I'm really good. He knows he can do it." He kept looking from one to the other of them, while Hunter sat silently on the other side of me, his head bowed. I felt such a deep sadness for him. And desperation.

I had hope but also trepidation. Maybe this was the thing

that could finally bring Hunter back. EADP had an outpatient model: Hunter would stay at home with us while he worked with the counselors. He was meant to go to the townhouse daily, and I'd join him there once or twice a week for therapy sessions, which would mark a fundamental change in my involvement with his addiction. It was the very first time that I was included in any substantial way in his recovery.

In our first therapy session, Hunter and I sat holding hands on a couch in a little room in the back of the lower level of the building. Our counselor sat in a chair across from us with potted ferns behind her on the windowsill. The room felt worn, like the rest of the building, but had a warmth to it. The counselor, slightly younger than we were, with long brown hair, looked at me with compassion and said, "The first thing we are going to do is set some ground rules." She was soft-spoken and kind, and I liked her right away.

"Hunter, you are going to sign an agreement that says you cannot stay in the house if you aren't sober." She looked somber as she made her point. "You both have to agree to it. It isn't good for anyone, especially the kids."

Finally he and I were in dialogue about the actual disease. Finally I was seeing the struggle up close. Over the past few years, as Hunter lost his hold on sobriety, I hadn't seen any options for me other than to endure it. Now I was being told I had choices. It was an utterly foreign concept to me, telling my husband that he couldn't stay in our home. For years to come, I'd cling to this rule.

"Kathleen," she went on. "You are no longer policing Hunter. No more smelling water bottles or rummaging through his things looking for alcohol. Okay? He's going to be tested here every day, so you do not have to worry while he is in this program." She smiled kindly but with a look that said, *You better be listening to me.*

It was as if she lifted a fifty-pound weight off my chest. "Thank you," I said, and Hunter and I both nodded our agreement. I knew his commitment to sobriety was real, but I also sensed a deep frailty in him.

During our next session, Hunter talked about how foreign travel was a trigger for his drinking, how it had caused his relapses in the past. Now he was being truly honest about his addiction in a way I had never heard before. He looked more like the Hunter I knew, wearing his suit, ready to go back to the office after our meeting. At one point he turned to me and said, "I'm not going to travel outside the country until I've been sober for a year. I need to get back into my routine. I know what I need to do."

Slowly, I was beginning to believe this could work. He knew better than me what he needed, and I pushed away any doubt about his sobriety because he was being tested daily and building his routine of going to the office and exercising. I felt protective of him during this time, because I was seeing it up close now: how hardworking the program was.

We talked about Beau every day but never once mentioned that he was, in fact, dying. Instead, we talked about treatments and logistics. At night, when Hunter came to bed, I'd wrap my arms around him, desperately wanting to comfort him. He took my affection but there was a sadness that I couldn't lift from him. The only laughter and smiles we shared came from being with our girls.

At another therapy session in the EADP brownstone, Hunter's dismissal from the Navy came up. He repeated to the counselor his story about not knowingly taking cocaine. "I honestly have no idea how cocaine got in my system," he said with a look of real bewilderment.

She didn't push back on it, and I sat there, stunned. Hunter's story had never made sense to me.

"The only thing I can think of," he added now, "is that a cigarette someone gave me was laced."

I looked to the counselor, but she didn't say anything. I wanted her to challenge him, but maybe that's not how recovery worked. When she sat quietly, seeming to accept his explanation, I followed her lead and let him stick to his story. But I knew, too, that this was part of the pattern Hunter and I had of not talking about things, as if to erase them.

More than anything, we didn't criticize each other. Sometimes I'd look at other marriages and feel shocked at the way they worked. On more than one occasion, I had told Amy and my sister-in-law Michele that they were too hard on their husbands. They yelled and they got mad. They criticized. But Amy and Michele were completely comfortable in their marriages, and when they were upset, they vocalized it. Hunter and I kept our negative thoughts to ourselves. And what may have started as a kindness, not wanting to hurt each other, ended up creating a relationship filled with secrets and lies.

But I sat in that little room in the EADP brownstone and watched as Hunter explained how the positive cocaine results were a mistake. The counselor simply took in the information without judgment. I tried to follow her lead and let it go too.

"He's good, right, Kath?" Beau asked me on the phone each week. "I'm talking to him every day. He sounds great."

"He is great," I answered, wanting to comfort Beau. I could no longer burden him with my worries. Now I only wanted to make him feel better. And I had started to believe that maybe Hunter really was great, or on his way to great.

I let go of his Navy story and of some of the tension I'd been carrying. I followed the counselor's instructions and stopped searching his closet and pockets for alcohol. I looked forward to our weekly sessions together. And I began to feel connected to him again.

It was April when Hunter announced during our session at EADP that he had to go to Paris on business. Instantly, I felt my entire body tense up. "Kathleen." He turned to me on that tired couch. "Everyone I'm traveling with *knows* I quit drinking. I'm going to be talking to my sponsor every day. It's only *three* days. You have nothing to worry about."

"You told us you weren't going to travel abroad until you'd gotten a year's sobriety," I said, feeling, in that moment, as though I'd already lost him. I turned to the counselor. "Right? Didn't he say he needed a year's sobriety?"

The counselor seemed caught in the middle.

"Listen," Hunter said now, taking my hand, "you don't have to worry. My addiction has gotten so bad, if I relapse, I'll die. It isn't going to happen. I *promise* you."

The counselor sat there quietly. Maybe this conversation

seemed like a marital issue, not one for an addiction counselor. But Hunter had promised no foreign travel for a year. He'd said it was his biggest trigger. I felt as if he was already taking a drink right there in front of me.

Hunter left for Paris a few weeks later. But it didn't stop there. Soon he was traveling abroad frequently. He was going to AA meetings, so I tried to keep my worry at bay. He was no longer testing every day. Of course, daily testing couldn't last forever, but now my fears started creeping back. We were going to EADP sessions together less and less, and those words he'd told me on that couch in that little back room haunted me now: *If I relapse, I'll die.*

TWENTY-FOUR

DO YOU KNOW WHERE HUNTER IS?

A few months later, in June 2014, I found my husband sitting on the deck off our bedroom at the lake. Maisy and I had just arrived from D.C., having stayed back for a basketball tournament. Maisy hopped out of the car and ran up the hill to my parents' house to see her cousins while I carried our bags into our house. I smelled cigarette smoke as soon as I opened the door, and my stomach knotted. He was smoking inside, something that he'd never do sober.

I dropped the bags in the hallway and walked to our bedroom at the back of the house. When I opened the door, the room was filled with smoke, and Hunter was sitting, glassy-eyed, on the little back porch with the sliding door open. He could barely hold his head up.

"What are you *doing*?" I said with anger. "The whole house smells like cigarettes. Why did you leave the door open?"

"I know that, Kathleen. I *know* the door is open. You're so goddamn dumb. You walk in yelling at *me*?" He put his cigarette out now. "Are *you* drunk, Kathleen? Why don't *you* go get drunk with your *cousin*!"

I was now accustomed to his turning the tables on me this way, but each time he drank, the process of getting him to admit he wasn't sober took longer and was more exhausting. The denials grew angrier and more bitter too. For the first time, Hunter was calling me names.

I recognized this man standing before me. This was Hunter B. The cruel version of my husband. The Mr. Hyde to his Dr. Jekyll. His drunk persona no longer pretending to be sober. He was simply mean. Some part of me understood that it was the addiction talking, but his words still cut.

"I'm going to my parents'," I told him, trying to keep my voice calm. "You have to be gone when I get back." That was the agreement we'd made at EADP, and I clung to it.

As I walked up the hill to my parents' house, I pressed my eyes shut. I remembered how Hunter, Beau, and I had sat together on that beat-up couch during the EADP intake, and how I cried in my parka while Beau assured the counselors that Hunter was finally and truly ready for recovery. And later, in that same room, Hunter and I had agreed he could no longer stay at home if he wasn't sober.

I found my mom in her kitchen and sat on one of the blue wooden chairs near the window as I watched her prepare soup. "Hunter's drinking again," I told her. The first time I'd told my parents about Hunter's drinking was back when he'd gone to Crossroads the second time, in the fall of 2012. I'd told them quickly, in a way that made it sound as if it was his first time in rehab. I also told them something I'd repeat for years to come: "I don't want to talk about it." Now, as I sat slumped in the chair in my mom's kitchen, I just wanted her to know the facts, and I still didn't want to talk about it. I felt the whole story was too complicated for my innocent mother.

She came over and kissed me on the forehead. "You're going to be okay, sweetheart."

"What are you making? I'm starved." Sitting in the kitchen watching her cook, I felt comforted, even though I knew it was only temporary. The house was full of my brothers' kids and my cousins' kids and my own three girls, and I stayed through dinner, happy to be distracted. I didn't want to think about what was going on back in my house, didn't want to imagine what my husband was doing. Could he even pack himself up to leave when he was this drunk? And where would he go? Where would he sleep? But he had to leave. That was our deal.

It felt like a new low. Why was he so mad at me? What had I done? I began to question myself in a new way. Was I making it worse? The only thing I could hold on to was the rule that he had to leave if he wasn't sober. He couldn't get mad at me for that. We'd both agreed to it.

When I got back to our house that night, Hunter was gone, and I felt relieved. The next morning, I woke up alone, and my relief turned to worry. Where was he? I walked quietly into the kitchen, careful not to wake the girls. The early morning sun cast a warm glow through the large front windows. Quiet mornings when I woke first were normally a great comfort,

but not that day. I made myself a cup of coffee and took it out
to the front deck. The lake was calm, and the street was empty.

Sitting across the street in their black SUVs were our Secret
Service detail. I waved to them as I sat down on the sofa in my
pajamas, self-conscious as they waved back at me, smiling.
But the Secret Service couldn't help it. They had a job, which
was to know where my girls and my husband were at all times.

I thought, *If only they knew what's really going on in our
lives*. Though in truth, they probably knew far more than me.
They'd been following Hunter since 2008. Surely they'd seen
him drinking. Surely they'd seen his darker side.

The coffee tasted bitter, but I drank it. I watched a jogger
slowly making her way along Lake Shore Drive. I wanted to be
her, to run and listen to music and not sit on the porch, wondering where my husband was. I wanted things to be normal.
I wanted to worry about sunblock and who was coming to
dinner.

I called EADP. They didn't answer, so I texted his counselor: "Hunter relapsed and left last night. I don't know where
he is. I don't know what to do."

I set the phone beside me and looked out at the lake that
had brought me so much comfort in the past. Hunter's anger
the evening before was seared into my brain. I did tell him he
had to leave. I did accuse him of drinking. But I had to remind
myself, it was all true. I was not crazy.

I picked up my phone again and stared at it. There was no
one else to call. I couldn't call Beau. It was too much to put on
him now. I felt more alone than ever before, so I finally called
Hunter.

He didn't pick up.

"Hunter," I said into his voicemail. "Please call me and tell me you're okay. I'm scared. Just let me know what you're doing."

While I was sitting there staring at my phone, it rang. I almost screamed.

"Hey, I've got a plan," he said quickly, sounding manic and not at all sober. "I'm going to Mexico to a program I told you about. Remember how I told you about this drug, ibogaine? I feel really good about it, and I want you to research it. I think it will work. I believe it will work."

I didn't remember us ever talking about this program or about ibogaine. The idea that he had to go to Mexico to take it made me skeptical and scared. "You're doing *what*?" I asked him. Nothing was ever simple with Hunter. Nothing.

But it was as though he hadn't heard me: "My friend from AA, Bobby, said he'd be happy to talk to you about it. He did it and it worked for him. I want you to support this. I need you to support this." He was talking with a slight slur that let me know he'd probably been up all night drinking.

Going to Mexico to take an experimental drug sounded like a really bad idea. I didn't want to talk to Bobby about it, whoever he was. "Can you call EADP and see what they think?" I didn't want to fight. "Please, can we talk to EADP?"

But Hunter just said again that Bobby would reach out to me, and then he hung up.

Not long afterward, his counselor called, and I told her about Hunter's plan. "If he believes it will work," she said, "then I think you should support him. Everyone's addiction is different." Another counselor from EADP called and suggested we hold an intervention at the lake, asking Hunter's family to come, specifically Joe and Beau.

"Hunter isn't here. I don't even know where he's staying." I was exhausted by the thought of trying to arrange an intervention. EADP didn't have the answers I wanted, and my faith in the program was gone. I didn't know what I expected them to do from D.C., with Hunter on his way to Mexico. But now I had nowhere to turn.

Hunter's friend Bobby did email me. I wrote back to him that I was scared and didn't want Hunter to do it. Bobby wrote that he'd tried literally everything and ibogaine was the thing that got him sober. Bobby was kind and patient. Because ibogaine had worked for him, maybe it could work for Hunter.

The girls would be waking up soon, and I finally acquiesced. "Okay," I texted Hunter. "Go. I will be praying for you."

Later that morning, I heard a knock on the side door of the lake house, and I opened it to two men standing in khakis and button-down shirts.

"I'm sorry to bother you, Kathleen," the taller one said. As much as the agents tried to be not only discreet but casual, there was always a great seriousness to their expressions. After all, these were men and women with guns hidden under their shirts, responsible for the well-being of the vice president's family. "Do you know where Hunter is? We can't reach him."

"I don't," I said. "I'm sorry. I'll try to reach him too." I knew my husband was on his way to Mexico, but at this point I had no idea where he would be staying there.

The agents covered the vice president's family "loosely," which allowed the girls and Hunter to drive on their own while the agents followed, but this type of coverage required us to be very proactive about our movements and to tell the agents everything; their jobs were on the line.

Having spent his entire life in the public eye, Hunter could be obsessive about his privacy. Like many addicts, he was even more secretive about his addiction. And I knew that the stigma of his addiction was, ironically, yet another degree of difficulty in his struggle to stay sober. He didn't want the agents to know he was going to Mexico to try yet another recovery program. But I'm sure they knew more than they wanted to about his difficulties.

I texted Hunter now and told him he had to call his Secret Service detail. He told me he was going to ask to be released from coverage. After almost six years of Secret Service protection, Hunter would now be on his own.

When the girls got up that morning, I told them that their dad had to go back east for work. Maisy started to cry. "Why?" she asked. "I just got here. I didn't even get to see him."

I couldn't stand to see her cry, so I did what I always did in a crisis: I went to work. "Maisy, you need to help me clean the driveway. Come with me now," I said, dragging her into the garage. "Here, take the blower and blow all the dirt and twigs into a pile." I put an old pair of sunglasses on her, smiling.

"I don't want to," she said, still crying.

"I don't care," I answered, a forced smile on my face. "Blow the driveway, Maisy!"

She rolled the blower into the driveway and started working.

Hunter finally called me from Mexico that evening and said he planned to stay at a clinic for a few days while he detoxed. After that, he'd be monitored while he took the drug. He wanted me to understand the treatment, but I couldn't summon the attention to really listen to anything about it on the phone. I didn't want to read about it either. The idea that there was a medicine that could safely erase Hunter's addiction and yet was illegal? It sounded insane. But I chose my words on the phone very carefully, trying to sound hopeful. "You do what you need to do, and we'll be here when you get back. When will it be over?"

"I don't know," he answered. "I'm not sure how long it will take, but I'm allowed to use the phone, so I'll call you. I love you, Kathleen. I'm sorry. This is a good thing and I really believe it will work." I could barely muster a goodbye.

It was our anniversary just a few days later. July 2. We'd been married for twenty-one years. The year before, we'd taken a twenty-mile hike for our twentieth, and I decided to take another hike now in honor of our twenty-first year. I set my alarm for five and dressed in the dark of my bedroom: my old Nike running shorts, a T-shirt, and my sneakers. I strapped on a backpack with a bottle of water and headed north toward Michigan.

I didn't have a plan. I didn't have a route mapped out. I just texted Amy that I was doing it and told her I'd call her to pick me up around ten. My adrenaline and nerves turned the hike into a run. I stared up at the gray sky, looking for a sign that Hunter and I were going to survive. When the road dead-ended, I turned in to the neighborhoods and wove my way through the cottages until I came upon train tracks. I climbed up the small berm and continued running along the tracks.

After two hours, my stomach began to hurt. I hadn't packed any food, and now I was mad at myself for not planning better. I'd never be able to make twenty-one miles without something to eat. How had I left the house without thinking of this? Somehow I felt that Hunter's sobriety rested on my making the full twenty-one miles.

I ran, hopping from one wooden tie to the next, until I saw a road up ahead and a shop off to the side of the tracks. Subway. Subway sandwiches! They would be open at seven. This seemed like a gift from the gods.

I sprinted the distance to the front door, and I think I scared the hell out of the young girl working behind the counter. "Hi! I'm so excited you're open! I'm so hungry! Can I have a turkey and cheese sub with everything you've got?" I asked, grabbing a bag of potato chips. I was more excited about this meal than anything I'd ever eaten before. This little shop, this oasis, was my sign.

I left with my sandwich and returned to the train tracks. That first bite was magic. The best freaking bite of food I'd ever taken. I walked along the tracks eating my sub. Why *couldn't* this drug work for Hunter? Ibogaine in Mexico was radical, with a dangerous side to it—perfect for Hunter.

Okay, I thought as I devoured my sandwich, *I'm all in now. I'm an ibogaine believer. This is going to work. Hunter is going to get sober because too much is hinging on him. I need him. The girls need him. His brother needs him. He knows what's at risk.*

My mood lifted. I took the last bite, shoved the empty potato chip bag and wrappers into my backpack, and picked up the pace. I looked up at the sky one more time, just as the clouds parted and the sun shone bright. "I see you, God," I said as I skipped over the railroad ties. "I see you."

TWENTY-FIVE

THE PHOTOGRAPHS

After Hunter had been in Mexico a little over a week, I hosted my family for the Fourth of July. For just that one day I wanted to forget about his drinking and our problems. I'd grill shrimp and steak for my entire family and give myself over to the fireworks. As I was prepping the food, my oldest brother, Michael, sat down at the island and picked up Hunter's iPad, which was lying on top of a pile of books.

It has been said that my three brothers and I were divided into two categories growing up: Easy and Not Easy. My younger brother Johnny and I fell squarely into the Easy category, while Michael and Jimmy fell squarely into Not Easy. But Michael made every family gathering more fun. He had my mom's auburn hair and the same jutting chin as me. "I can't wait until tomorrow," he'd so often say to me, "because I get better-looking every day." Having him around meant a lot of laughing. I gave him the password that Hunter and I both used for everything, and he started swiping through family photos on the iPad. He paused on one. "Where was this taken?"

I wiped my hands on my apron and walked over to take a look. The screen showed a photo of a hotel courtyard taken from a balcony a few floors above, and I recognized it instantly. "It's the Four Seasons courtyard where Hunter and I stayed in Paris a few weeks ago."

In early June, we'd gone to visit friends who were living in Paris and were able to spend some time alone, just the two of us. A pause from the worries: romantic dinners and walks through the city holding hands. One day Hunter came back to the hotel with a beautiful little leather purse for me. It had been a long time since he'd spontaneously bought me a gift. That trip had been such a tender moment outside of time. I swiped to see if there were more photos to show my brother. But then a new one came up on the screen, and my body froze.

"I'll be right back," I said, and pressed the iPad to my chest as I walked to my bedroom in the back of the house. Stevie Wonder's "Isn't She Lovely" was blaring over the living room speakers, but all I could hear was my own head pounding. Somehow my legs were carrying me, but I didn't feel in control of my body. What had I just seen?

I sat on the edge of my bed, the iPad clutched to my chest, and closed my eyes. I didn't want to see it again, and yet I had to. The picture was of a woman on the stone balcony of a hotel room much like ours in Paris, wearing a white Four Seasons robe. She was young and pretty, mascara dripping from her eyes. The photo was a little blurry, but she had a heart-shaped face with red lips and dark hair. The next picture hit me like a full-body wave. Hunter. My Hunter. My partner. My love. Sitting in a matching robe, looking down at something, and seemingly unaware that his picture was being taken.

Like a robot, I opened the drawer of my bedside table now and put the iPad away. I took a deep breath and stood up. I knew my life was forever changed, but I couldn't face it then. I wanted to hide the truth in a drawer. Of all the fears, one thing I never worried about was Hunter's fidelity to me. In our twenty-two years together, I'd never once questioned his faithfulness to his vows. And in my darkest days, I never considered that he'd ever be with someone else.

There was a houseful of people to feed. I didn't have time to curl up in a ball the way I wanted to. Nor did I have the luxury of screaming. I rubbed my face, tucked my hair behind my ears, and went back to preparing dinner. Did I look different now? Of all the secrets I'd held tight, none felt as heavy as this one. And yet there was Michael, still sitting at the island with a smile on his face. No one seemed to notice that I was only pretending to be me.

Carly Simon sang "You're So Vain" through the speakers now, while the kids ran around and around in circles. I was thankful for all of it. Amy and Michele were pulling the salads we'd made earlier out of the fridge. I picked up the steaks and the platter of shrimp and headed out to the grill. I knew I had a whole evening in front of me before I could get back to that iPad, and I resigned myself to it.

I can't believe that I not only served dinner but visited with my family after the meal for hours. I talked and listened to their stories and jokes. No one could see that my life had been turned upside down. I held my nephew in my lap for as long as he would let me, playing with the curls on his head and bouncing him on my knee.

It was close to eleven by the time the last guest left. I put away all the dishes, rearranged the couch pillows, and turned off the lights. I brushed my teeth, put on my pajamas, and climbed into bed. Then and only then did I pull the iPad back out of the drawer.

I stared at the photos for hours, looking for clues, though the pictures were dark and so close up that it was hard to see much. I lightened them and enlarged them until the Four Seasons emblem and the intricate brickwork of the balcony were unmistakable. Hunter and I had stayed at that very hotel back in June, but these pictures clearly weren't from that visit. I remembered how weeks before our trip, he'd gone to Paris alone on business. It was the trip that I'd worried so much about his taking.

A month later, I'd stood on the balcony and asked Hunter which room he'd stayed in on his earlier visit. He'd walked over to me and looked to his right. "Over there," he said as he pointed to another room. "It was just like this one," he said casually, as we both looked out across the hotel.

I wondered now whether he'd felt guilt or shame when I asked about the room. He hadn't shown a hint. I couldn't imagine what it felt like to so deeply betray someone you loved. I never went to sleep that night, just sat hunched in bed in my pitch-dark room, staring at the iPad.

I know now why it's called heartbreak, because that is just what I felt: a deep searing pain in my chest. I tried to remember how Hunter had behaved when he got back from that

Paris trip. Nothing stood out. We must have kissed, because that's what we did whenever he came home. Could he have held me, just hours after being with another woman? And what did those pictures mean? He was an introvert who never seemed to notice when women showed him attention. He wasn't a flirt. But these pictures destroyed everything I'd believed in.

The next morning, I met Amy for our daily walk. She stood on the side of the road waving in her running shorts, her red hair tied up in a knot. Her face was probably more familiar to me than my own. It would be impossible to keep my secret from her. Hunter was my husband, and Beau was my partner in all things Hunter, but Amy was all things Kathleen.

I hadn't slept, and I hadn't cried. My emotions felt as if they were pushing up against my skin. "What's wrong?" she asked within seconds of seeing me.

"Hunter cheated on me," I spat out. "I found pictures on his iPad. He was with another woman." I was crying now, and Amy held me by the side of the road and rubbed my back. She showed neither shock nor anger.

"What I don't understand," I continued, "is that—I still *love* him. How? How can I love him? I don't even feel . . . angry, just *sad*. Sad and drained."

Why wasn't I screaming and raising my fists? I stood there under a clear blue sky, before the great expanse of Lake Michigan, and felt only a deep sadness. I didn't want my life to change, but it kept getting distorted, pushed further and further from what it had once been, and I couldn't see how I was ever going to get it back.

"There's no right or wrong way to react," Amy told me, holding my face between her hands. "You do what works for you and I will be here."

"But why am I not mad?" I asked, genuinely confused.

"Marriage is about forgiveness," she said.

I decided then that I could forgive him if I wanted to forgive him. But I still felt ashamed that I wasn't angry. And shame, too, that I still loved him. Amy took my hand, and we started a slow walk in silence. I didn't have any more energy to talk. She simply held my hand and walked by my side.

The only other person I told about the photos was Hallie. She'd been calling me, and I avoided answering as long as I could. Finally, after a few days, I gave up. "What's going on?" she asked. "Why haven't you called me back?"

Hallie and I had found common ground as Biden daughters-in-law, mothers, and runners, and with Beau's illness, I saw her strength, dedication, and loyalty. But when I told her about the photos, I'll never forget what she said: "If you leave him, Kathleen, he'll find someone else, and then you'll have to live with that." Her words hit at the core of my fear. Losing Hunter.

I was avoiding Hunter's calls, too. I didn't want to confront him over the phone about the pictures. For one thing, if he was sober, I didn't want to risk a relapse. Our whole life, it seemed, hinged on his sobriety, and there could be no real discussion if he wasn't.

But if you had asked me the previous morning, before I found the pictures, what a woman should do if her husband cheated, I would have said, "Kick him out." And yet now I just wanted to find a way back to him. I was desperate for answers.

Was he in an ongoing relationship with this woman, or had it been a one-night stand? And how many others had there been—how many others were there?

A few days later, I flew to Chattanooga with Maisy for a basketball tournament. Every morning I ran along the Tennessee River. I rode a bike-share around town to the gyms where Maisy's team played. I organized the team dinners. I never stopped moving.

One evening, as we were walking into a barbecue restaurant, Hunter texted that he needed to talk. I stayed out on the sidewalk and called him. He answered in a clear and optimistic voice. "Hey! How are you? How is Maisy playing?"

I paced in front of the restaurant. "The competition is tough, but she's having fun."

He said he was exhausted from the treatment but felt good. He wanted me to know that he was leaving Mexico in a rental car to drive to Arizona to work with a meditation instructor.

I didn't understand. Why couldn't he just come home?

"A woman from the recovery program is going to stay with me in a condo while I work with a meditation teacher," he said.

The absolute absurdity of what he was telling me let loose a torrent. I couldn't hold back anymore. "You've got to be kidding me. You're going to stay with a woman in Arizona?"

"Kathleen, she's a part of the *program*. She's my *recovery* counselor." He sounded so surprised at my reaction. As if there was no reason a married man shouldn't share an apartment with another woman.

I'd always prioritized Hunter's sobriety in every way, but this was too much. Maybe before I'd found the pictures of

Paris, he could have convinced me that staying with this recovery counselor was part of the plan. But not now. The pretending was just too hard. The mountain of secrets I was holding, too high. I broke.

"No," I said, my hands shaking as I walked back and forth on the sidewalk. "No. You cannot stay with a woman in Arizona." I wasn't screaming, but anger was behind every word. Hearing his plan to stay with a woman finally turned my sadness into something stronger. I couldn't stand still.

A couple stared at me as they went into the restaurant. I bowed my head and walked around the corner. "I know what you did in Paris," I whispered into the phone. "I know you were with another woman. I saw the pictures on your iPad." Saying it out loud drained me completely. I leaned against the brick wall of the restaurant and slid down to the ground. "Hunter, I've never been so sad in my entire life."

Silence on the other end. My heart was pounding. I didn't have the energy to keep talking. "You can't stay with a woman in Arizona, Hunter. You can't do that to me."

"I love you, Kathleen." This was all he said. He didn't deny the photos. How could he? "I love you. I promise."

"You can't promise me anymore, Hunter, because I don't believe you. I don't know how I'll *ever* believe you again."

This moment outside the restaurant in Chattanooga may be when I lost any semblance of self-respect. Because he didn't listen to me. He drove to Arizona and did share a condo with that woman.

I sat on the sidewalk and felt my own weakness and shame and fear: I was afraid of life without Hunter. Plain and simple.

TWENTY-SIX

MY SHAME

I went back to Indiana with Maisy and waited for Hunter at the lake. I hardly slept while he was gone, and when I did sleep, I had nightmares of losing the girls and finding myself in a house of mirrors, unable to get out. The pictures of him and the woman were stuck in my head. I couldn't concentrate, my stomach hurt, and I was clenching my teeth all day. I decided to talk to Dr. Levy, the therapist I hadn't seen since I was pregnant with Naomi.

When I drove into Chicago to see him, he looked exactly the same as he had back in the eighties and wore a placid expression that still said, *You cannot know what I'm thinking.* Now that he was older, his slight frame seemed enveloped by his yellow shirt and tan suit. I imagined he had one cup of coffee a day, two glasses of wine a week, and read the entire paper every morning, folding it neatly into his recycling bin. To me, Dr. Levy held the wisdom and diplomacy needed to set me straight. His sessions lasted forty-five minutes and not a minute more. I had to be strategic: I wanted answers. I was still desperate to believe Hunter and needed a path forward in my marriage.

I told him about Beau's diagnosis, Hunter's addiction, and finally, the infidelity. Dr. Levy was blunt. He said that Beau's diagnosis meant he would most likely die within the next few months. Hearing Dr. Levy say this made my body freeze. As a family, we never *ever* spoke about Beau dying. Never. He had spoken out loud the most unspoken secret of them all.

Dr. Levy also told me that he didn't think Hunter would be able to handle losing Beau and me at the same time. While he expressed serious reservations about Hunter maintaining his sobriety, he gave me the verified excuse I needed. I couldn't in good conscience leave Hunter. Dr. Levy said he wouldn't survive.

Dr. Levy also gave me permission to let Hunter come home. On the day that he actually drove back to the lake, I couldn't figure out what to wear. Not since we'd first started dating had I worried about my outfit. But I needed him to see me and feel overwhelming love for me. Searching through my closet, I pulled out a summer dress. How humiliating to care what you look like when you confront your husband's infidelity.

I left him a note on the counter telling him to meet me on the beach. I sat in the sand, staring out over the water, trying to put my thoughts in order. I wanted the truth. I wanted him to tell me everything.

When he came and sat down next to me, my heart hurt. He looked straight into my eyes and took my hand. "I love you. I will always love you," he said. "I'm so sorry. I will never stop trying to earn your trust. Never."

I looked back into his eyes, feeling a deep pull toward him that somehow made me feel worse. Turning toward the dune grass that ran along the beach, I tried hard not to cry. I wanted him to hold me, but I knew I couldn't let him. Wanting his affection seemed like such weakness.

Dr. Levy had given me cover for letting him come home. And Amy said I could forgive him. But I didn't know yet what he'd actually *done*.

"Tell me everything," I said, turning to him. "I know this can't have been the only time, Hunter. If you want me to trust you again, I need to know it all."

He put his hand on my knee, and I felt a charge. "I didn't have sex with the woman in the picture," he said. "I promise. I met her at a club. I was drunk, and a group of people came back to my room to party. She stayed after everyone left. We fooled around but we did not have sex."

Hearing him talk about being with another woman made me feel physically sick. They "fooled around"? What did that even mean? Of all the bizarre lies he'd tried to convince me of, this one seemed the most absurd. Of course they'd had sex. And yet he stuck to his story. I couldn't even look at him as he spoke. I didn't know what to feel. Was I actually trying to convince myself that if he admitted he'd cheated, then I could somehow trust him?

From the outside, it seemed perfectly clear. He could not be trusted. But emotions aren't always rational. "Tell me everyone you *have* slept with," I said. "Each one."

The beach was quiet now, and the sun was starting to set. "There were five times," he said with conviction. "All prostitutes. All outside the country. The first was in Spain. A business friend sent a masseuse up to the room and she turned out to be a prostitute. I wasn't sober. It happened."

The pain of that admission was crushing. But wasn't that what I was asking for? Wasn't I asking to be crushed? Next was a prostitute in Mexico or maybe China, or Argentina or Italy. I can't even remember. His delivery was strong and unwavering.

I could hear the absurdity of his stories, and yet I didn't push back. According to him, these weren't emotional infidelities, they were only physical. And he'd only cheated when he traveled outside of the country. He only cheated when he was drinking.

I didn't state the obvious: how strangely convenient it all sounded. There was still one question inside me that hurt my whole body. Did he still love me? That was the sharp-edged uncertainty I carried with me, deep in my soul. The question I never found myself able to ask.

I now know that you can love someone and still expect them to take responsibility for their actions. I could have loved Hunter and still said, "I need you to stay with your family while I work this out." But I didn't, because I didn't think I could be without him. I didn't feel strong enough without him.

He swore to do whatever it took to earn my trust back; he needed me too much. He couldn't live without me. On and on it went. I looked at this face for signs of the real Hunter. His angular face. His strong jawline. His stubble. I'd looked at this face since I was twenty-three. I knew he'd cheated, so why did his face look the same to me? Even his voice—that sweet low timbre—sounded the same. His rough hands with the silver cuff—these were the same hands I'd been holding for more than twenty years. No one knew us as well as we knew each other. How could he love me and so easily betray me?

Our conversation on the beach went in circles. "I can't talk anymore," I finally said. "You have to promise to go to therapy with me. I just . . . don't know how to come back from this."

"I'll do anything. I'll never give up."

Only it turns out that lying is an addict's most reliable defense.

TWENTY-SEVEN

THE NAVY

On a sunny weekday afternoon in October 2014, as I was starting to make dinner, I received a call from the White House, saying what Hunter and I had feared for over a year. *The Wall Street Journal* was publishing a story about Hunter's discharge from the Navy for testing positive for cocaine, and the reporter had called the White House for comment.

They were kind but direct: "I'm really sorry you all have to go through this. We tried reaching Hunter, but he didn't pick up."

I took the phone outside to our porch and started pacing. My dad, who was visiting for a few days, sat at the kitchen banquette, reading the paper. I was intent on making sure that he couldn't hear my conversation. Even though soon the entire world would know.

I didn't bother telling them about the truthfulness of the

story. The actual story wasn't the point. We needed a response from Hunter. "Hunter is in Northern California at a yoga retreat," I said, hearing an edge in my voice. "The reception is spotty up there." I sat down on the patio couch.

Our dog, a giant goldendoodle named Brother, sat at my feet. We'd bought Brother as a surprise for the girls a few years earlier, but he'd soon become my partner. I picked up the dirty tennis ball he'd dropped and tossed it to the end of the yard, watching him bound down the deck stairs after it. "The *Journal* is looking for a statement from Hunter and they need it soon in order for it to be a part of the story."

When we'd returned from the lake, Hunter's infidelity hung over our life. It was always with me. This latest yoga trip was in the name of sobriety, so I hadn't pushed back. What I had done, though, was look up this latest retreat online. The Esalen Institute sat on over one hundred magnificent acres of Big Sur coastline. Often described as a retreat center for the wealthy, it offered yoga classes and workshops, but its storied history was more often known for psychedelic drugs and sex. Hunter told me he was going for the yoga workshops. Did I believe him? Not really. Did I try to stop him? No. Anything having to do with his sobriety was still beyond questioning.

I wanted to find a way to trust him again. To move on. But we hadn't even found a therapist yet, so this giant mountain remained in our marriage. I texted Hunter now: "Please call me."

Then I thought about what I'd want Hunter to say in a statement to the press. I wanted him to take responsibility. I wanted him to admit, apologize, and move on. No denials. No excuses. No promises. Just an honest acknowledgment. With the phone still in my hand, I got up and started pacing again. I didn't want any of his excuses.

By tomorrow, the Navy story would be everywhere, and I'd have to tell the girls while Hunter was far away, practicing yoga.

In the end, a statement I desperately wished were true was released: *Mr. Biden said in a statement that it was "the honor of my life to serve in the U.S. Navy, and I deeply regret and am embarrassed that my actions led to my administrative discharge. I respect the Navy's decision. With the love and support of my family, I'm moving forward."* Of course, the words "cocaine" and "addiction" were not part of the statement. That level of honesty was still far away.

When the call ended, I sat back on the couch. The sun was setting, and the sky over our neighborhood looked like an abstract watercolor of orange and pink. I didn't want to go inside and do what I knew I had to do: Tell the girls that their father had been kicked out of the Navy—a year ago—for testing positive for cocaine.

Anger started to build inside my chest again. He'd cheated on me. He'd lied again and again about drinking. He'd so often made me feel I was crazy. Here I was handling the painful act of telling our girls about their father getting kicked out of the Navy while he was on a retreat in Big Sur. I knew I wouldn't tell them the whole truth. I'd tell the bizarre story that Hunter had told me: that he didn't know how cocaine got into his system. I'd say it quickly and keep moving. No long discussions. "Hunter!" I wanted to scream now. "Why aren't you home? Why aren't you home helping me?"

I went inside and found my dad reading his book in the basement guest room. "Dad," I said, "a story is coming out tomorrow about Hunter. It's going to be all over the news. He was kicked out of the Navy last year because he tested positive for cocaine." I spoke the words quickly, wanting the news out.

"Ah, honey," Dad said. He was always wonderfully unperturbed, so calm and unflappable. "I'm sorry. Cocaine. That's tough. How is Hunter now? What can I do?" Of course, my dad had no judgment against Hunter. I knew he wouldn't.

"Before I tell the girls, I'm going to take a quick run," I told him. "My nerves are a mess." I dreaded the task ahead of me.

After changing, I ran out of the house toward the canal. My legs seemed to be moving automatically. I looked out over the serene Potomac River and tried to calm my mind. I needed to support the girls and let them know they would be okay. That was my mantra: Tell the girls we are going to be okay. Their dad will be okay. I turned around to head back home.

I opened our front door and ran upstairs to my bedroom, calling out to Finnegan and Maisy. "Wassup, Mother?" Maisy said as she flopped on my bed, her thick blond hair falling out of her ponytail. She still had on her soccer uniform, and I could see her knees stained green from the grass. Finnegan came and jumped on top of her sister, pinning her down with her hands and knees.

I stared at their laughing faces and felt physically exhausted. "I have something to tell you," I said, looking at them with what I hoped was a reassuring face.

I told them quickly and directly: Their father had been released from the Navy because he'd failed a drug test. It was a vague retelling of Hunter's story: He didn't take drugs and didn't know why the test showed otherwise.

I sat quietly on the bed after my announcement and watched both their faces crumple. I felt as if I'd torn their innocence away. Maisy started to cry, and Finnegan had a contemplative look, as though she was trying to absorb my words and really understand what I'd said.

This was not a strong parenting moment for me. I didn't comfort them as much as I tried to downplay the news. How incredibly scared they must have been. But I didn't acknowledge their fear. I just tried to brush it aside. "Your dad is *fine*," I said. "It happened a year ago. He's healthy and sober now. And he's so sorry." It was then that I felt the weight of the lie. Their dad was *not* okay. Nothing was okay. I had little faith in his sobriety and no faith in his fidelity and yet I clung to our former life. Still I said, "Your dad is going to be okay."

Screw *The Wall Street Journal,* I thought. I wasn't letting go of my life that easily. I'd fight for it. I'd defend it. I started rubbing their legs and said, "Look, your dad is working really hard right now to stay healthy. I'm not worried, so you two don't need to worry. Okay? Go do your homework. Dinner will be ready soon. Come on, let's go."

I nudged them off the bed and then called Naomi at school. That conversation was also short. She was sitting in the library with a paper to write, and I could imagine her on the other end of the line, squeezing her eyes shut to block out the reality of the news. She whispered into the phone that she was fine, and I knew that she couldn't allow herself to fall apart.

Start to finish, these conversations with my daughters lasted less than ten minutes: This bad thing happened. But now it's over. Now we move on. No discussions about addiction. No discussions about Hunter committing a crime. Just, go do your homework and I'll let you know when dinner's ready.

After dinner, I went back out to the porch. From there, I could see the neighborhood beyond our hilly backyard. Darkness descended, and my dad opened the kitchen door and came and stood against the railing with me. "I just checked on the girls," he said. "They're going to be okay."

I felt such relief that Dad was there with us. The girls knew that he loved Hunter as much as he loved all of us, and they trusted my dad. He couldn't tell a lie if he tried. "I told them their dad loved them and that life is hard," he said to me now. "It is hard. Life isn't meant to be easy. They'll survive this and be stronger because of it. I love you. I'm heading to bed."

I didn't have the words to say what I really wanted to say to him at that moment. How much he meant to me. How much he meant to the girls.

I went upstairs and climbed under the sheets. Then Hunter called: "Hey. How are you?"

"Hi." I kept my eyes closed. "Did you talk to your dad?" I was so tired of the pain.

"Yeah. I just got off with him. I'm sorry, Kathleen. Did you talk to the girls? I want to talk to them when I get home." He sounded strangely calm. I knew he'd worried about the Navy story breaking all year, and maybe there was a little sense of relief now that it was finally happening and would be over.

I lay on my back in bed, the phone to my ear, trying to hold on to the sleep I knew was coming for me. "I told the girls," I said quietly. "They'll be okay."

"I'll be back on Saturday," he said. "I love you, Kathleen."

"I love you too," I answered, believing it and yet finding no comfort in our words.

The next day, I drove the girls to school, then headed to the canal for another run. Again, I ran to feel some relief from my spinning thoughts. My legs felt strong while my emotions felt weak and scattered.

Dr. Levy's words continued to echo in my head: "Hunter can't survive losing you and Beau." What did that mean in a practical sense? That I should stand by, let Hunter tell me what he needed, and just support him? What Dr. Levy's marching orders did, in a way, was give me an out in terms of having to confront the reality of my life. And I have always liked to follow orders.

When I got back to my car, I checked my phone and saw dozens of messages: "Here for you" and "We love you" came from family members and friends, along with many different iterations of "The press sucks." The story was out.

Hours later, I picked the girls up after school, and they looked like they'd just come out of the boxing ring. "Mom, it was literally on TV all day." They still had on their team uniforms, and their faces were flushed. I had something concrete I could be mad at now. Why was this story even news? Leaking Hunter's private file was unethical.

My co-dependency had grown so big that now I was the one giving Hunter cover. I was mad at the cable news, not at Hunter for doing cocaine and lying about it and causing our girls this pain. It was the cable news networks' fault for airing it and Sidwell's fault for showing it.

"I'm sorry. I really truly am," I said to the girls as we pulled out of the school parking garage. "You haven't done anything wrong, and you have nothing to be embarrassed about. Every family has addiction. Your dad had a problem and now he's sober. This happened over a year ago."

"Mom, everyone was acting so weird around us," Finnegan said.

"I know," I answered. "But your friends love you, and I know they want to be there for you. They just don't know what to say." I simply wanted them to be okay, to stop being sad.

Now I wish I'd just held them in my arms that afternoon and told them that it was okay to be sad and to be scared. My mantra: Keep busy and you can ignore the trouble mounting in your life.

The next morning, I ran up and down the stairs, trying to get the girls out the door to school for their homecoming celebrations. I grabbed Finnegan's tennis skirt out of the dryer and ran it up to her bedroom. Next, I grabbed a tennis ball off the floor. We'd be gone for hours, so I called out to Brother and took him into the yard and threw the ball again and again as I watched him bound down the stairs after it. I put my head back into the doorway and yelled, "Finnegan and Maisy, we are leaving in two minutes!" After a few more tosses to Brother, I walked inside. "Finn and Maisy. Now!" Dad sat quietly in the living room, reading his book through it all.

The girls came down, and we all headed outside. "Shoot. My car keys," I said, turning back toward the door and the ceramic bowl that held all the keys. But the bowl was empty.

"Has anyone seen my keys?" I called out to the car, and started running through the house. Why did this keep happening?

"Mom," Maisy called to me. "Mom, they are in your purse! In the car!"

I climbed into the driver's seat and thought I was losing my mind. *Okay,* I told myself. *Calm down.*

When we got to Sidwell's campus, I told the girls, "Let your friends be there for you." They both ran off, showing no sign that they'd heard me. "Come on, Dad," I said, putting my arm around him, "let's get a hot dog and watch the football game."

I'd always loved homecoming at Sidwell, and as we walked through the crowd, I smiled at the parents I'd known for years, determined to show a strong front. Several friends asked me how I was. "Oh, just smiling my way through the day," I told them with an exaggerated grin, and it was true. I was smiling my way through it. The girls and I had nothing to hide, no reason to be embarrassed. No news cycle was going to say that my family was broken.

When one woman I barely knew walked up to me and said, "I saw the news about Hunter. What happened?" I was dumbfounded. Did she really expect me to answer her question? To say, "Thanks for asking! Hunter relapsed, got drunk at a bar, and did a few lines the day before his first weekend with the Navy." No. I just smiled and turned away. What had really happened? Even I wanted to know the answer to that.

When we got home, I braced myself. Hunter was expected back that night, and when I heard the front door open, I met my husband in the front hall. He looked healthy and rested, and my body relaxed. He was sober.

"Are you okay?" I asked him.

"Yeah. Yeah. I'm okay," he said, pulling me into a hug. "I'm sorry, Kathleen. I'm sorry I wasn't here for you."

I let my body ease into his embrace. Sober Hunter, healthy Hunter, gave me strength. How strange, in the midst of everything, to still find comfort in him. But I did. I still felt that longing for him. We stood in the front hall holding each other, my head on his chest, that muscle memory of intimacy erasing, if just for a moment, the anger and fear I'd been holding.

He dropped his duffel bag at the foot of the stairs. "Where are the girls?"

They were both upstairs. I didn't want to go through it again, and Hunter walked upstairs to see them on his own. He didn't seem nervous or worried at all. He never did.

Afterward, he went out to the kitchen porch to smoke, and sadness came over me. I longed for the time when we sat and talked about everything. But the infidelity had put up a wall between us.

Come back, I wanted to say. *I'm still me. I'm still the same person you married. I'm waiting for you.*

Later I found Hunter, my dad, and Maisy in the family room watching a football game. My dad was sitting in a chair with his feet up on the coffee table while Hunter was lying on the couch, Maisy snuggled under his arm. "I'm going to bed. I love you all," I said as I bent down to kiss Maisy. I felt comfort seeing them together on the couch, but then a wave of heartache hit me.

I used to climb onto Hunter's lap like a cat. We always fitted together perfectly. This was my madness. Moments, glimpses, of normality followed by the realization of all he'd done. My mind carried the photos of the women in Paris. My sadness was always just below the surface.

When I felt Hunter climb into our bed a few hours later, the weight of the bed shifted, but we didn't move to the middle and put our arms around each other the way we used to. We each lay alone.

As the days passed, the distance between us grew greater. When he was away, I could hear myself talk about how much I loved him, and what a great person he was. I could pretend that he was still the man I'd married. But when we were together, it became harder to pretend, because Hunter seemed a shadow of himself.

He always seemed tired now, as if it took an effort to be with me. If he wasn't out on the kitchen porch, reading on his iPad, he was on the couch with the girls, watching TV. I felt him avoiding me, this man that looked like my husband but carried a weary, aloof sadness.

Soon I began to feel a strange comfort whenever he left the house. If I was with my friends, I could push away his addiction, his infidelity, and Beau's illness. I could smile and laugh and pretend that everything was okay because I hadn't shared all my secrets with them. In my mind, I was protecting Beau and Hunter. The truth, though, is that I was protecting myself.

TWENTY-EIGHT

ABIDING LOVE

My internist had given me the names of three therapists, but I didn't call anyone for months. In some ways, I felt detached from Hunter's infidelity, as if my mind couldn't truly process it. Finally I reached out to a therapist named Debbie, who was at the top of my doctor's list.

Debbie practiced out of a basement room in her brown-shingled house, which had a warmth and charm to it. The slate walkway leading to the door was uneven, with giant hostas planted along either side. Hunter and I began seeing her together and separately. She was nothing like pragmatic Dr. Levy.

In loose-fitting clothes and no makeup, she'd lean forward with her long salt-and-pepper hair pulled back in a ponytail and talk about our trauma as a big *T* and a little *t*. I'd never even thought about what I was going through as trauma. Yes, Hunter's infidelity was a big *T*, but she told us our love for one another was real and that our love was "special."

With Debbie, the goal was to save this "special" marriage of ours. She was on our side. Debbie had lost a child to the same horrible disease that Beau was dying of, and this hard fact bound us all together even more. Debbie was also deeply spiritual—often speaking about being open to receiving grace. Her spirituality and optimism were a great comfort to me.

I went all in with Debbie. She had the serenity and peace that I wanted for myself. Every week, sometimes for hours, I'd sit on her couch and take notes in the little black book that I carried everywhere now. Hunter opened up to Debbie in a way I hadn't seen with Dr. Levy or almost anyone else before. It seemed that he really wanted answers to what had happened in our marriage. He seemed sober for a while too. But as Beau's health continued to deteriorate, Debbie told Hunter and me that we needed to put our infidelity on a shelf and turn our attention completely to Beau. Now my mind went back to Dr. Levy's words: Hunter wouldn't survive losing both of us.

At a certain point that spring, any semblance of Hunter's sobriety seemed gone, but his denials once again made me feel as if I was losing my mind. There didn't seem room in our life to talk about it. Beau was scheduled to return to MD Anderson Cancer Center for another surgery, and Hunter and I flew out to be with him. The three of us sat on the bed in Beau's hotel room, which was attached to the hospital, and watched a travel show on Ireland. This night was a rare moment, just the three of us, before everyone else arrived the next day. We talked about how we'd all go to Ireland soon, and I held on to each moment, loving and somehow also missing the two men sitting right there next to me.

. . . .

After Beau's surgery in Houston, his health continued to decline and he was moved to Walter Reed hospital outside D.C. He was slipping away, and I saw Hunter struggle in a way I'd never seen before. The man who could fix anything, the person everyone turned to for answers, couldn't stop his brother from dying. It seemed like every day that Beau was at Walter Reed a medical emergency arose, and we lived in daily fear and worry. Now Hunter's drinking was obvious in the darkest, angriest way. One night I called Hunter to check in, and he said he was sitting in his car in the hospital parking garage. But he wasn't making sense, and his speech was garbled. It scared me.

I drove to Walter Reed and walked up to Beau's room, where I found Hunter standing in the corner—all the lights off except for the glow from the machines. I cannot imagine the pain he felt as he stood against that wall, seeing his brother lying motionless in the bed. When Hunter looked up and saw me in the doorway, his broken expression turned to anger. He wove past me and down the hall.

I followed, asking him for the keys to his car. There was no way he could drive in this condition.

"Get away from me, you idiot," he said as I followed him through a confusing maze of corridors and stairways.

"Are you trying to lose me, or are you lost?" I asked in frustration.

"Shut up" was all he said.

At one point, he stopped at a soda machine and rummaged in his pocket.

"Are you kidding me?" I yelled. Was he really stopping for a Coke right now?

He jumped back in surprise. He seemed to have forgotten I was there.

When we got to his car, he opened the door and climbed into the driver's seat. I jumped in with him, squeezing myself into the space at his feet, frantically searching for his keys.

"Kathleen, you are the dumbest person I've ever met," he sneered at me.

I got out of the car shaking, holding the keys I'd found. In that moment, standing in the darkened garage, I believed my husband hated me.

I walked toward the exit and he followed me, repeating the whole way: "You think you're so perfect? You're an idiot."

My car was parked out on the street. I got in and locked the doors and watched Hunter weave his way across the hospital green toward the street.

Then I called an old friend of ours who lived in D.C. John had known Hunter and Beau since college, and I trusted him completely. When he answered, I said, "Can you call Hunter? He's in a bad way and just stormed off."

I didn't know what to do except try to get Hunter somewhere safe. John ended up taking him to Hunter's uncle Jim's house, where Hunter spent the next two days sleeping and detoxing. When Jim finally drove him back to the hospital, a sober and broken Hunter never left his brother's side.

And on the day Beau died, we all stood holding one another's hands, surrounding Beau in his bed. Hunter was right next to his brother, kissing his head and whispering in his ear, "I love you."

TWENTY-NINE

THE GOOD WIFE

We'd all known Beau's death was coming, and yet on the day he actually died, May 30, 2015, everyone seemed stunned. I couldn't see what life would look like without him. The extraordinary thing about Beau was that as loved as he was by so many, he returned all that love in the most authentic and beautiful way. When you talked to him, his eyes were only on you, and you knew you were heard. He loved not only my daughters, but my parents, my brothers, my nieces, and my nephews. He never said "Goodbye," always "See you later." For years, I replayed a voice message he left me shortly before his illness took over: "Hey, Kath. Just calling to say I love you."

The day after Beau died, Hunter went to Delaware with his family to make arrangements for the funeral while I stayed back with the girls, who were finishing their last week of school. I spoke to Hunter every day, and he seemed strong and focused in a way I hadn't seen in a long time: sober and in charge of Beau's memorial service and funeral. I knew he wanted to make it a truly special occasion to honor his brother.

On the day of the funeral, Hunter and I held hands outside the church and walked in together, but I felt I was grieving alone. I knew that the alcohol turned him into a different person, but I didn't know if I had fully forgiven him for what he'd said and done in that parking garage.

Then, the night after Beau's funeral, I found him sitting outside his parents' house, looking at a video of his eulogy on his cellphone. "Are you watching yourself?" I asked him. It was mean of me. Pure and simple. Perhaps he was watching the footage to feel as if he was back at the funeral—as if he was closer to Beau and the pain of losing him.

He looked up at me with a mixture of embarrassment and anger. It is one of many moments I wish I could take back. But I returned his look, and I knew we were both breaking.

Driving home the next day, Hunter told me he was considering running for office in Delaware. I was shocked. "What are you talking about?" I looked at him closely. "You've only been sober a few days. We live in D.C., Hunter. This is insane. Please don't mention anything to the girls."

He stopped talking, and I knew that I'd hurt him deeply again, but I refused to entertain the idea of his running for office. He was acting as if his addiction were over. As if the last year hadn't even happened.

After the funeral, Hunter's focus was on Delaware. I saw a purpose in his work to set up the Beau Biden Foundation, which he was creating with Hallie and his parents. But he started spending most of his time at Hallie's house. When I'd see our therapist, she'd tell me that Hunter needed to be up there, helping Hallie.

"But what about his sobriety?" I asked her. "He needs routine. He needs to be home with us."

Debbie held firm that being with Hallie and her kids was an important part of Hunter's grieving. I didn't feel that I was entitled to be upset about it, and I struggled to get my emotions in check. How could I begrudge him this time with his family?

As crazy as I'd felt in the year leading up to Beau's death, now I truly spiraled. I didn't recognize this version of Hunter: He was sober and clearheaded, yet he treated me like an intrusion. When I'd call Hunter at Hallie's, he'd take my calls but he seemed removed. He said it was his duty to take care of Hallie and her kids, because when Hunter's own mother and sister died, his aunt Val had moved in and helped raise him and Beau.

I tried to explain the differences in the situation. "Val was Joe's sister," I told him, "not his sister-in-law." Val had been young and lived nearby and didn't have any children of her own yet. "You have your own family two hours away," I said. "Val needed to be there to take care of you and Beau. You were babies. You're just recovering from a terrible relapse. Don't you need your routine?" On and on I'd go, trying to persuade him to come home. But he seemed to hear it all as a rebuke. He didn't want to talk about the trouble we'd faced in the year leading up to Beau's death. I seemed to only be pulling him down.

When Father's Day came that June, the girls and I drove up to Delaware to be with him. The pain of losing Beau was still palpable, and we all seemed raw and hurting. After Mass and a family brunch, the girls and I sat outside with Hunter on the patio at Hallie's house. It was a beautiful day, but also strange and sad. Beau was really gone.

After an hour or so, Hunter stood up and told me that he and Hallie were leaving to drive our niece to camp.

No was my first thought. I felt a sharp pang of anger. What was *happening*? I was a terrible person to feel this way, I told myself. How could I be angry that Hunter was helping? How dare I? And yet, strangely, they really did seem like . . . a family. Guilt coiled itself around my anger as if to crush it. I loved Beau's children deeply.

My jaw tightened, and my face felt flushed. "Why do you have to go?" I stood and walked over to him. "We drove up here to see you and you're just—leaving? Why can't they go without you?"

Hunter looked furious—as if I was the problem. We all stood in the driveway in awkward silence: my girls, Hallie, and her two kids. Who was this man? This man who looked like my husband but was utterly unfamiliar to me.

"Why are you going?" I asked him again.

"She asked me to go, Kathleen," Hunter snapped. He was speaking to me as if I was an insolent child, and in many ways, that's exactly how I felt.

I wanted to stamp my foot and say, "No! Okay? You can't go. No." Instead, I just stood in the driveway, my arms crossed, anger written all over my face.

"The kids just lost their father a few weeks ago," he said. "Please—you're being ridiculous. You know I'd rather stay with you."

Except I didn't believe him. He looked as if he couldn't wait to get away. I stood in the driveway and watched as they climbed into his car and drove off. I was still crying when I turned to face my girls, and Finnegan tried to save the moment. "It's okay, Mom," she offered. "We're not mad. We understand why he had to go."

"Well, if you're okay, then so am I," I said. But I didn't mean it. I could tell the girls saw anger on my face, so it seems I wasn't fooling anyone. Now I was lying again.

A few weeks after Father's Day, Hunter's parents took everyone to Kiawah Island in South Carolina for a much-needed vacation. But once I got there, I felt lonely in a whole new way and didn't want to get out of bed. Hunter couldn't seem to comprehend why I was upset. Was I now a trigger for him?

One day in Kiawah, I watched from an upstairs window in our rented house while Hunter and Hallie climbed into the car to take the kids for ice cream. Why did the sight of them together upset me? I must be crazy. Why couldn't I make myself go down and join them? Why couldn't I smile and be relieved that Hunter seemed healthy? Where did I get off acting like this? Beau was my brother-in-law, not my son or my own brother or my husband. Why couldn't I do better at putting on a brave face for the kids? Everyone else seemed to be doing it, while I lay in bed. I didn't deserve to grieve in the same way as Hunter and his family. I needed to support my husband. But I wasn't sure I could be the "good wife" anymore. I didn't have the energy to pretend everything was okay.

THIRTY

FIREWORKS

Back in D.C., I decided that my husband's anger toward me must have some foundation. Some real cause, some plausible reason. It had to be my own craziness. Somehow I'd gone from being the one to help him to the one who was triggering him. Maybe, I wondered, I represented too much baggage from his relapses. Maybe I had come to signify only pain to him. Maybe I only reminded him of his addiction. And maybe spending time with Hallie allowed him a clean slate.

Then, in early July, Hunter drove down to D.C. to take a twenty-two-mile hike with me for our twenty-second anniversary. It was July 2 when we walked toward Virginia on a trail along the Potomac River and I saw the old Hunter again. It was the most surprising, wonderful thing. He'd been sober only a little over a month now, but somehow everything seemed different on this day. We talked for six hours straight.

At one point, while we were reminiscing about Beau, a

young deer stepped out of the woods and stood a few feet in front of us, staring. We both froze. "Hi, Beau," I said.

Hunter took my hand and smiled. I felt in that moment that I had my husband back.

Later, we sat on a bench and took our shoes off and ate the grilled cheese sandwiches that I'd packed, and I felt something like forgiveness for the first time. For the past year, I'd loved my husband but hadn't trusted him. Loved him but hadn't felt confident that he loved me. I'd sniffed so many of his water bottles and checked so many coat pockets and watched him so many times to see if I could catch him in a lie, I had turned into someone I didn't recognize, or even like. But now we spoke openly about his infidelity and his addiction.

Hunter actually talked about the guilt he'd felt the first time he was with another woman. How shocked he was by his own behavior. I could hear the earnestness in his voice. We talked about our future, too—a future that we would have together—and I felt the weight of my years of fear start to lift. We would spend more time at the lake, just the two of us.

It was the first time in so long that he seemed to speak honestly and with self-revelation, and I sensed that he, too, was trying to understand it all. We laughed and joked and finished each other's sentences the way we used to, and I could feel myself letting go of my anger and suspicion. I began to believe we might survive it all—Beau's horrible death and the scourge of Hunter's addiction. We'd made it through the past two years, and it hadn't broken us.

He was showing such strength in his sobriety that I thought maybe Beau had passed his strength on to him. Maybe, too, the strength Hunter had shown toward Beau while he was dying could now be a source for his own health. I was so full of hope on that walk. So full of love and forgiveness.

We went home afterward and lay in bed, holding each other, and I knew that he loved me and I loved him, that this love would carry us through.

The next day, I couldn't wait to get to our therapy appointment. I felt I could finally forgive him and stop ruminating on the same questions: Had he not been happy with me? Had he wanted out of our marriage for years? Were there others he hadn't told me about? And the biggest question of all: Could I trust him again?

I arrived early for our session at Debbie's house. Hunter was coming directly from his office. "I can forgive him," I said excitedly to her. "I truly feel it. I can't wait to tell him."

"Kathleen, that's wonderful. I am so happy for you," Debbie said, smiling. We were sitting in the second-floor sunroom—a room filled with afternoon sunlight now.

A few minutes later, Hunter walked in, gave me a kiss, and sat down next to me. Together, we told Debbie about the deer on our hike and about all the miles we'd covered. I turned to him with a smile. "Hunter, I forgive you." I was so full of emotion. "Yesterday's hike was a turning point for me. You spoke so openly and honestly that I really feel I can forgive you. We never need to discuss your infidelity again." I stopped now and waited for him to take me in an embrace.

We had crossed a bridge that I hadn't known we'd ever make it across. I felt overwhelming love for him in that moment. But he looked blank, as if a curtain had dropped. A long, silent minute passed before he answered.

"Thank you," he finally said. "I'm sorry. I have to get back to the office. I love you." He bent over to give me a kiss and left.

I was stunned. What had just happened?

"What was that?" I asked Debbie.

"Maybe he's in shock," she said. "Give him time to digest it."

But there was a knot in my stomach. His departure was so strange. Within minutes I went from a sense of healing to one of impending doom. Something was not right.

Hunter didn't come home for dinner, and I wasn't able to reach him by phone. That night I went to bed alone. Later, I was awoken three times by accidental calls from his cell. Each time I answered, I could hear him down on the kitchen porch moving around, oblivious that he'd dialed me. I stayed in bed. I didn't want to face what I knew in my heart.

When I finally got out of bed around six the next morning, I went down to the porch. He wasn't there. The ashtray was overflowing, and I picked it up to take it into the kitchen and empty it. That was when I saw a broken piece of glass pipe in the ashes. I held the pipe up close to examine it. It was such a small piece, shattered on one end. My heart started pounding, and I held it in my hand as I went to look for Hunter.

I walked into the family room and found him on the couch with his headphones on, watching something on his iPad. He looked up at me with a blank stare and took off his head-phones, as if I were just coming in to say good morning on any ordinary day. His eyes were empty now. He wasn't there.

I held out the broken piece of glass. "What is this?"

"A crack pipe," he answered without hesitation. He sounded as though he was telling me what time it was.

Crack? What did I even know about crack? Except that people who smoke crack die. And if he was smoking crack, was he also doing other drugs? I felt like a passenger in a car whose driver was blindfolded. Cycling through my head was his warning to me back in EADP: "If I relapse, I'll die." I knew it would be just a matter of time before he went over the edge.

"But where was it?" I'd searched his closet and his car for alcohol. How did I miss it?

"I hid it in my Bose headphone case," he said flatly.

"You have to leave," I said and turned away. After years of thinking it couldn't get worse, I'd lost the ability to be surprised by him.

He didn't respond. He was still high.

I needed to get out of the house. Throwing on sneakers and shorts, I walked out the front door, wanting to run as far away as possible. I drove to the canal and ran hard toward Maryland. My mind and body craved the pounding repetition of my feet hitting the ground. I could have run forever that day. It was the Fourth of July. Naomi was in California work-ing, and Finnegan and Maisy were both home sleeping and wouldn't be up for hours. Their parents' problems were just a blip on their teenaged minds.

Just yesterday I'd forgiven Hunter for everything. I'd felt real hope in our future. How long had he been smoking crack?

I thought back to the drug test for the Navy. Had he been using it for years? Could I really not have realized it?

When I got back from my run, I found Hunter asleep on the sofa, and I knew he'd probably be down for the whole day. When the girls woke up, I told them their dad was drinking again. I didn't tell them about the drugs. I knew how much it would scare them. We'd been invited to the White House for a barbecue and fireworks later that night, and as was my habit, I focused on the future and kept the secret.

By the time the girls and I left to go to the White House, Hunter still hadn't woken up. We got to the party, and I watched as the girls ran around with their friends. My phone kept buzzing. It was Hallie calling. She'd come down from Delaware to watch the fireworks. But I didn't pick up. She and her kids were on the balcony of Jill's office next door with Joe and Jill. I couldn't fathom showing up there without Hunter. What lie could I tell them about his absence?

Midway through the party, Finnegan walked toward me with her phone, saying Hallie was trying to reach me again.

I took her phone and walked away from the crowd. "Where are you guys?" Hallie asked.

"Hunter relapsed," I whispered. "I left him sleeping in the family room."

"I'll get him" was all she said. Then she hung up.

I dreaded going home to him, so part of me was relieved that she was helping. She went to my house that night and took Hunter to Delaware with her, and in a way, he never came back.

THIRTY-ONE

IT'S NOT ABOUT THE CHICKEN

The morning after Hunter left, he texted me, "We are in DE—I love you." I went to Mass by myself after that, and the priest's words seemed delivered specifically to me: He said God is with us more profoundly when we are in our darkest, most difficult times. I prayed that this was true for Hunter. A few days later, I learned that he had flown to Los Angeles.

I called him over and over again, leaving messages that I was scared and worried about him. When he finally answered, his anger shot through the phone. "Why are you acting so crazy?" he said, irritation in his voice. "I'm finally in a good place and you're acting like I've done something wrong. I'm here to work on my sobriety. Stop questioning me."

He then explained that he was working with a sober coach named Dan in a ten-hour-a-day program and staying at the Chateau Marmont, the hotel where John Belushi overdosed and from which Lindsay Lohan was barred. To me, staying at the Chateau Marmont to work on your sobriety was like going to an ice cream shop to work on your dairy-free diet.

When I called Hallie to ask her about it, I heard exasperation in her voice. She said she'd already talked to Hunter in L.A. and he seemed *fine*. For the first time, she seemed truly tired of me. Soon she'd stop responding to me at all. One of my last texts to her said that I didn't understand what was happening and that I felt like I was being punished. I didn't hear back.

When Hunter returned from L.A. a week later, he came down to D.C. to see the girls at the house and barely looked at me. Debbie wanted me to give Hunter *space*. She said that he'd never forgive himself if he wasn't in Delaware for his family now. When I told her how it felt to see Hunter and Hallie looking like a family, she said that this was also hard work for Hunter. He was doing what he had to do.

Hunter and Hallie continued to spend most of that summer together, and the whole thing felt surreal. They went on vacation to the Hamptons and stayed at our lake house when I wasn't there.

Earlier in our marriage, I had a recurring dream that Hunter was leaving me. In the dream, he was always indifferent. I'd chase him, screaming and crying, grabbing hold of his jacket, and he'd look at me with no emotion at all. In the morning I'd wake up feeling betrayed and tell him about the dream, regarding him with suspicion. He'd just tilt his head and smile, saying with a low, throaty laugh that I couldn't get mad at him for things I dreamed about. But now it felt as if the dream was coming true. It was eerie how familiar it felt and how calm Hunter appeared.

Sometimes that summer he texted me how much he loved me. Other times he angrily told me that he was sober and I should let him be with the girls whenever he wanted. He said I was driving a wedge between them. Our conversation went in circles. I wanted to stick to our rule: He couldn't be in the house with us if he wasn't sober. But the girls missed their dad, and I struggled to explain to them why I was keeping him away. They still didn't know about the drugs.

Later in July, he insisted again that he was sober and told me that he was coming to see the girls at the lake and that I couldn't stop him. His anger scared me. Before he got there, I left and stayed at my parents' apartment in Chicago. The girls wanted to see their dad, and as long as they didn't get in the car with him, I felt like they were safe. I'd been firm with them since his relapse that they were not to drive with their dad. When I went back to the lake after he'd gone, bottles were stashed everywhere. Empty vodka liters in the laundry, in the garage, under the bed. When I found a bottle in a drawer of our bathroom vanity, I couldn't help thinking he wanted me to see it.

When I asked the girls how the weekend had gone, all they said was "Fine." I had the sense that they felt talking about their dad to me was a betrayal of him. I didn't tell them about the bottles. Maybe, I thought, I could still protect them.

In early August, Hunter told me he was planning to take Maisy to Norway on a business trip. They would fish on a lake, he said. There wouldn't be any driving, and the Secret

Service would be with them the whole time. Although Hunter had signed off on coverage, Maisy still had a detail that traveled with her. She was excited, but I was worried about Hunter's sobriety. I told her that I didn't think she should go. But she wanted to be with her dad. She begged. In the end, I quit fighting.

Each decision I made that summer felt fraught. I kept second-guessing myself. After Maisy returned from Norway, Hunter texted to say he was flying the girls from the lake to Philadelphia, where they'd meet him and Hallie and her kids and drive to the Hamptons for the weekend. Hunter still denied that he was using and wouldn't address the bottles of alcohol I'd found at the lake. He sent a text message saying that if I continued to try to keep him from the girls, I would see "the full power of his sober rage." His anger toward me was as clear as the vodka bottles I'd found.

We were coming up on Maisy's birthday, and I told him I didn't feel comfortable with his coming to the lake. "It was our deal," I reminded him on the phone. "You can't be around us when you are using."

Hunter continued to tell me he was sober and talking to our therapist, but I believed he needed more. Some type of recovery program. I called a doctor that we were close to and asked for advice. He suggested I call the Charles O'Brien Center for Addiction Treatment in Philadelphia. I reached out and told a doctor there about the crack and Hunter's haunting words: *If I relapse, I'll die.* He agreed to see Hunter, and surprisingly, Hunter agreed to see him, but he was seething. He said I was forcing this appointment on him so that he could see the girls. In a way he was right—I wanted someone unattached to our family to tell me Hunter was okay. I wanted something that you can't get: certainty.

When I told Maisy that her dad would not be coming to the lake to celebrate her birthday, she broke down, and I felt like the source of everyone's pain. But I didn't know how Hunter could possibly come to the lake without making a scene.

The day before her actual birthday, Hunter had an appointment at five in the afternoon to see the doctor I'd spoken to at the O'Brien Center, and I was on edge from the minute I woke up. I'd told them about Hunter driving under the influence, and that it was my hope that they would ask Hunter to go back into some type of recovery program. If everything went according to plan, Hunter might be heading to rehab by sunset.

I sat at the glass dining table at the lake, chatting with my cousins and nervously looking at my watch: only two more hours now until Hunter would be sitting with the doctor. Just then Maisy came up from the beach holding her shattered iPhone. The screen wouldn't turn on. She was crying, and I knew her tears were about a lot more than the cellphone.

She called a store forty-five minutes away that said they could fix it that same day. Would I drive to the town of Valparaiso with her broken phone? I drove to Valparaiso, where I was told they could not in fact fix the phone and that I'd have to take it to an Apple store in a mall in South Bend, another hour away. I got in the car again and started driving, my mind consumed with Hunter's appointment with the doctor.

It felt like the culmination of my whole manic summer.

Finally, I'd get him sober, and he'd come back to us. Five-thirty passed. Then five-forty-five. I kept waiting for him to call and tell me he was on his way to rehab.

I couldn't wait any longer and called him at six. He was furious. He'd passed all the tests they'd put him through at the hospital. He was in great health, he told me, completely sober, and "had the liver of a thirty-year-old." But because of me, he now had to live at his uncle Jim's house outside Philadelphia and go to the addiction center every day to prove he was sober.

I sat in my car in the parking lot of that South Bend mall and truly felt out of my mind. Was I crazy? Had I been wrong all summer?

"Are you happy? Are you happy now!" he yelled at me.

My head hurt. How could this be? I called the doctor, who said he believed this was the best plan: Hunter would live at his uncle's house and be monitored daily by him.

"Staying in an apartment above the garage at his uncle's house, alone all day?" I asked him. "How in any way is that good?" He seemed taken back by my words. "Know this," I told him. "You bear responsibility for what happens to him now. I told you that he was smoking crack and that I believed he'd overdose or get in a car accident. You have to live with the decision you've made." I hung up the phone, shaking. How could anyone think this was a good plan? Then again, why was I trying to blame a doctor who had just met Hunter? This doctor received the venomous anger and frustration I felt, and he didn't deserve any of it. He didn't do what I wanted him to do and so I blamed him for making the wrong decision. I barely recognized the woman I'd become, sitting in my car while I yelled at a doctor who was trying to help us.

I got out and walked into the mall, stopping at a kiosk where I bought a box of tissues, because I could not stop crying. A dam had finally broken inside me. I found the Apple store and went inside and told a smiling clerk with a Dorothy Hamill bob that I needed to fix a cracked phone. Could it be done while I waited?

The woman put her hand on my shoulder and said it could be done that day, but it would take an hour or longer.

I handed her Maisy's phone and said this wasn't why I was crying.

She just nodded at me with a knowing smile.

I walked out of the store and sat on a metal bench in the center of the mall and cried some more. Hunter must be right. It was all my fault. I was the crazy one. I was unfair and unkind.

Every so often, one of the Apple folks came out to the bench with a look of worry and let me know they were working as fast as they could.

"It's not about the phone," I told them. "It's not about the phone." I didn't care how long the phone took to get fixed. I had no energy left. I was finally on empty.

The Dorothy Hamill look-alike came out an hour later and gently handed me the phone. I was pretty certain that she wanted to hug me. But I couldn't do any hugging.

I thanked her and walked out to my car in the pouring rain. When I got home, it was close to ten and I could barely keep my eyes open. Finnegan and Maisy met me in the kitchen, and Maisy smiled. She couldn't wait to get her phone back.

She pulled it out of the plastic bag and turned it on. "It still isn't working."

Now I was slobbering and hiccup-talking. "I'm sorry," I said. "I can't do anything right. I should have checked. I keep messing everything up. I didn't let your dad come for your birthday, and maybe I was wrong to do that. Maybe I'm the problem. If no one thinks Dad needs help, then why do I?"

The girls were sitting at the kitchen counter, legs dangling. They stared at me wide-eyed while I had my breakdown. Then Finnegan spoke first. "Mom, no. You aren't wrong. Dad isn't sober. Maisy, tell her about Norway."

Maisy spoke hesitantly. Since Beau's death, all three girls understandably felt very protective of Hunter and put in the middle. But now Maisy told me that yes, her dad had been drinking in Norway. "You're not crazy, Mom," she said. "Dad needs help."

I felt a flood of relief. I wasn't crazy. These two girls, barely teenagers, were carrying all this weight by themselves. I took them both in a hug. I felt I hadn't been there enough emotionally for them because I was so consumed with trying to keep up the charade that everything would be okay.

Later, after I'd kissed them good night, I went into my bedroom and called Patty and told her to grab as many of her nieces and nephews as she could in Chicago and come up to the lake in the morning. Maisy was going to have a real birthday party.

The next morning, Amy and I drove to Al's Grocery Store to get fried chicken for the party. As we waited for our number to be called at the deli counter, I told my cousin about Hunter's appointment with the specialist. "He has the liver of a thirty-year-old," I said. "And because of me he is now forced to live above Uncle Jim's garage and submit to daily sobriety tests."

Amy stared at me, speechless. When our number was called, I stepped up to the counter and asked for fifty pieces of fried chicken.

"Are you crazy?" the gray-haired woman behind the counter shouted, looking as if I had asked for her firstborn. "You can't just walk up like that and order fifty pieces. I can't give you all my chicken."

I started crying again, and the woman looked at me with bewilderment.

Now she spoke to me with a touch of compassion in her voice, as well as outright worry. "I can make you fifty pieces, but you'll have to wait. It'll take about twenty minutes."

I nodded. "I can wait."

Amy and I stood by the counter, and every few minutes the woman came over to give me updates on the chicken. While I stood crying, Amy rubbed my back and told her, "It's not about the chicken."

When the woman finally brought out an enormous box, she put her arm around me. "I told you I'd get you the chicken," she said with a smile.

Amy and I both started laughing. "Thank you!" I said as I took the box. "But seriously, it's not about the chicken!"

THIRTY-TWO

WHY DO YOU KEEP LEAVING US?

When the girls and I returned to D.C., the tabloids released a list of men who were on AshleyMadison.com—a dating site for married people looking to cheat. Their motto was "Life is short. Have an affair."

I was sitting on the side porch when I saw Hunter's name on the list. It almost felt comical.

When we spoke on the phone about it, Hunter was angry, not apologetic. "This is obviously untrue," he said.

I sat silently. Arguing the point would be screaming into the air.

When the girls found out about the article, they asked me what I thought, and I answered with a straight face that I believed their dad. But I could feel them staring hard at me, hearing the absurdity of my lie.

About a week later, in early September, the doctor in the Philadelphia outpatient program told Hunter he felt the best thing for him to do was admit himself to the Caron Treatment

Center in Pennsylvania. Hunter agreed to go, but he told me: "I'll go to Caron and prove my sobriety. But you are not the person I married, and I'm done apologizing to you."

I responded with my own anger: "And you are not the person I married. How can you be finished apologizing? You haven't apologized yet."

But once he was in rehab again, I wanted it to work. I wrote him a letter telling him I loved him, and I asked my family to do the same. I wanted him to know that we all loved him.

My parents sent a little handwritten note:

Our dear Hunter,
There isn't a day that goes by that you're not in our thoughts. We wish we could hug you and tell you how much we love you.

There's so much more we could say, but the most important thing to tell you is that you're our son and we love you.

Knowing how much you love us in return has been your gift to us.

                              Love, Gramma and Grandpa

I'd promised Hunter that the minute he was in a program, I'd bring the girls to see him. But he was adamant that the Secret Service not discover that he was in rehab—he was still trying to keep his addiction a secret. I'd have to sneak Finnegan and Maisy out of the house to avoid the agents parked outside.

On Hunter's second day at Caron, I had Finnegan and Maisy crouch down in the backseat of my station wagon.

I drove slowly past the Secret Service car and waved at the agents, so they could see I was alone.

Caron sat in a peaceful, country-like setting in suburban Philadelphia, a spray of buildings set apart by wide lawns. We met Hunter in the large upstairs office of an old home that may have been the original building on the property. He'd entered a program that allowed him access to the Internet, and he'd already emailed me about how miserable he was there and how it was all my fault. Now his counselor sat across the table from the girls and me, but Hunter asked him if we could all have some time alone. The counselor smiled and got up and left.

I felt unprotected after that. I'd thought there would be some sort of program with the counselor that day, some kind of guidance for the girls. Instead, we all sat awkwardly, the tension palpable between Hunter and me.

He talked about the history of alcoholism on both sides of our family and about how the girls would need to be careful with their drinking because it was hereditary. He didn't talk about the last year or his own struggle with addiction.

He never looked at me while he talked, and I sat silently on the couch. Every ounce of my energy went into not crying.

As he walked us out to the car, he told the girls how much he missed them. They clung to him in the parking lot as I stood by the car.

Later, I went back to Caron for a weekend workshop with Hunter and his therapists, and this time I walked into that same meeting room with several folders containing printouts of my text and email exchanges with Hunter. I was going to prove to everyone how he had refused to answer me about whether he was drinking or doing drugs. I'd actually high-lighted lines of the texts and emails in which I'd asked him directly to explain the bottles I'd found at the lake. In the mar-gins of the pages, I noted the messages to which he never re-plied.

He sat as far away from me as possible and stared at me with what looked like hatred.

I'd honestly expected remorse from him now that he was back in rehab. Maybe that is what I most wanted from him—that he would admit what he'd done and apologize. I reasoned that when we'd visited him the first time, he hadn't fully de-toxed yet. But by now I'd expected to see the old Hunter again.

I'd also brought the little black book that I used to track everything that happened to us each day. The book I normally used for grocery and to-do lists had turned into a diary of all things Hunter—my attempt to hold on to some kind of real-ity with him, as if my record-keeping of the facts would some-how point us toward safety.

When Hunter saw me pull out the notebook and my pile of printed text messages, he became furious. "What do you think this is? A courthouse? You think you're going to prove what an asshole I am?"

The therapist sat quietly nearby. "How much do you un-derstand about addiction?" she asked me.

I wanted to scream. Was she kidding? I felt certain I under-stood my husband's addiction intimately.

When Hunter was midway through his time at Caron, Fin-negan and I stopped to see him on our way up to Delaware to celebrate her birthday. But this visit was no different from my previous two, and when we got there, he was just as angry at me as he'd been the last time. The three of us sat outside in a covered portico near his room. I'd brought him coffee and doughnuts, but he seemed only irritated.

I stood up and told Finny and Hunter to visit alone while I took a walk, but he said I wasn't allowed to walk on the property.

Then I said I'd sit a bit away from them, but he told me I was only making it worse by trying to give them space. To Hunter, I was always making it worse.

We stayed only twenty minutes, but the visit was painful from start to finish. As we pulled away in the car, I started to cry. Finnegan, with her brand-new license, offered to drive. I got out of the car and walked around to the passenger side.

This was her birthday, and I was ruining it. My desire to get Hunter into rehab seemed to be backfiring. I didn't want to admit that I might be part of the problem. In my mind, the only problem was Hunter's addiction; that's all I focused on. Get Hunter sober, and our life could return to normal. I wasn't thinking about how I might be making it harder for Hunter. I believed that he knew, in his heart, that I was trying to save him.

I began to worry about what would happen when Hunter came home from Caron. We were not communicating at all. It was as if we were strangers to each other, and Debbie suggested it might be best if he didn't move back home right away. She thought we both had too much unresolved anger. It was decided that he'd stay at his parents' house for a few weeks while we continued in therapy.

He also had a new sober coach in D.C. now, whom Hunter and I met on our porch on Hunter's first day back. The coach explained to us that Hunter would take a Breathalyzer test on a video screen every day, so his sobriety could be monitored.

I was so anxious that day that I didn't stop talking to the coach about all my opinions on Hunter's sobriety. I wanted the coach to know not only the things Hunter had done over the summer—the bottles of alcohol stashed everywhere—but also my efforts to get him into rehab.

All the while, Hunter just sat there looking at me as if I'd lost my mind.

At one point his coach turned to me. "Excuse me for saying this, but it feels to me like you think you're the only one who can help him."

I sat speechless. How dare he say that? Who else was trying to help? He didn't even know us, and he definitely didn't know Hunter as well as I did.

"I'll be working with him now," the coach said. "His sobriety isn't your job." I didn't hear him.

This return from rehab was nothing like Hunter's earlier returns. As I looked over at Hunter, I didn't see the anger anymore; I saw indifference.

Now whenever I knew I'd be with him, I dressed up and put on makeup. I hoped to see in his eyes that he wanted me again. We'd meet at Debbie's for therapy, and he'd sit at the other end of the couch, as if he couldn't get far enough away from me. I would come with my little black notebook filled with questions, and Hunter would cringe at the sight of it. The book held the same questions I'd been asking since Beau died, mainly: How could Hunter maintain his sobriety if he was dividing his time between Delaware and D.C.?

"He needs his routine and his AA community," I'd say. "He can't get that if he's going back and forth to Delaware." What I didn't say was: *It's my turn. It's our marriage's turn.*

I also wanted to take our marriage off the shelf now and find a way to rebuild our relationship. I wanted to see in his eyes a wish to be with me. Instead, he was closed. When he answered my questions about Delaware, the answers never satisfied me. "I will go to Delaware to help my family for the rest of my life," he'd say. "I'm working hard on my sobriety, but I'm not going to stop helping my family." I bristled every time he acted as if I wasn't doing enough for his family. I'd spent my entire marriage loving and genuinely trying to do whatever I could for them.

Sometimes he'd come to the house for dinner with the girls, and it would almost feel like old times. He'd seem present and happy, and the girls were thrilled to have him there. One night we were standing in the kitchen cleaning up after dinner. It felt like we were almost a family again. I spontaneously told him he could stay overnight at the house with us.

"Thank you, Kathleen. I'd love that," he said. "I'll come back tomorrow. Tonight I have to go up to Delaware."

My anger exploded. Why didn't he take me in his arms? And why did his telling me he was going to Delaware trigger such strong emotions? "Are you kidding me?" I shouted. "Why? Why can't you stay here for the night?" My voice was barely under a scream. "You can't keep this up."

He calmly answered with the same line again: "I won't ever stop going up to Delaware, Kathleen."

He turned away from me and walked into the family room to kiss the girls goodbye. They kissed him back, unfazed. They didn't understand what was happening. But I did. It felt like a before-and-after moment. For the first time since I'd found him smoking crack, I'd asked him to stay at the house with us, and yet he was leaving to stay at Hallie's in Delaware.

When he grabbed his keys and walked outside, I chased him up the driveway. "I can't believe you're going," I screamed as he climbed into his car. "Why do you keep leaving us? Just stay up there! You obviously don't want to be here with us!"

He didn't turn around or answer me. He just shut the driver's-side door and drove away.

THIRTY-THREE

DETECTIVE WORK

When Hunter wasn't at Hallie's in Delaware, he was at the Holm, a building in Logan Circle where he'd rented a two-bedroom apartment. The day that he explained he was moving into the apartment, I covered my face with my hands in Debbie's office. It felt like a body blow.

He looked at me from the other end of the couch with a mix of sympathy and defiance. He couldn't stay at his parents', he said. The security and staff at the vice president's house in D.C. made him uncomfortable. He told me the new apartment would be furnished and was rented on a monthly basis. As soon as we worked through our anger and mistrust, he said, he would come home. But in his eyes I saw the look from my recurring nightmare—that look of cold indifference. "This is only temporary, Kathleen," he said again, this time with mild irritation.

"But you're moving out of our house!" I cried. "Why?" An

apartment felt a world away from staying with his parents. An apartment had a sense of permanence—a dramatic break from our family.

"As soon as we get to a better place," he said, "I'll come home. I want to come home. I don't want to do this. But you were the one who kicked me out."

"You weren't sober," I said, exhausted by the argument. It had followed us since I'd found him smoking crack. "You left" versus "You kicked me out" got repeated over and over again. But I'd told him I fully forgave him for the infidelities. I'd said he could move home now that he was sober. So why was he moving out?

Even when things were difficult in the past, we'd always maintained our intimacy and could always rely on our affection and physicality. But now I didn't feel like I could even touch him. The last time we'd held each other was the night of our twenty-second anniversary, and since then, we hadn't so much as given each other a kiss, much less slept in the same bed. For so long our physicality had felt like the foundation of my life. Now his body was off-limits to me. He became a stranger to me, even as I became a stranger to myself—unable to recognize the manic, consumed person I was turning into.

In the fall of 2015, I called and texted Hunter compulsively. Every day I had things to tell him and questions I wanted answered. Any excuse to communicate with him, I took it. Multiple times a day I'd text. When he stayed in his D.C. apartment, I dialed his cellphone, and if he answered, I stayed on the line without speaking, trying to hear if someone else was in the room. Some people might call what I did "stalking," but I prefer to call it detective work.

After taking the girls to school, I sat at my desk and pored over our bank accounts, tracking where Hunter was going and what he was doing and, to the best of my ability, with whom. Within a few months of his return from Caron, I began to see the signs again that he wasn't sober. I kept a tally of his daily charges to liquor stores in D.C. and Delaware, and large cash withdrawals. Whenever he was in Delaware with Hallie, his parents said how great it was to have him nearby. I knew they all desperately needed Hunter. They were all struggling to live without Beau, while I was constantly poking them with my calls and texts, always bringing bad news. In their grief and need, they must have looked at me as insensitive for trying to bring Hunter back home to D.C.

From my computer at my desk, I watched his every move. There were charges at Lake Tahoe at a nail salon and a charge for two lift tickets. I found a credit card charge for $10,000 at a hot tub store in Los Angeles and called the store, trying to find the address where it had been delivered: "Hello, my husband and I bought a hot tub for friends, and I can't remember the address. Can you remind me?" No, they could not. That mystery remains unsolved. I couldn't keep up with all of his movements. He traveled often. I'd call the front desk at his hotel, certain he was staying with some woman, and ask for Hunter's wife to see if they had a name. I found thousands spent on clothes at Tom Ford. Hundreds at liquor stores and strip clubs. And the whole time, he kept telling me that he was healthy and sober, and that I was a crazy person.

I continually told him that I was the one person actually

trying to get him sober. It became my own kind of addiction. He said I wasn't there for him or his family when they were mourning. He said I didn't come to Delaware enough to see him and his parents and Hallie. Back and forth it went. Determined to defend myself, I sent him the dates showing how often I went to Delaware. My little notebook became the repository for the mad scribbles of a woman losing her mind. I didn't want to admit, to myself or anyone else, how unhealthy our relationship had become, so my struggle was just one more secret.

"Where's Hunter?" someone might ask me, and I'd respond with a quick "Oh, he's up in Delaware helping his family." But deep down I knew we were out of control. Both of us.

When a friend wondered, "What are you up to?" I never answered with, "Well, I went for a run and then I tracked my husband's every move for hours while he did drugs, drank, and had sex with prostitutes. What are *you* up to?"

I was trying to prove to Hunter what he was doing, which makes little sense now. He was there, after all. I'd text him the bank statements and ask about his charges. He'd never answer, just get angry that I was tracking him. What did I hope to get from him? My expectations were as far away from reality as a dream.

"See?" I told myself. "He's sick, and I'm sane, and I'm trying harder than anyone to help him." Yet I could not stop to really look at what I was doing to myself. I refused to see how I was contributing to my own madness.

"Are you drinking?" I asked him again and again.

He never answered. He said my texts tortured him. I knew I should stop, but I didn't let up. I could no longer prove my support to him, just as he could not prove his sobriety. He even asked me if I ever visited Beau's grave. If I even missed Beau. He knew how to hurt me the most. Still, every now and then he'd write about how much he loved me and needed me, yet couldn't be near me.

One day he wrote: "I love you and I always have and I always will—more than anything or anyone anywhere at any time in my life. You are my end all and be all—period."

But what about the charges? I'd ask. *What about the drinking? What about the infidelity?* We were simply throwing our words at each other.

I'd call his addiction coach and say, "No one else understands his addiction. No one has been around it like me. I know what he needs." That is what I truly believed.

"I don't mean to offend you," the coach said to me again, "but it's pretty arrogant to think you're the only one who understands him." Again, I couldn't hear what he had to say.

Just give me a little more time, I thought, *and I'll figure it out.* But I didn't understand how much an addict has to want to help himself. As much as I wanted to complain that Hunter wasn't listening to me, was I really hearing *him*? Maybe I was desperate. Or maybe I suffered from a case of acute stubbornness that had turned into obsession. But that addiction coach was right: I was arrogant in a very specific way that was damaging both to Hunter and to myself and my girls.

I was mostly in a defensive crouch, explaining my actions ad nauseam. Each month I became a bit more unhinged. I still believed that Hunter would eventually want to get better because I needed him. His girls needed him. His parents and his whole family needed him. Everyone needed him. This view left him no room for error. No time for him to exhale or learn how to get better on his own terms and of his own volition.

I thought I could be his savior, by sheer determination and love and need. Being a savior can give you a false sense of purpose. It did for me. And like picking a scab, I couldn't stop myself.

By now, I'd hit a new low point in my manic and irrational behavior. Whenever Hunter was in town, I'd stake out his apartment from across the street in my station wagon. I'd sit for hours staring up at his balcony, willing something to happen. Just wanting a glimpse of him. The Holm was across the street from a beat-up liquor store, a remnant of the old neighborhood. I'd watch as cars drove through the alley behind the store. A man in the alley would lean down into the car window and pass the driver something, then the car would pull away. Did Hunter get his drugs from this guy, too? I knew he bought liquor at the store because I'd seen it on our bank account. I knew where he ate, and where he shopped and got his gas, too.

One night, I pulled up, turned my car off, and got out. I didn't have a plan, but I was tired of just watching his balcony. I wanted more. Without allowing myself to stop and think about what I was doing, I walked up to the front door of the apartment building and pressed my face to the glass to see inside the lobby. Someone was coming down the stairs to leave, and when they opened the door, I smiled and slipped inside. They didn't seem to notice that I had on pajamas under my coat. They didn't glance down to see my beat-up slippers.

I took the back stairs up to his floor. I hadn't actually been to his apartment, but I knew everything about it, having studied the floor plans on the building's website. I knew that his kitchen sat to the right of his door, and that straight ahead was the living room with floor-to-ceiling windows. Outside that window, right across the street, sat my parked car.

I walked up to his door silently, my heart pounding. What was I doing? What did I think was going to happen? Nothing about my decisions that night made any sense, but neither did the fact that my husband was in this apartment across town and not at home with us. I pressed my ear to the door, but I didn't hear anything.

Still, I needed something. With one ear still pressed against the door, I turned my phone to "unknown"—he was more likely to pick up the call if it came from "unknown" because this often meant it could be his father. I called his number and brought the phone up to my other ear.

When he answered, I could hear him on my phone, but I could also hear him talking just on the other side of the door. I jumped back, afraid he might open it. I stood there in the hall with my heart racing. Then the elevator door opened. Someone stepped out, and before they could get a good look at the unhinged lady standing there in her pajamas, I turned and walked quickly to the staircase, running down the steps, fearing I was seconds from being caught.

When I reached the bottom level and opened the door, I found myself in the parking garage. I stopped to catch my breath and turned to go back into the stairwell and up to the lobby. When I grabbed the doorknob, it didn't budge. I put all my weight into turning the knob, but nothing happened. The door was locked. I rattled it, willing it to open. *No. No. No. I am not locked in the basement of this building. I am not standing in his dark garage in my pajamas.*

Finally, I hid behind a truck, slumping down on the cement floor. *Shit.*

There was no one to call and say, "Hey, it's Kathleen. I'm locked in Hunter's parking garage. Can you break into the building and come down the stairway and let me out? Great. Thanks."

I couldn't call Hunter and say, "Hey, so, funny thing. I was just checking out your place as I was on my way to . . . you know, in my pajamas, and . . . well, now I'm locked in the parking garage. Crazy, right?"

Maybe someone would come down soon to get their car, and I could pretend I'd just pulled my own car in and slip out the door. I felt like I was in there for a day, but it was probably only twenty minutes. How did I come to be hiding in this garage? When did it turn into *this*? Was it the day I found the crack pipe? The night I stared at pictures of Hunter with another woman? Or had it been a slow burn for years?

Finally I stood up and started looking around. I walked over to the garage door and tried to see if I could lift it. No luck. Then, just as I was turning to walk away, I saw a panel off to the side. Flipping it up, I found the button to my freedom. The garage door came to life, and as the cold air hit my cheeks, I felt myself smile. I had escaped what would be my last stakeout. I ran down the alley toward my car, cackling and smiling as if I'd won.

THIRTY-FOUR

EMOTIONAL LIFE SUPPORT

Hunter and I had always maintained a united front, but now the girls were firmly in the middle of his anger and my hysteria. "You're trying to keep the girls away from me," he'd yell at me on the phone. "You keep putting them in the middle! You tell them lies about me and I've never said a negative word about you to them!"

"I'm not saying anything bad about you to the girls!" I'd yell back. I continued to defend myself and held firm to that long-ago rule of ours that he couldn't be home if he wasn't sober. But why couldn't I just hear his words, without the need to continually justify my behavior? If only I could have responded with "I hear you." Or better yet, not responded at all. Instead, my heart would race as I yelled back at him and the predictable pattern continued. I let myself get pulled down this rabbit hole and stayed there for a very long time.

The girls just missed their dad and didn't understand what was happening. Debbie also thought Hunter needed to spend time with them. Finally I gave up, and Hunter spent the night alone with the girls at the house for the first time since he'd left the day after our anniversary.

But I hadn't told anyone about our separation yet—not a single friend. I was still keeping my vow of secrecy, holding out hope that we could save our marriage. Maybe if I didn't admit our problems, we could pretend they didn't exist. So I couldn't ask anyone if I could sleep over while Hunter stayed with the girls. Still, the thought of staying alone in a hotel nearby seemed too sad. While running on the canal, I had noticed the little houses that dotted the pathway. Sixty-four cottages, built in the 1800s, available to rent from the park district. A cottage on the canal felt less sad to me than a room at the Embassy Suites. I went home and booked Lock-house 10.

On the day of our actual switch, Hunter and I were both at Maisy's soccer game, standing on the sidelines together, barely speaking to one another. "Where are you going to sleep tonight?" Hunter asked as the game ended.

"You don't need to worry about it," I said, smiling as I walked away, feeling a satisfaction that now he wouldn't know *my* whereabouts for a change.

By the time I was heading out of the city, the sky had turned black. I couldn't even see the rental house from the parking lot. With my phone light leading the way, I walked into the woods on a small trail in the pitch dark. The trail opened up to a little field, where I could finally catch sight of a stone house a few yards away. The place was probably sweet in the daytime, but in total blackness it seemed the perfect place to be chased by an ax murderer.

"If anyone's here," I announced as I walked into the house, "I have a gun and I'm crazy." What was I doing out here? I felt like the wide-eyed blonde from a horror movie, walking into an empty old house in the woods. The audience would be shaking their heads.

But when I woke up the next morning, the sun was streaming in through the window, and I felt a new sense of strength—the beginning bud of independence. I'd survived the night in the woods on my own.

Hunter and I were rarely alone together now. With the exception of a few meetings at Starbucks to go over schedules, I saw him only on the sidelines of the girls' games. Couples therapy had devolved into our seeing Debbie separately. Hunter was still splitting his time between Delaware and D.C., and I continued to question his sobriety. I decided to give him a year to come around.

This one-year grace period wasn't totally arbitrary—or at least, I told myself that. While watching Finnegan play lacrosse at a tournament one day that fall, a parent I just slightly knew found me sitting alone in the stands, crying. He knew about Beau's death and told me he'd lost his wife to cancer a few years earlier, leaving him to raise their young children on his own. He knew loss. He understood why I was sitting alone, crying as I watched the game.

"I don't know what's happening," I said, "everything is a mess." How bizarre that I could open up to this stranger while holding my own family at bay. But grief seems to work in the most unexpected ways.

"I know what you're going through," he said, sitting down on the bleachers next to me. "When my wife died, a friend told me to imagine that we were all on emotional life support. We can't be there for one another. We just have to wait until we are breathing on our own."

I knew he was looking at me from the other side of grief. He'd survived. Now he said, "Give your family and yourself a year in the ICU."

I took his words to heart. It helped to think of Hunter as being on emotional life support in the ICU. It made sense to me. I'd give him a year in the ICU. A year in which I'd stay with him and try to help him.

When Christmas came that winter, I drove up to Delaware with the girls and met Hunter at his parents' house. Every year since Hallie had come into the family, she and I had spent the days before Christmas shopping, but this year she said she'd finished her shopping already. Hunter wasn't speaking to me, and I felt like an outsider in a family I'd long thought of as my own. "Emotional life support," I kept telling myself.

On Christmas Eve, the entire extended Biden family met at St. Joseph's on the Brandywine for Mass. This would be our first Christmas without Beau, and the mood was somber. We all sat in the upper level of the church where the choir normally sat, Naomi between me and Hunter. As the ceremony began, Hunter leaned over Naomi and whispered in my ear, "Everyone knows what you've done to me. Do you even miss Beau? Have you even visited his grave?"

I sat motionless.

"Everyone knows what you've done to me," he whispered again.

I never answered him. I didn't have the energy—it all went into not breaking down. I couldn't wait to leave.

Hunter never came to bed that night; I didn't expect him to. The next morning, we all woke up and watched the kids open their gifts. I barely made it through. I sat exhausted and defeated on the couch, trying to smile as the kids showed me what they'd unwrapped. I couldn't wait to get out of there.

But in January, I decided I would make one final push to get Hunter sober. I contacted an outpatient program in D.C. called the Kolmac Clinic and went in to see the doctor who'd founded it. Dr. Kolodner was an older, former military psychiatrist who ran one of the best-regarded programs in the area. He agreed to try to help Hunter and told me to also call Babette, the director of the alcohol and drug abuse program at Georgetown University Hospital.

Babette was another story. I wanted to talk about Hunter's addiction, but she wanted to talk about *me*. I didn't understand at first when she said that I needed to take care of myself. Nor did I understand when she tried to make me see that I couldn't force Hunter into recovery. "Your addict has to make the decision to get sober," she said. "You cannot force him."

But the more it seemed Hunter was moving away from me, the more I tried to assert control. I felt a new sense of purpose now—constantly emailing and calling Kolmac, and our therapist Debbie, and Hunter's addiction coach. I felt I had pulled off something remarkable: an entire team of professionals devoted solely to helping Hunter.

Babette also talked to me about the girls. She wanted them to focus on taking care of their own health and to cede responsibility for their parents' well-being. But in my self-consumed fear, I still wanted the girls to understand how hard I was trying to help their dad. *Do you see how good I am? Do you see my efforts?*

I didn't understand what a heavy, unreasonable ask I was making of my children. They were stoic and strong—in so many ways stronger than me. They were simply trying to love both Hunter and me and to stay out of our mess. But I wanted them standing close beside me, telling Hunter he needed to get sober. In my mind, I was helping the girls, but in many ways, I was making it so much harder for them.

Hunter finally agreed to enter Kolmac, if only because I wasn't allowing him to see the girls until he began another recovery program. I had no reason to believe Kolmac was any better than the half dozen places he'd already worked with. Maybe I thought taking control of his recovery might bring him back to me in some way. What I wasn't seeing was the damage I too was now causing our family by forcing everyone to play a role they weren't ready or willing to play. I wouldn't accept that I wasn't helping him. I wasn't helping at all.

David Sheff wrote in *Beautiful Boy:* "Caring about an addict is as complex and fraught and debilitating as addiction itself."

While Hunter was working with Kolmac, I emailed the staff and called them constantly. Could they please tell me if Hunter was actually sober? They didn't know what to make of me and my constant requests.

"Are you talking to Babette?" Dr. Kolodner would ask me.

He knew I needed to work on my own issues of co-dependence, but he never said it directly.

I didn't hear him.

Eventually, Hunter said he couldn't take it anymore and stopped going. My persistent and manic outreach didn't help things one bit. He left Kolmac, and there was nothing left for me to do. I'm not sure if I was any more reasonable than Hunter at this point.

Now if the girls borrowed Hunter's car, I searched the entire thing in our driveway. One day, I found a little Jack Spade canvas case containing a crack pipe and a baggie with white crystal powder, plus a strange assortment of copper wire, wooden sticks, little scissors, a pocketknife, tweezers, and a lighter. With a strange mix of fear and vindication, I took the whole bag and put it in my purse and drove to the school to get the girls.

I called Amy on the way and told her what I'd found. I had the proof: Hunter was still smoking crack.

"What did you do with it?" Amy asked.

"It's in my purse."

"Kathleen! You can't drive around with crack! Throw it away *now*. Take a picture of it and then throw it away. *Now!*"

I panicked and pulled over and threw the bag into a city trash can. Then I got back into my car and panicked some more. Why hadn't I gone farther away to toss it? What if someone had seen me? What in the world was happening to me?

THIRTY-FIVE

NO MORE SECRETS

On the first anniversary of Beau's death, I had to admit defeat. Hunter wasn't talking to me. I tried to stop tracking his every move. I still loved him, but I could finally acknowledge that I wasn't helping him, that our relationship was damaging to both of us. My role as his sobriety police had turned me into a sick version of myself.

I needed to try to take care of myself and get back to the person I was before addiction and infidelity took over. Each day it was a struggle to fight to reclaim myself. My friend Karen gave me the name of a lawyer who volunteered at DCVLP, and in the summer of 2016 I went in to see her and ask about a legal separation.

Even if Hunter was still hooked up in the emotional ICU, I knew we couldn't keep living the way we were. The girls needed stability and so did I. They needed to know what to expect from their home life. Rebekah was a young associate at a family law practice, and when we met at her office, she looked to me like a teenager dressed up in her mother's suit. But she volunteered at DCVLP, which to me meant she was a good person. "I still love my husband," I told her. "We just can't live together anymore."

She handed me a box of tissues and listened. I still believed we could find a way to rebuild our life together if Hunter got sober. If we could agree on a collaborative separation, I'd wait it out until he came back. That was my hope. "I don't want a divorce," I said. "I just want the fighting to end."

Over the course of the next few months, Hunter and I went back and forth. Every step toward separating was exhausting. I loved him still, but I couldn't live in this strange in-between place. Then on a crisp, bright Sunday morning in November 2016, I walked out of a coffee shop around noon and received the kind of call that tightens every parent's chest.

"Mom, I need to talk to you," Finnegan mumbled through tears, barely able to get the words out. "I'm at Debbie's. Please just come here."

As I ran to my car, my mind went to intense fear. "Are you okay?" I asked Finnegan.

"I'm okay. Please, just . . . come here," she said.

I'd taken all three girls to see Debbie a few times to discuss Beau's illness and Hunter's drinking. "I'm coming now. What happened?" I asked again, so scared. "Please just tell me what's wrong!"

"I don't want to tell you over the phone."

I'd been enjoying coffee with my friend, and in less than a minute, my mind had turned to abject fear. Why did this keep happening—these frightening surprises? When would our life become calm again? Was Hunter in the hospital? Had there been an accident? I knew little about what he was doing. He'd given up his apartment at the Holm and now lived mostly in Delaware with Hallie, and I had resigned from stalking him.

I jumped into my car and called Naomi, who was working in New York City. "What's going on?"

"Mom, just wait until you get to Debbie's. I'll be on the phone with you and Finnegan when you get there." She sounded calm, but that was Naomi.

Now I called Maisy. "Hello, Mother," she answered with joking theatricality.

Whatever had happened, she couldn't have known yet. I didn't mention Finnegan's call to her. I'd know soon enough. Whatever was wrong, I now assumed it had to do with Hunter. There had been so many times over the last year I'd thought he would die. His own words from a few years ago still rang in my ears: "You don't have to worry about me relapsing. My addiction has gone far enough, I know I'd die if I used again." He'd told me that to comfort me, I suppose, but his words were far from a comfort now.

Three miles later I was at Debbie's house, sprinting across her front lawn. She stood at the open door, a small, apologetic smile on her face. I went straight through to the sunroom and found Finnegan curled in a chair with her feet tucked underneath her, holding a pillow while she wept.

I climbed into the chair and wrapped my arms around her. "Everything will be okay. All right?" I told her. "I love you." I kept repeating this as I kissed her head again and again.

"Debbie," Finny said once we had Naomi on speakerphone, "can *you* tell her? We can't do it."

Debbie looked me in the eye and calmly said, "Kathleen, Hunter's having an affair with Hallie."

"Oh my God." This was all I said.

Then for several minutes I sat in total silence. There was no anger or sadness. Nothing, really, just—shock.

Finnegan stared at me. Waiting.

"I don't know what to say," I finally whispered.

From the moment Hunter had started spending time up in Delaware, the sight of them together had hurt my heart. I had thought I was crazy. When I think back now to the most seminal moments in my life, this one in Debbie's sunroom stands out for my lack of any immediate emotional response.

Hunter's relapses, Beau's diagnosis, the cheating—each of those moments had brought a powerful, visceral wave of emotion. But this news, in some ways the very most damning, seemed to sit placidly on the surface. Was this what shock felt like?

"How do you know?" I finally asked them all.

"We found his phone," Finnegan said.

"There were text messages between them," Naomi added.

I could see Finnegan's face relaxing now that the secret was out and I was okay. I hadn't fallen apart.

If anything, I felt a strange sense of vindication. Not only had I not been crazy, but it was so much worse than I could have imagined. I was shocked, but not heartbroken. Heartbreak had already flattened my self-esteem that past year during all those times when he'd chosen to be with Hallie rather than us.

I sat curled next to Finnegan, holding the phone with

Naomi on the other end. I wanted to wrap my arms around both of them. I didn't cry. I knew in some way that he couldn't hurt me anymore.

Could a change like that happen this quickly? Had it happened while I sat there, stunned? It was a wholly new place for me. After so many years of pain from even his smallest slights, I was okay now. I wasn't that crazy woman chasing after a man who no longer wanted her. Somehow, during those minutes in that sunroom with Finnegan, I became someone else. Someone stronger. Or maybe on that bright November day I just returned to my former self.

How could our children possibly navigate this? Children who'd already suffered and lost so much in their young lives? I thought then of how Hunter kept telling me that he had to be in Delaware *for his family. Family is the most important thing,* he'd argued. But weren't our kids his family? Wasn't I? A cool anger started to rise up in me.

"I saw Dad's phone this morning," I said then.

The previous night, I'd attended a friend's wedding in Chantilly, Virginia, and Hunter spent a rare night at the house with the girls. When I came home, I went straight to bed and assumed he was down in the guest room in the basement, sleeping. In the morning I went out for a run, and by the time I returned, his car was gone. Later, I went down to the basement to change the bedding and saw his phone on the wooden table on the porch just outside the bedroom. I actually picked it up and looked at it. But it was dead. I still can't believe I didn't charge it and try to see what was on it.

I'd spent the last year stalking him and losing my mind, but now I left his unattended phone alone? What if I'd been the one to find the texts instead of the girls? How differently it all might have turned out. Some greater power must have held me back from charging his phone. Or maybe I was just exhausted at this point. Either way, it was serendipity that the girls had found it. Because finally I didn't have to keep another lie from them. As painful as finding the phone was, it set us free from all the secrets.

Only right now, Finnegan's beautiful face was full of such sadness.

"We called Hunter," Debbie said to me then with a look of compassion. "We told him we found the phone and that we knew." She paused now and looked directly at me. "From now on, Kathleen, no more secrets. I told the girls that from this day forward, you will tell them the whole truth."

No more secrets. The idea was a relief. I spent the rest of the day suspended between feelings of betrayal and a bizarre sense of giddiness. The phone seemed to give me power. In this sense, it was a gift. I could stop the secrets. The ones I'd been keeping that had distanced me from the girls, and my closest friends, and my mother and father, and my in-laws, and most important, myself.

Finny and I drove home in silence. Being the bearer of such awful news is a weight, and I wanted it off me. We walked into the house and found Maisy coming out of the kitchen. "Maisy, Dad's having an affair with Hallie," I told her quickly.

Finally, maybe we could move on and rebuild. First, though, the girls needed to mourn, and there was no way to make it feel better. I could let go of Hunter, but that wasn't true for them. He was their father. They would turn to one another for support. Their tight bond was a silver lining in those terrible days. And so it felt right when Finnegan turned to Maisy now and said, "Let's go up to my room."

In a very real way, they were on their own to navigate this mess. They needed to find a way to forgive their father, and I couldn't be the one to help them.

As the afternoon light faded and evening settled into our quiet house, I kept trying to process it all, as if it were a math equation I could solve. None of it made sense, and yet it also made complete sense. I felt restless and called my closest girlfriends, who came over to be with me as if it were a death. Sitting on my porch, I told them everything I knew.

I thought they'd be as shocked as I was. I anticipated looks of horror. Instead, I heard very little surprise.

"How could you have not even suspected? You may have been the only one not to," they said, shaking their heads as they sipped their wine.

"Well, none of you bothered to tell me! How could I have even gone there?" I answered, with my face scrunched up in disgust.

"Call your accountant and your lawyer tomorrow" was followed by a lot of "Uh-huh" and "Make that your first two calls of the day."

"Do you think he just did it to get me to finally leave him?" I asked them, smiling.

How could I have missed the truth when it was right there? Was I too scared to face it? Could I have been lying to myself? I thought back to the signs: All the weeks and months that he'd lived with her in Delaware. Their trips. The pictures I saw of them online that made me cry.

When I went to say good night to Finnegan and Maisy later, they both looked exhausted. "Mom, can we please stay home from school tomorrow?" Maisy asked. "I don't think I'll make it through the day without crying."

"I think finding out your dad is having an affair with your aunt warrants a personal day," I told her, smiling sadly.

After I turned out their lights, I sat in the kitchen with Hunter's phone in my hands, and I found so much more than his affair. While I'd felt as if I was losing my mind, he'd been living a strange new life I didn't recognize at all. The texts were filled with curses and graphic sexual references. He was mean at times, and then strangely tender, with dozens of women—none of whom I'd ever heard of before. I was struck by the number of them who clearly thought they could save him.

After searching for so long, the answers were finally here. How long had it been since I truly recognized the man I'd married? There weren't just Hunter A and Hunter B; there were a dozen different Hunters. Were there any remnants left of the authentic person I'd known? How long had he been sleeping with Hallie while we walked into our therapist's office together and talked about healing and saving our marriage?

Eventually I went upstairs and lay in bed. Something shifted in me. For so long I'd held on to some idea of love for the man I'd married. But that night, I felt no love for him at all.

In the morning I drove to Home Depot and bought dozens of boxes and lots of bubble wrap and tape. Maisy came down into the family room and saw me going through the books. "What are you doing?" she asked. I smiled at her. "I thought it was time we packed up Dad's things."

"I think that's a good idea," she said, surprising me.

We went upstairs, and I started filling the boxes with his clothes. I walked around the house after that, pulling his things from the cabinets, closets, and kitchen shelves. The process was cathartic. I didn't feel sentimental. I just wanted to close this painful chapter.

Everything he'd brought into the marriage, every painting he'd picked out, his books—I boxed it all up. The broken grandfather clock that we'd moved with us to every apartment and house, I carried into the garage. I didn't want to see him anywhere in the house. By the end of the day, I'd piled dozens of boxes, bags, and furniture pieces out there with the clock.

"It's time to file for divorce," I told my lawyer, Rebekah, that evening on the phone. "Tell Hunter's attorney he has until the end of the week to pick up his things before I call Goodwill."

I could almost feel the power seeping back into my veins.

PART III

AFTER

THIRTY-SIX

A NEW BATTLE, A NEW PLAN

When Hunter and I began the work of ending our marriage, a new battle started: blame. "You kicked me out," he'd often say to me.

"Because you relapsed," I'd shoot back. "You weren't sober, Hunter. That was our rule."

I felt a new sense of strength and purpose. I wasn't fighting for Hunter or my marriage anymore, I was fighting for myself. But I grasped too hard at the things I could control, one of them being my children. Naomi was in college, but Finnegan and Maisy felt the full weight of it.

I had already established a rhythm as a hypervigilant mom, but now I became intolerant of the slightest missteps. I didn't want them to use our situation as an excuse to not work hard, because I was afraid those excuses could snowball. I would not bend on homework, chores, or curfew. "If you don't want to be late," I'd say, "aim for early." Anything I felt I could control, I held on to with a death grip.

It was as if my obsession with Hunter was replaced by an obsession with the girls. My mantra to them now was: We will not break. These words were my response to their complaints over my strictness. In my mind, we needed to show that we were more than okay. We were strong.

Finnegan was a junior in high school that fall, and she now found herself grounded almost nonstop.

One night I woke to my alarm clock at 10:55 and headed downstairs to see if she would make it home for her eleven o'clock curfew. The car wasn't in the driveway, so I sat on the front hall stairway and waited. At 11:15, the car's headlights shone through the front door as she pulled into the driveway. When she flew through the door, flushed and breathless, I stood up and announced she was grounded again.

"Mom," she said, her face instantly filled with tears. "Please, no! The traffic was stopped on the bridge, and I had to go around. Mom, please don't ground me again. Please!"

I walked into the kitchen and leaned against the counter, holding firm. Maisy heard Finnegan crying and came downstairs. By now, the girls were both exhausted by my rules and punishments. "Mom, what are you doing? Stop making Finnegan cry," Maisy said, looking pained.

"You both know the rules," I said, with no sympathy. "I'm not making exceptions. I know things are hard for you right now, but we will not be broken." Every day I carried this intense fear inside me that the chaos in our life would somehow destroy us.

Maisy looked at me with such exasperation. "Mom," she said, "it's okay if we break a little."

Her words hit me like a punch.

"Go up to my room, please," I told them. "I need a minute to think." I went outside and sat down on the patio couch. The kitchen lights illuminated the yard, and I watched leaves drift down from the trees.

Since they were toddlers, my girls had been teaching me how to be a better person. Maisy's words that night seemed like an epiphany. It's okay if we break.

I sat and stared at the sky and saw that I'd been so focused on the idea of not breaking that I hadn't allowed us to mourn the broken family that we already were. Because we really were broken now. Sitting on that porch, I accepted Maisy's challenge: I could try to become less controlling. More willing to show the cracks. More willing to break.

I went inside and found both girls lying on my bed, tears still in their eyes. I wrapped my arms around them and pulled them close and kissed them.

"I'm sorry," I said. "You're right. It is okay if we break a little."

We lay in silence for a while, holding one another. "I'll be more patient with you if you'll be more patient with me," I said. "And I promise, I'm only trying to do what I think is best for you."

It was a relief to let go of some fear. We were living a different life now, and I needed to change with it. The girls needed to trust me more than to fear me. They needed my compassion more than my rules. I pulled the comforter up over us, craving their bodies close to me. We all fell asleep.

·   ·   ·

Now I needed a plan. At the age of forty-eight, I hadn't received a salary in twenty-three years. While I may have been intimidated to look for work before, now I had no choice. I was forced to understand my finances and take control of them. With each additional responsibility I took on, I felt more powerful. I had a hill to climb, but sometimes I could see the top: living on my own and on my own terms.

Soon another bomb landed. One bright day in March, as I was picking up our dog, Brother, from the groomer, I received a text from a friend that read: "I'm so sorry. Let me know if I can help in any way."

Something must be in the news. I took Brother and sat on the steps outside the shop and googled "Biden." The story was everywhere, and it sent me spinning: BEAU BIDEN'S WIDOW HAVING AN AFFAIR WITH HIS BROTHER.

Page Six had called me for a comment about the affair the day before, but I'd hung up. So I knew there'd be some story— I just didn't know when it would come out or what it would say.

As I read the article, anger consumed me. "Hallie and I are incredibly lucky to have found the love and support we have for each other in such a difficult time, and that's been obvious to the people who love us most. We've been so lucky to have family and friends who have supported us every step of the way." That was the statement from Hunter Biden.

They were *lucky*? Supported every step of the way? No mention of the family he'd left behind? As I drove home, the statement played over and over in my head. Why hadn't he at least warned us?

Now the tabloids began staking out our house, following me on my runs, leaving notes in our mailbox. Walking out after a lunch with friends one day, I saw a photographer across the street, crouched by a garbage can. I never spoke to the press, but it didn't seem to matter. Hunter still blamed me for all the stories about him. It was a constant accusation of his. I sent him every request that came to me to show him how diligently I was trying to protect our privacy, but I was screaming into the wind.

Now my focus was laser sharp. During the four months between the filing and the actual court date, I treated my pending divorce like a full-time job. It brought me clarity. Every morning I woke up and spent the day poring over bank statements and credit card bills and ATM receipts. No longer was I trying to keep Hunter sober or to save him. My aim was saving myself and my girls. For the last year, his spending had scared me. He was spending money erratically, but somehow we were still covering our bills. Now I was tracking our finances through a different lens. I couldn't count on him anymore. I couldn't close my eyes to our situation and hope that Hunter would figure it out. Now I scoured our bank statements because I was leaving him and needed to understand how the girls and I would live. For so long, really from the beginning of our marriage, I'd pushed away the warning signs that we were living above our means. Now I sat at my desk and realized my fear was true: We didn't have any savings. Both of our houses had a double mortgage and no equity. We had credit card debt and medical bills. We were in terrible financial shape. The sheer amount of our debt overwhelmed me. We owed as much for both houses as when we'd bought them. We were underwater.

I became dogged about getting every last scrap of financial

information. And as the court date approached, for the first time in a really, really long time, I felt highly competent. *He can't hurt me anymore,* I told myself. He will not have control over me. And he is not going to hide money from me.

For months, Hunter and I fought through our lawyers to reach a legal settlement. He said the tabloid stories had destroyed his business and wouldn't sign the agreement. In the end, it was my mother who persuaded him. She called him. "We love you, Hunter," she said. "And we know you and Kathleen loved each other. Sign the papers so you can both get on with your lives."

The next day he signed the agreement.

THIRTY-SEVEN

GOOD FRIDAY

The actual divorce proceeding fell on April 14, 2017, a beautiful sunny day that happened to be Good Friday. After sixteen years of Catholic school, albeit without much of the religion sticking, I took the court date as a good sign, the beginning of a rebirth. While my divorce felt like a death to me in many ways, I was determined to honor my marriage to the man I'd loved so deeply. I also wanted to celebrate my hope that I had another life in me yet.

Some iteration of my family always came to D.C. for Easter. It had been the one holiday that Hunter and I celebrated with both sides of our families. In the past, Amy, my brother Johnny, and Beau had always come to D.C. with their families and we'd spend the weekend together. So when I received my court date in the mail, I called Amy and Michele to make sure they were still coming. My cousin Mo also came with her husband and baby son. As somber as a divorce could be, I knew there would be laughs that weekend as well. "It's perfect timing," I told them all on the phone. "We'll go to court and get divorced, then we'll have a celebratory lunch and toast my marriage."

My family had all loved Hunter. He was godfather to Amy's youngest son and Michele's oldest. Knowing that my family had truly known and cared for Hunter, and that they would be there with me at the courthouse, gave me great peace. Some of my friends had castigated Hunter after they found out about the affair, and I got it. But right now, I needed to be around people who knew what the end of my marriage meant to me. There was no need to dwell on the pain. The marriage was over, but I refused to dismiss the twenty-four years of my life that I had spent with Hunter. My marriage deserved a send-off celebration.

The morning of court, Amy and Michele got ready with me in my bedroom. "What are you two wearing?" Michele asked. "I brought a dress, because I predicted you two would get dressed up." She laughed.

"A divorce is way more relaxed than a wedding," I told her, smiling. "You can wear whatever you want!"

I ended up choosing the black dress I'd worn to every funeral over the last ten years. It seemed fitting to wear something that reminded me of mourning but also made me feel good about myself. I put on the little diamond cross the girls had just given me for my birthday so that they'd be with me in the courthouse in spirit.

Later, I stood in my kitchen and watched everyone gather. Johnny came down in jeans and a button-down shirt. Chris walked in wearing a blue blazer. My parents never came for Easter, and I was relieved, really, not to have them with us.

Their love felt too strong for this day; I knew their hearts would break for me.

The kids were scattered around the house, still sound asleep, while the adults in my kitchen were all nerves. This was everyone's first time in divorce court, and none of us knew what to expect. We stood around the island laughing nervously, and in the end we were so determined to get the whole thing over with that we left for the courthouse two hours early to make the fifteen-minute drive.

We parked the car and met my lawyer, Rebekah, across the street from the courthouse at Cosi, a little coffee shop. We grabbed coffees and teas and sat around one of the tables in the back corner. "This should be quick. I don't anticipate any issues," Rebekah said. "We'll ask that the settlement agreement not be included in the divorce filing, so as to keep it out of the public record. We know Hunter isn't coming, so hopefully this won't be too hard for you." We'd already learned through his lawyer that Hunter wouldn't be in court. Now she smiled at me and added, "I should mention that I already went over and looked around, and I didn't see any press. We can go in the back way if you want, but I think it's safe to go right in through the front doors." I nodded, and we all followed her outside and across the street.

When we got into the courthouse, we all sat down on the plastic chairs that lined the hallway. Chris made an identifiable sound out of the corner of his mouth. "Did you fart?" Chris said, leaning over to me.

"Chris!" I said. "Please don't."

Then we all burst out laughing. Chris did it again and we continued snickering like ten-year-olds.

When it was finally our turn to go into the courtroom, we stood and walked single file, with me in the lead. I sat with Rebekah at the long oak table in front of the judge's bench. I turned around and smiled at my family, who were in the front row of the gallery directly behind me, separated by a partition.

The judge entered, and we all stood until he took his seat. He was tall and imposing but had a kind face.

"Have you lived apart for the past six months?" he asked me.

"We have," I answered as the tears started falling.

"Is there any reasonable prospect for reconciliation?"

"No," I said.

The judge paused, lifted a box of tissues from his desk, and handed it down to the court clerk. She got up, walked over to our table, and extended it to me.

"Thank you," I said weakly.

"I appreciate the emotion that is often present in matters such as this," the judge said now with real compassion.

Start to finish, the case took just a few minutes. When the judge approved the divorce and we were dismissed, I turned around again to see everyone in my family crying—all mourning the loss of the Hunter we'd known and loved for so long.

Back in the hallway, I thanked Rebekah and gave her a hug.

"I wish you the best," she said. "While I've loved getting to know you, I really hope you never have to call me again. And I pray Hunter abides by the agreement he signed."

I prayed for that too.

As we walked out the door, a photographer jumped in front of me and took photos inches from my face. We all kept walking and bumping into one another as we tried to ignore the spectacle of the tall, disheveled man walking backward as he continued to take pictures. When we finally made it to the car and climbed in, we all burst out laughing.

"That was crazy!" I said. "Who really cares about our divorce?"

We drove to Chez Billy Sud, my favorite neighborhood restaurant. With its light green and gold painted walls, it reminded me of a brasserie in Paris. The tables were covered in white linen, and antique portraits and mirrors hung everywhere. We settled into our table—Amy, Michele, Mo, and I snug on the upholstered bench along the wall.

The waitress came over to take our order. "Champagne," I announced and smiled at her. I wanted to toast a successful marriage. I wanted to acknowledge that I'd loved my husband and that for a long while I'd loved being married to him. It was neither easy nor smooth, but for years and years, we had a true, mutual love. And for almost as long as I'd loved Hunter, I'd felt his love back for me.

When the champagne arrived, I raised my glass. "My marriage had a twenty-four-year shelf life. I think twenty-four years and three kids sounds like success to me."

Bibb salads, pâté, steak, French fries, and a lot of wine later, the table was filled with empty glasses and plates. We sat there for hours, reminiscing.

"Remember when Hunter would take the kids out on the paddleboard?"

"Remember the mustache he grew that one Christmas?"

"How about the Fourth of July parades?" I said, smiling. "I can still see Hunter walking with Johnny and Dad, each of them with a kid on his shoulder, Hunter's face painted by the kids with stars and stripes." For so long, Hunter was part of the fabric of our lives, and no matter what happened in the end, we had these happy memories.

When the dinner crowd started to arrive, we unfolded ourselves from the table and headed home. I didn't want to leave. I wanted to stay in that in-between place for as long as I could, before I had to start the hard work of actually building a life of my own.

We went back to my house and the kids stormed us, asking what was for dinner. They were starving. Naomi wrapped her arms around me in the front hall. "Are you okay?"

Finnegan slipped herself under my right arm and hugged me around my rib cage. "How are you feeling?"

"I love you, Mom," Maisy said next and pressed herself into the group hug.

"We toasted my marriage to your dad," I told them. "I'm good." And I meant it.

After my divorce, I quickly sold the big house and the fancy car. I went full-time at DCVLP and rented a little row house. For the first time in my life, I felt in control. I was moving on. I wanted to start this new chapter and let go of all the anger and hurt that the dissolution of my marriage had caused me. What was the point of revisiting the details? We needed to figure out what this next chapter looked like for our family, and I was determined to make it work.

On the first Christmas after our divorce, I invited Hunter to join the girls and me for dinner at our new house. We needed to make new traditions for our family, and I knew it wouldn't be easy. I decorated the house with garlands and lights, and we put up our Christmas tree with the ornaments we'd collected over the years, the white porcelain ornament reading HUNTER AND KATHLEEN'S FIRST CHRISTMAS 1993 tucked into the branches with the many homemade ones from the girls.

When Hunter arrived, I gave him a hug. I knew we wanted to forgive each other and let go of all the pain and hurt. When he stepped back and smiled, I saw a man I didn't fully recognize. He'd had his teeth straightened. I'd always joked that his teeth made him more relatable. "You're too good-looking," I'd joke. "Your crooked teeth make you more human." For some reason now, his new teeth made me sad.

We sat down to our family's favorite: spaghetti and meatballs. Then we talked and laughed throughout the meal, telling stories about the girls when they were little. After dinner, everyone broke open the party favors I'd placed at their seats and put on the gold paper crowns inside them. Hunter and I sat across from each other, smiling. Still, there was a heavy weight of nostalgia in the room, and sadness hung over all of us. It wasn't the same. Nothing would ever be the same. We knew he was leaving and going back to Delaware. When we said goodbye to him and he walked out the door, the girls cried.

THIRTY-EIGHT

SAY YOUR LIFE IS GREAT, AND SNAP, SOMETHING BAD HAPPENS

Long ago, I inherited a superstition from my grandma Ann about acknowledging any good fortune that comes my way—maybe because it feels like bragging, or not showing enough humility. Say your life is great, and snap, something bad happens. But when my divorce was finalized, and I found myself living in a small rental house that I loved, with a new career, a sensible car, and control over my finances, I couldn't hide my contentment. For the first time in so very long, I felt happy with my life. I was doing it.

Nine months after my divorce, I visited my doctor for an annual checkup at which we discussed my recurring stomach pain. I could point to my diet heavy on greens, and my long runs, and the stress of the last few years as possible causes. But regardless of all that, Dr. McBride wanted me to get a colonoscopy, even though I was only forty-eight. I'd already gone through different tests for my stomach, and I wasn't worried.

The gastroenterologist, Dr. Kirk, didn't seem worried either. My health record was strong. There was no family history of colon cancer. I could count on one hand the times I'd had the flu, and I rarely caught a cold. As for the actual colonoscopy, everyone told me it wasn't that big a deal. The prep was simply inconvenient. The actual procedure was even somewhat enjoyable, as they knocked you out and you slept through the whole thing.

My appointment was scheduled for an early morning in January. The night before, I went to a women's therapy group we called "wives of narcissists." I loved the women in this group. I got to play the role of sage elder. I was on the other side now, while the rest of the group was either still married or newly separated. They hadn't known me during my crazy years. Now I seemed calm and relaxed as I doled out advice.

Of course, I wasn't completely on the other side. And I was still slow to admit my role in the breakup of my marriage. On my way home from the meeting, I started taking the awful prep drink, trying hard not to vomit. The rest of the night I had cramps, headaches, and chills. I went from the bathroom to the bed, covered in sweat, while my body shook. When the bathroom visits stopped, I lay awake, counting the minutes until I could get the procedure over with. I took a taxi to my appointment, having arranged to be picked up afterward because of the anesthesia I'd be given. When I arrived at Dr. Kirk's office, I couldn't wait to get into my gown and be wrapped in blankets and put under. I hadn't eaten in twenty-four hours, and I went to sleep thinking about the cheeseburger I would get on my way home.

I woke up in the post-op room still feeling sick. I was given juice and crackers, but I couldn't touch them. A nurse helped me out of bed and led me to a small sitting room, where Dr. Kirk came and sat down in front of me. "Is there someone you'd like to join our talk?" she asked me, looking serious. Why would I want someone with me? My friend Bettina was picking me up because I couldn't drive after the procedure, but I didn't need her in the room to talk about my colon.

"I'm okay," I said, smiling. "But I still feel really sick."

Dr. Kirk put a pile of papers down on the table between us. The top sheet held about sixteen little square pictures of what I assumed was my colon. "Kathleen, you have cancer. We found a major block in your colon," she said, turning to the second page of photos.

Amid the rows of bright pink pictures sat two that were completely black. Even I could have made the diagnosis. It was an ugly, burnt-looking section of an otherwise pink colon. If this was why I'd been having stomach problems, that meant I'd had cancer for years.

After focusing on Hunter's sobriety and my dissolving marriage for so long, I'd never considered my own health as an issue.

"Am I going to die?" I asked her. I'd spent years worried about Hunter dying. Now I was the one dying?

She leaned over and took my hand. "No, I don't think you're going to die. This does explain why you felt so sick doing the prep. It's blocking your colon. First thing you need to do is get a CT scan so we can get a better understanding. I'm so sorry. I wasn't expecting this." Then she told me the next step was to see a surgeon. She suggested Dr. Paul, a surgeon at Johns Hopkins who specialized in colon cancer.

When I walked out to the waiting room, Bettina saw me and stood up, smiling. "I have cancer," I said to her flatly. She took me quickly and strongly into a hug. "I can't talk about it now," I said, "I need to sleep." I was dying. My girls were losing their mother. I couldn't process it.

Our little house was quiet as I walked up to my bedroom and pulled the covers back and climbed in. I was still wearing the sweatsuit I'd worn for the procedure, and I curled up, bringing my knees to my chest. With my eyes closed, I imagined I could feel the cancer moving in my gut like a devil baby. Sleep was not going to happen.

I sat up and grabbed my phone and called the surgeon's office. "Can I make an appointment with Dr. Paul?" I said. "As soon as possible. I had a colonoscopy this morning and they found cancer." Tears started to fall for the first time.

The nurse said he could see me in two hours. I climbed out of bed and did what I'd been doing my whole life: I kept busy. With an hour still before my appointment, I left the house and ran errands. I dropped off dry cleaning, went to the hardware store, and stopped at the post office. As I stood in line to send a package, I wondered if anyone else around me had cancer, if anyone else in line was dying. Because even when we're dying, we still have mail to send.

Afterward, I sat in my car outside the hospital and texted my friend Denielle. She had two children who were best friends with Finnegan and Maisy. We came from completely different backgrounds and yet we were as close as family now. We jokingly called her Google, because there wasn't a question she couldn't answer. She was calm, competent, and smart, and I knew she would be there for me in exactly the way I needed. My text simply asked if she'd meet me at the hospital.

She didn't ask any questions except the room number, and when she arrived, I simply said, "I have cancer." She gave me a tight hug, took out her notebook, and sat down next to me. I felt instantly held and supported.

Dr. Paul looked like he'd stepped out of a 1950s ad for a hospital—everything about him was pressed and spotless. He was also soft-spoken and earnest. He told me the first step was a CT scan, and then the surgery would be scheduled based on what they found. The best possible outcome would be that the cancer hadn't left the colon.

"What should I tell my daughters?" I asked him, as again tears started falling.

"You're not going to say anything until we know more. I'll call you as soon as I get the results of your CT scan, and then we'll make a plan," he said. "Until then, I'm going to assume the cancer is only in the colon and surgery will be the end of it. You do the same." If it had left the colon, that was bad. If it was in another organ, that was really bad.

"Can she get her scan today?" Denielle asked him.

"You can try," he answered, "but they normally schedule a few days out. Why don't you go down and see if you can get her in, while I call them too."

Denielle took me down to radiology, where I sat slumped in a chair as I watched her talk to the receptionist—whispering to the woman and pointing at me. Denielle was magical. "I got you, girl," she told me with a wink as she put her arm around me and gave me a squeeze. They were going to fit me in that day.

When I got home, Maisy was sitting at the dining table

doing her homework. With Finnegan off to college, Maisy was the only one left at home. She was in her junior year of high school and I was working full-time at DCVLP now. It was a very different life from the one her sisters had known at her age. As I watched Maisy studying, a terrible ache washed over me. I wanted to take her in my arms and hold her and share my news with her, but I knew I couldn't. She was in the middle of her finals and Dr. Paul had told me we didn't know enough yet. Plus, I still hadn't truly wrapped my own mind around the diagnosis.

She looked up at me and smiled. "Hello, Mother."

"Hi, angel," I answered, giving her a kiss. "How about we order Chinese food for dinner. I'm too tired to cook." Exhaustion had overtaken me. It took every ounce of energy to get through the meal.

Afterward, I couldn't change my clothes or brush my teeth. I felt numb and depleted. I'd been sad in the past, I'd been angry and scared, but this feeling was different.

"Maisy, will you tuck me into bed?" I called down to her. As she came into my bedroom, I turned to look at her. "I barely slept last night."

She sat down next to me, leaned over, and gave me a kiss and a hug. "I love you, Mother," she said, getting back up. She had no possible way of knowing the sadness I held.

"I love you, daughter," I said, my heart aching.

"Kathleen!" Dr. Paul said, sounding excited, when I answered the phone early the next morning. "Great news! The cancer is only in your colon!"

I burst into tears of relief. I'd been so certain that it was everywhere and that I'd had it for years. Just yesterday I'd felt certain that I was dying. But now, twenty-four hours later, I had hope. "You have colon cancer" had destroyed me yesterday, but this morning, "You only have colon cancer" saved me. I literally felt giddy.

"What should I tell the girls?" I asked Dr. Paul.

"Tell them you have colon cancer but that you are going to live a long and healthy life." He said this with such conviction that I believed him.

In my mind, I'd just received the greatest gift. First, I called my parents. "Jim, it's our girl!" my mom said, putting the phone on speaker. I had practiced how I would tell them: "First, I want to assure you that I will live a long and healthy life," followed by the news of the diagnosis and impending surgery.

My parents responded without showing their own fear, although I knew they felt it. "Okay, honey. Dad and I will be there. We will do whatever you need us to do. We love you."

Next were the girls. I told them with Maisy sitting next to me on the couch and Finnegan and Naomi on the phone. As I gave them my rehearsed speech of reassurance, Maisy stared hard at my expression. I wasn't pretending to be happy; I *was* happy. "I'm really lucky," I told them. "And I'm not scared. I'm relieved. Thank God they found it. I'll have surgery and that will be the end of it."

I know they were scared. How could they not be? As reassuring as I tried to be, you can't tell your kids you have cancer and expect them not to be scared. "I promise I will tell you everything," I said. "You can ask the doctor whatever you want. You'll all come home for my surgery in a few weeks and hopefully that will be the end of it."

Naomi asked the most questions. She wanted details on the surgery and diagnosis, and I realized my baby was a twenty-four-year-old adult. "Mom, is it okay if I talk to the doctor directly?" she asked. My heart swelled as I listened to her.

I still really believed my surgery would be the end of it. I hadn't so much as googled "colon cancer." I only wanted to listen to Dr. Paul. After surgery and a two-week recovery, I'd be back to normal. It was when I called Amy that a feeling of vulnerability hit me. Yes, there was relief that the cancer wasn't in another organ, but it was still cancer. I was still going to have part of my colon removed. "Can you come down and be with me and the girls for the surgery?" I asked Amy. "We all need you."

"Are you kidding me?" she said. "I'm moving in with you for as long as you'll let me." And she did, arriving from New York with new pajamas for me, along with a blanket, slippers, and boxes full of homemade meals.

When the day of surgery arrived, my parents stayed at a nearby hotel while Amy and the three girls crowded into our little row house. On January 23, nine months after my divorce, we all went to Sibley Hospital for my operation. I gave the girls a kiss, then went back to a room to be prepped.

After the surgery, Dr. Paul came into my room, smiling. He said the surgery was a great success and that he'd removed seventy-two lymph nodes. I didn't know what that meant, but he explained that he'd taken out all of the nodes attached to the cancer and was sending them to the lab. I now began to understand that there was a chance the cancer had left the colon and was in a lymph node. We'd know the results in a few days. If they showed any sign of cancer, that meant Stage III and chemotherapy. Now I went back to worrying.

When he called two days later with the results, Amy was sitting next to me in bed. "We found cancer in two of the seventy-two lymph nodes," he said. "It's a small amount, but it means the cancer did leave the colon."

Tears started streaming down my face as Amy put her arm around me. I'd need to find an oncologist. Stage III colon cancer meant chemotherapy for six months, daily oral medication, and an infusion every two weeks. I hadn't let my mind consider this possibility. From the CT scan until surgery, I'd comforted myself with the certainty that it wasn't going to kill me. Now the rehearsed speech I'd given my family didn't ring true. Suddenly I didn't really know if I'd live a long and healthy life anymore.

I found my doctor at Georgetown University Hospital. Dr. John Marshall was a leader in gastrointestinal cancer research, and he explained that treatment for Stage III colon cancer was relatively straightforward. I'd end up getting two more additional opinions from other hospitals, but the treatment was universal: six months of an oral chemotherapy and three months of an infusion chemotherapy.

First, I had to have a port put under my skin, below my right collarbone. That was a quick surgery, although again I had to be put under anesthesia. For six months after that, my fingers continually went to the little raised square port, tracing its outline. The worst part of my cancer treatment was the infusion. Every two weeks, I'd walk the mile from my house to Georgetown Lombardi Comprehensive Cancer Center, and

I'd be put either in a little room or behind a curtain in a recliner. Even though they'd numb the area around my port, the
needle often hurt going in. The sight of other patients, at different stages of their treatment, always made me sad for them
and for me. We were a quiet community, smiling to one another as we passed in the hall.

I continued working at DCVLP throughout my treatment,
but for days after each infusion, I'd be in bed, curled into a
ball, nausea pounding my body. There was no relief from that
misery. Bettina put together a meal train, and Maisy and I
found our dinners packed neatly into a big cooler outside our
front door. There was no cooking or housekeeping or busy-
making for me during this time. All my energy went into trying to keep working, and with her sisters away at school,
Maisy took on the role of full-time nurse. When I was sick
from the infusions, she'd massage my feet until I fell asleep.

Unlike addiction and divorce, there was nothing to solve
with cancer. Now it was simply a matter of enduring it. In a
strange way, cancer simplified my thoughts. While my mind
had raced during the years leading up to my divorce, now my
thoughts were basic. On good days, when nausea was at bay, I
focused on work. On bad days, I simply lay in bed, waiting for
the nausea to pass.

Throughout this time, I didn't talk much about my cancer or
my treatment to the girls or to my friends. Maybe I thought I
could minimize cancer's importance by keeping quiet about
it. And for a while, I clung to the worn-out idea that I had to
be strong. Naomi recently told me that she had asked my par-

ents if they ever worried about me. She said my mom answered her with conviction: "I have never needed to worry if your mom would be okay. She's strong. She's a survivor."

Amy said you get a universal pass when you're going through cancer treatment. I thought differently. While I'd accepted the idea that it was okay if the girls broke a little, I hadn't allowed that for myself. I was a few months out of my divorce and just starting my new job, and I still thought I needed to prove myself. I don't know how I was able to keep my emotions hidden, or whether I actually did. But I definitely wasn't honest with myself about them. I wanted to be able to handle it all—parenting, working, and cancer. A scene in *Monty Python and the Holy Grail* often came to my mind. A traveling knight encounters the Black Knight and a sword fight ensues. When the traveler cuts off the Black Knight's arm, he responds, "'Tis but a scratch . . . I've had worse." When three limbs are scattered on the ground, the Black Knight, now just a bouncing torso, continues to taunt his antagonist, shouting, "I'm invincible!" That was me. Addiction, you can't conquer me. Infidelity? Bring it on. Divorce? Still standing. Cancer? Puh-*lease*.

Eventually, I began to accept my limits in a way I hadn't before. The need to prove myself while I had cancer just became too heavy a lift. I didn't have the energy to care as much. Without my realizing it, cancer had reprioritized my life. It cleared a lot of the clutter and self-doubt and slowly put everything into new perspective.

I remember walking to the hospital one day for an appointment and thinking, *I can't believe how upset I was about divorce.*

THIRTY-NINE

TRUST ME ON THIS

After the cancer treatment was finished, my life took on a new lightness. I swore never to forget the nausea I felt from chemotherapy and to appreciate every day that I lived without treatment. It was over a year since my divorce, and my life didn't feel lonely as I had feared it would. I now cherished the quiet. When I woke up in the morning, I'd slip out of bed and tuck back the sheets, making it as I got out. My days were scheduled and my life organized, predictable, and calm. When my friends began suggesting I get out there and start dating, I didn't know if I was ready. Finally, after so many years of chaos, my life had started to feel calm and routine. Dating seemed like an anxiety-inducing prospect. I hadn't been in the game since my early twenties.

But that August, I received a text message from a friend, and I decided to be brave. He asked if I was ready to date because he had a newly divorced friend who was just getting back out there too. I answered yes. Why not? His friend was tall and good-looking, working in New York City in finance.

First we texted, then we sent pictures of ourselves. In short order, we made plans to have dinner. I was at the lake, so Amy and Michele were able to review every text and picture before I sent it. Hat on or off for the photo on the beach? Hat on. How do I answer his last text? Do I send an LOL or does that make me sound stupid?

At dinner my family wanted to know all the details. With about twenty-five of us sitting at three long tables stretched out on Amy's screened-in porch, her daughter Clare took my phone and read the text exchange out loud, playing his part in a deep alto and mine as a breathy Marilyn Monroe.

A few weeks later, before my date, Finnegan had advice for me. "Mom, don't be too silly," she said. "Be mysterious. Hold back. Don't talk about Dad or cancer, not on the first date."

"Finnegan, I actually know what I'm doing," I told her with raised eyebrows and a tight smile.

"Do you, Mom?" she asked with heavy sarcasm. "I think I've dated more than you. Trust me on this."

The truth was that I had no idea what dating would look like at forty-nine. Since my divorce, I'd been navigating a life I'd never imagined for myself. After twenty-four years of marriage, I was still figuring out how to live on my own.

We met in New York City, where he lived. I agonized over my outfit.

"Sexy!" a friend insisted. "Show off your tight body."

"I'm not a sexy person," I answered. "The attempt at sexy will make me uncomfortable."

I took dozens of pictures of myself and sent them to Amy. In the end, I wore a little black dress with a scalloped hem, and sandals. We met at a restaurant in midtown, and when I walked in, I found him standing at the bar, smiling at me with a wave.

Oh, shoot, I thought, *he's cute, and now I'm nervous.*

We sat down at a small round table in the back of the restaurant. Within the first fifteen minutes, he asked me how I was feeling toward my ex-husband.

"My daughter told me not to talk about him on the first date," I said with a smile, "but I guess it's okay since you've asked. I had a husband I loved for twenty-four years. No regrets and no anger for me." By then I'd worked on countless iterations of how to respond to questions about my divorce, so my answer was quick.

"Do you ever imagine you'd get back together with him?" he asked, looking genuinely curious.

"He slept with my sister-in-law," I said, still smiling. "That's kind of a deal breaker for me."

He told me about his divorce. It would prove to be a story I'd hear over and over again from other dates: His marriage ended years before they actually divorced. They stayed together for their kids.

At this point I definitely did not heed Finnegan's wise advice and hold back. Sex? I told him I hadn't had any since my husband left. Hadn't so much as kissed anyone. I also let him know that he in fact was my first date.

When dinner ended, he offered to walk me home to the friend's apartment where I was staying a few blocks from the restaurant. As we walked along the sidewalk, I began to panic. *How do dates end for middle-aged people? Will he try to kiss me?* I felt like a complete novice. We were talking but I cannot remember what we said because my mind was focused on how the evening would end.

We finally arrived at the apartment building and stood looking at each other. I imagine that my face was pinched, and my shoulders were up somewhere near my ears—my entire body felt wrapped in tension. When he leaned down and gave me a soft kiss on the lips, I felt a shock.

"There," he said with a smile, "you've had your first kiss."

Embarrassed, I gave him a bear hug, my head falling somewhere near his armpit. I felt I was doing absolutely everything wrong.

"Thank you," I said quickly, and walked away.

The minute I got into the apartment, I burst into tears. The utter foreignness of being with another man, even just a peck on the lips, overwhelmed me. I hadn't known how hard it would be. But I wasn't going to give up. That night, I felt something I hadn't since I first met Hunter—an actual attraction to another man. It was as if this first kiss flipped a switch. I saw a whole new chapter in front of me. Hunter hadn't destroyed my heart, because that night, I felt it flutter.

When we were in the middle of our divorce, Hunter often taunted me about having kept the Biden name. "Are you enjoying your last name?" he'd ask on his worst days, when he was tired or using or both. He called me many names and accused me of many awful things, but the idea that somehow I wasn't entitled to the name that had been mine for twenty-four years hurt me in a deep and personal way. It was as if he wanted to erase all evidence of our marriage. It felt like a slap.

By the time I turned fifty in December 2018, I'd been a Biden for twenty-six years, which was longer than I'd been a Buhle. I'd always felt proud when people asked if I was related to the vice president. But now I answered no to checkout clerks. "Too bad," they'd say. "We love him." And I'd smile in agreement.

When I first got divorced, I felt embarrassed to tell people about it. It felt private and personal. I stopped wearing my wedding ring, but I still didn't really consider myself single. I wasn't sure how to think of myself then. But the stronger I felt, the more thought I gave to changing my name. But I was still apprehensive. I didn't know if I had that much strength yet.

Throughout my divorce, I had girlfriends pushing me. They said things like, "I'm not friends with you because of your husband. I barely know him. I'm friends with you because of *you*." On long walks along the canal, these friends talked to me in a way no one had before: "You need to take that job, because you haven't worked outside of the home for pay in twenty-three years." They scared me and gave me a sense of urgency. I needed to pivot. I needed to be stronger, because I didn't have a choice. "Take control," they'd say to me. "No more excuses and no more talk about Hunter. We don't want to hear about him anymore. What are you doing to take care of yourself and your daughters?"

These women had been there for me when I divorced and when I had cancer, and they helped me see that I needed to pick myself up and keep moving. I needed to reclaim my identity and learn how to make it on my own. "Get moving," they said. "You've got this."

FORTY

RECLAIMING MY NAME

Everyone knew me as Kathleen Biden, and I understood the benefits that the Biden name brought me. From the minute I got wheeled into that private hospital room after delivering Naomi, I'd felt the change. People treated me differently. That was an undeniable fact.

Biden was my name. I'd taken it so we could be a family. It was my daughters' name, after all. In many ways, my last name became a crown and shield to me; it wasn't easy to consider giving it up. For a while I had tried to think of ways to get around actually changing it. "What if we pronounce 'Biden' with a different accent?" I'd joked with the girls. "What if we are now the 'Be-*dens*'? Or maybe we are the 'D.C. Bidens,' a very different branch of the family?"

Their refrain: "Oh my God. Seriously. Stop!"

Each time I got close, I'd end up deciding I just wasn't ready, was still too scared to let it go. Then one Sunday morning in August 2019, while I sat at the kitchen island drinking coffee and going through mail, I finally felt certain. I felt the strength that my girlfriends and my family had given me. My identity no longer needed to be tied to my ex-husband.

With one bank account and a handful of bills, my life was finally streamlined. Every month I could predict my income and costs. There were no more surprises and no more fear. I was ready to say goodbye to Kathleen Biden. After agonizing over it for two years, I wanted my maiden name back. I had a job that could support me modestly without alimony. I could take care of myself. I had a home for myself and the girls and was ready to close the chapter on Kathleen Biden and start the next one as Kathleen Buhle. I set aside my coffee mug, went online, printed out the form, and dropped it off at the courthouse the next day.

A month later, on September 27, 2019, I drove back to D.C. Superior Court, wearing the same black sheath dress and heels I'd worn for my divorce. I parked in front of the imposing limestone building and walked through the front doors. My heart started beating loudly while I stood in line to pass through security. When I finally got inside the main lobby with all its gray stone, I glanced to my right down that first-floor hallway where so many lawyers and clients sat on plastic chairs, waiting. Two years earlier I'd sat in that very hallway with my own lawyer and family. When the memory came to me, I tried to shake the sense of mourning that accompanied it. Today was a good day. A positive day. I was taking my identity back.

I rode the escalator up to the second floor to find the "judge in chamber," and was surprised by the fluttering in my stomach. I walked slowly down a long hallway to find the right room. Inside was a small waiting area where a handful of people sat quietly, staring at their phones. Without looking up at me, the young clerk behind the counter handed me a clipboard to sign in.

Why had I chosen to come alone this time? I hadn't anticipated my racing heart or the tears I was now holding back. I barely understood those tears. Suddenly I felt all the old uncertainty creeping back into my head. My daughters and I would soon have different last names. Would they feel more Biden to me and less Buhle? I'd been proud to be a Biden, but now I thought I was strong enough to succeed without that armor. Or at least I'd felt strong when I'd gotten dressed for court that morning. But standing at the counter, I didn't feel so strong anymore. I felt scared. And sad.

After I signed in, I stared at my signature: K. Biden. Was this the last time I'd sign anything using that name? I handed the clipboard back to the clerk and said in a shaky voice, "I'm here to change my name."

The clerk took the clipboard, typed my name into the computer, and said, "Can I see your driver's license and the notarized letter from your credit card company?"

Panic gripped me. What was he talking about? What notarized letter? "I don't have a letter from my credit card company. I don't have a balance; I pay it off every month."

"It doesn't matter if there's a balance," he said flatly. "You need a notarized letter from all of your creditors before you can change your name." He spoke as if he'd told me this a thousand times before.

The words felt like a slap, and I started to cry. "Okay, I'll cancel the card right now," I said. "I just—I have to change my name today. I can't come back. I'll do anything. I'll sign an affidavit that there's no debt. Just—I'll cancel the card. Please. This has to happen today."

I didn't know if I'd have the strength to come back there and try again. And something in me knew that I couldn't go down that escalator as Kathleen Biden. I worked to get my voice back under control as I pleaded, and the clerk looked at me now with a slightly tilted gaze. I don't think this particular waiting room had seen a whole lot of tears, and my desperation must have been palpable.

"Let me talk to the judge," he finally said, realizing perhaps that I wasn't leaving so easily.

After he walked off, I slumped into one of the plastic chairs against the wall. An older man with a scruffy beard and a soft smile came and sat next to me and handed me what looked like a very old used tissue.

"Thank you," I said to him in a shaky voice as I took the tissue and wiped my nose.

"Honey, don't worry," he said. "Whatever you're crying about, it will be okay."

I smiled weakly at him, and we sat in silence after that, his kind eyes occasionally checking on me. Everyone else in the waiting room looked as calm as though they were waiting for their number to be called at the DMV.

When the clerk returned and called my name, I stood and walked toward him, willing him to say it would be okay.

"The judge reviewed your paperwork," he told me, "and she has enough information. You can have your name changed today." Relief washed over me, but the tears kept coming. In a way, the piece of paper I was after—the certificate of name

change—now felt more significant to me than my divorce de-
cree. The changed name was a physical manifestation of my
reclaimed sense of self. It signified that I was strong enough
now to stand on my own. At the same time, it was a farewell
letter to the old Hunter, the young man I had met in Portland,
Oregon, and the young woman who'd fallen so hard in love.

When the clerk came in and told us all to stand and enter
the courtroom, the older man and I walked in together. This
courtroom was not unlike the room downstairs where I'd gotten divorced, and I had to remind myself again that this wasn't
a day of grieving. We all took our seats in the gallery behind
the partition that divided us from the two tables and the
judge's bench: one table on the right, another on the left. During my divorce, I'd sat at the table to the left.

Today's judge was a slight woman in her fifties with brown
hair and a serious expression, and when she entered in her
long black robe, we all rose. A minute later my name was the
first to be called, and I quickly stood back up. The stakes felt
incredibly high to me now, and I worried that the judge might
have a change of heart and ask me for more documents.

"You are here to change your name from Biden to Buhle,
correct?" she asked me, pronouncing my maiden name perfectly.

"Yes," I said, the tears still falling, and the old tissue crum-
pled in my hand.

"Okay. Your reason is divorce, correct?"

"Yes," I answered again and saw my marriage so clearly for
a moment. Hunter had loved me. And I knew how much he
loved our girls. We were both flawed. I wanted to let go of the
blame and start anew.

"All right. The court approves your name change to Kathleen Ann Buhle. You will be mailed the official court documents regarding the name change. Until then, we can give you court-stamped papers. How many copies do you want?" she asked with a suppressed smile. "We normally give two, but you can have more if you'd like."

"I don't know how many I need," I said, unsure.

"How about ten," she said. "We'll give you ten copies."

Then she looked around the courtroom and announced with a full smile, "Everyone can have as many copies as they want today." Whether she was aware of my story, I don't know, but I believe she understood the gravity of the moment for me.

I bent down to pick up my bag and said goodbye to my seatmate. His kindness had let me know I wasn't alone that day. When I left the courtroom, I didn't feel happy. Yet I wasn't sad either. What I felt for certain was pride. Changing my name had been as frightening as anything I'd ever done before. I was no longer a Biden. I'd handed in my crown and shield because I no longer needed them. Maybe I never had.

ACKNOWLEDGMENTS

With the exception of being a parent, writing this book has given me the greatest sense of pride. The journey to write this book had many fellow travelers. In the beginning, as my marriage started to fall apart, I wrote alone and kept my thoughts to myself. When I finally unpacked that box full of papers and began the process of making sense of what had happened, I spent countless hours talking through my story with friends and family.

My girlfriends, my ride-or-die crew, pushed me to explore and understand my role. They held me up while pushing me forward. Without them, this book wouldn't have happened.

When I made the decision to take my personal writing to the next level, I reached out to Susan Conley, a brilliant writer and teacher who gave me the tools and the guidance to tell my story in an honest and authentic way. Without her advice and instruction, this book could have simply been a list of everything I'd done, without the reflection that truly gives it meaning.

When my writing started looking like a book, my agent, Rob McQuilkin, gave me the confidence to believe it could be. With his enthusiasm and sharp wit, he made my wildest dream come true. He brought me to my new family at Crown.

Libby, Gillian, David, Aubrey, Gwyneth, Annsley, and Susan gave me more support than I ever could have hoped for. Getting this book to completion was a group effort, and I had the best.

Of course, I wouldn't have been able to write this book, or even stand, if not for the support and love my family has shown me. Jim and Roberta, I am forever and always your girl. Your unfailing honesty and empathy guided me throughout this process. Amy, you have been my partner since birth, and there isn't a good thing I've done that doesn't also have your fingerprints on it. Your wonderfully accurate and colorful memory allowed this book its details. You are my North Star and I'll continue trying to be more like you for the rest of my life. Michele and Patty, how could I ever fail with two of the strongest women behind me. You've always reminded me to take pride in where we come from and shown me the beauty in authenticity.

Finally, I have to thank my three greatest gifts: Naomi, Finnegan, and Maisy. From the moment I became a mother, they have taught me how to be a better person. With patience, encouragement, and empathy, they've supported my struggle to reclaim my sense of self. I hope they know that my greatest role, the role I am most proud of, is being their mother.

ABOUT THE AUTHOR

KATHLEEN BUHLE has worked on women's issues in Washington, D.C., for the past decade. She was the director of strategic partnerships at the DC Volunteer Lawyers Project, a nonprofit serving domestic violence survivors. Presently she is the founder of the House at 1229, a collaborative space for women leaders, and the chair of development on the board of the Duke Ellington School of the Arts. She is the mother of three daughters, Naomi, Finnegan, and Maisy.

ABOUT THE TYPE

This book was set in Sabon, a typeface designed by the well-known German typographer Jan Tschichold (1902–74). Sabon's design is based upon the original letter forms of sixteenth-century French type designer Claude Garamond and was created specifically to be used for three sources: foundry type for hand composition, Linotype, and Monotype. Tschichold named his typeface for the famous Frankfurt typefounder Jacques Sabon (c. 1520–80).